D1483068

# NELSON ROCKEFELLER  A Biography

Books by Joe Alex Morris

NELSON ROCKEFELLER A Biography

DEADLINE EVERY MINUTE: The Story of the United Press

WHAT A YEAR!

THOSE ROCKEFELLER BROTHERS

*In collaboration:*

THE PRIVATE PAPERS OF SENATOR VANDENBERG

DEAR MR. PRESIDENT

# NELSON ROCKEFELLER
## A Biography

Joe Alex Morris

HARPER & BROTHERS

PUBLISHERS NEW YORK

NELSON ROCKEFELLER A Biography

Copyright © 1960 by Joe Alex Morris

Printed in the United States of America

All rights in this book are reserved. No part of the book may be used or reproduced in any manner whatsoever without written permission except in the case of brief quotations embodied in critical articles and reviews. For information address Harper & Brothers, 49 East 33rd Street, New York 16, N. Y.

FIRST EDITION

C-K

Library of Congress catalog card number: 60-7534

For Francis A. Jamieson

It seems clear to me that God designed us to live in society . . . and as our social system could not subsist without the sense of justice and injustice, He has given us the power to acquire that sense.

VOLTAIRE

# Contents

Two sections of illustrations will be found following
pages 82 and 146

## Acknowledgments

The author is grateful to the subject of this biography and to his father for making available many hitherto unpublished letters and documents.

He also wishes to acknowledge the assistance of a large number of friends and acquaintances of Nelson Rockefeller in preparation of this biography, including some who wish to remain anonymous. Special thanks are due to Martha Dalrymple, Howard Knowles, Louise Boyer, Donna Mitchell, Mary Elizabeth Buttfield, Ilene Slater, Nancy Hanks, Jane Magee, Beatrice Collins, Harry O'Donnell, Steven David, John R. Camp, Isabelle Savell, Bernardo Jofre, Henry W. Bagley, Stacy May and Barbara Bennett for assistance in research and assembly of material.

Source material, in addition to the daily newspapers, included *John D. Rockefeller*, by Allan Nevins, and *John D. Rockefeller, Jr.*, by Raymond B. Fosdick.

For historical accuracy, it is noted that the Prologue and Epilogue represent a synthesis of conversations on several airplane flights, the last of which was on January 13, 1960.

# NELSON ROCKEFELLER  A Biography

# 9:46 a.m., Wednesday, January 13, 1960...

The limousine rolled smoothly through the gates of the airport, turned sharply and cut across the apron to a big, two-engine private airplane where reporters and television cameramen had been waiting for an hour. Before the wheels stopped turning, a rear door was partly opened and the Governor of New York stuck his foot out toward the pavement. For a moment, he paused—his head turned back toward his secretary to give some final instruction, his wide hand gripping the half-opened door, his foot thrust out for the first long step toward the waiting plane—a frozen moment between finishing one task (for which there had not been enough time) and starting another (on which he already was behind schedule). Then he was in motion again, his foot striking the pavement firmly, his sturdy figure swinging athletically through the door and his attention wholly concentrated on what lay ahead of him.

He walked rapidly, his body relaxed and balanced and his shoulders slightly forward, almost as if he were a gymnast on the tanbark of a circus ring. He shook a few hands among the waiting newsmen. He slapped a few shoulders and called a few first names. His square,

1

mobile face was serious beneath a ruffle of dark brown hair across his forehead as he answered reporters' questions. His wide mouth stretched into a schoolboy grin and the skin crinkled at the corners of his eyes (one eye is slightly bluer than the other) as he exchanged jibes with a cameraman. After a few minutes, he signaled to the captain of the plane's three-man crew and motioned his traveling companions—including one interviewer as supercargo—aboard. He swung himself easily up the steep steps to the plane,[1] stopping by request to give the photographers one more shot of his famous smile. Then the plane door slammed shut and he spoke a familiar phrase: "Let's get going, fellows!"

Nelson Rockefeller is both a very direct and a very complicated man. Inside the handsomely furnished cabin, with its couches, its working tables, its television set and its big swivel chairs, only the fact that he is almost constantly busy on the contents of two bulging brief cases suggests that he is Governor of the nation's most populous state and a member of one of the richest families on earth. He is a man who, since childhood, has wanted and worked to be accepted for what he is as a person rather than for his family's wealth and position. It would be foolish to depreciate his efforts in this direction, because he has proved himself as much at home among the villagers of New York state or among the oil field workers of Venezuela as he is among the tycoons of Wall Street. He has understood and fought for recognition of the aspirations of the underprivileged, and his contributions to the social betterment of our times have been considerable, judged by any standard. Yet, in attempting to understand Rockefeller's character and career, the factor of great wealth cannot be ignored. The accuracy of estimates of his wealth at two hundred or three hundred million dollars is of slight importance. The fact is that he and his family command vast economic power when they desire to exercise it. That they have chosen to exercise it for the common good also is beside the point. The fact remains that the power,

[1] Jointly owned and used by Rockefeller and two of his brothers, Laurance and David.

while obviously not unlimited, is there and that it has been an important although not a decisive factor in the career of Nelson Rockefeller. The Rockefeller name and wealth open many doors, influence many persons and restrain many others. A quiet word from the Rockefellers may be heard at a great distance in the world of business and finance. If the family is interested in some civic venture, there will be many influential persons ready to help. If an advertiser offends good taste by using the name Rockefeller to signify wealth in a television commercial jingle, the word "millionaire" is pretty sure to be substituted upon request from the proper sources. The family influence reaches far and the Rockefellers, a close observer once remarked to a reporter, "lean heavily on their good will."

Nelson Rockefeller is not a humble man. There is no pretense about him and he despises pretense in others. He is able, deeply religious, tolerant, self-confident, highly ambitious, aggressive, persistent, extraordinarily competitive and, from a political standpoint, often recklessly courageous. But, despite his love of humanity and his universal good-fellowship, there inevitably remains in a man of Rockefeller's background a residue of arrogance—what has been called the "unconscious arrogance of self-conscious wealth." He has, owing to energy and fortuitous circumstances, achieved more than most of his contemporaries ever since he was a boy. He is now sure of himself and of his objectives and he pursues his course not just energetically but, when necessary, with a surprising toughness.

Rockefeller comes honestly by the complexities of his character. His immediate forebears were a varied lot. Great-grandfather William Avery Rockefeller was a tall, muscular farmowner in western New York state, a man who loved gaiety and adventure, who usually did as he pleased, sometimes without moral scruples. He became a peddler of patent medicines and herbal remedies in the middlewestern states, living at Cleveland. Perhaps more important in the lives of later generations of the family was William Avery Rockefeller's wife, the former Eliza Davison, a woman with red hair and blue eyes, with spirit and intelligence and with great religious devotion. She was a militant temperance worker who led groups of women into saloons to pray for deliverance of the nation from the evils of alcohol, and she passed on to her children and her children's children a powerful heritage of industry, thrift and piety. A son of this diverse couple was John Davison Rockefeller, Sr., who fought his way to the summit of the business world and, under the influence of his devoutly pious wife, Laura Spelman Rockefeller, gave away half a billion dollars as a philanthropist. Rockefeller's maternal grandfather, Nelson W. Aldrich, also was a strong character, a farm boy in Rhode Island who rose to political power as a United States Senator and a leader of the Republican party. But he acquired along the way a great love for literature, a keen judgment of good art, a taste for fine wines and an appreciation of the good life.

Any close observer will discover in Nelson Rockefeller a trace of all of these ancestors, tempered by the great influence of his parents. Nobody is likely to mistake him for an intellectual—an "egghead" in the political slang of the 1950's—but not a few students and technical experts have been surprised by the depth of his knowledge in specialized fields as well as the breadth of his study of social and political problems. One reason for their surprise lies in the fact that Rockefeller is not an abstract thinker, nor is he particularly articulate in expressing himself in philosophical terms. He does not have a broad intellectual background; he doesn't read much literature; he doesn't have any unusual knowledge of history. On the other hand, he is strong for direct action in terms of a concrete problem, he learns with amazing rapidity by seeing things and places and talking to people and he has a remarkable intuition for the right move at the right time. In addition, he can concentrate on what he is doing to the point where everything else is excluded, he is an irrepressible organizer and he knows how to bring together and make use of the "best brains" available for study of a problem.

"Rockefeller doesn't have an ideological frame of reference," one close associate explained. "He never gets tied up into philosophical knots because of a preconceived theory. He leaves his mind free to understand a problem and to focus on a practical, direct-action solution. His mind is on the future, not on the past.

"Anyway, it isn't a scholar's mind. For example, he is not a true authority on modern art although he has a highly cultivated aesthetic sense. He looks at a painting and likes it and therefore he wants to hang it but he probably couldn't tell you why. He likes jazz music—not progressive jazz—because it expresses something he feels but he can't carry a tune."

Rockefeller is a firmly entrenched businessman and capitalist, and he is a lifelong Republican, but he doesn't believe such designations can mean much unless businessmen and capitalists and Republicans are in a constant process of evolution to keep up with changing times and to contribute to the ultimate goal of a better and more harmonious world community. Such global phrases are not mere words to Rockefeller. More perhaps than any other American, he has worked at putting them into practice—in Latin America, for example—and he is convinced that the future of our democratic system depends upon our willingness as a nation to thwart Communism by taking vigorous, realistic action to help underdeveloped nations help themselves.

Rockefeller's political talents have sometimes been rather recklessly compared to those of Franklin D. Roosevelt, probably because both are examples of an ability to project a winning personality to mass audiences. As a young man, however, President Roosevelt was a sophisticated politician who knew where he was heading. Rockefeller matured slowly and charted his career only after a considerable period of indecision. The President was inclined often to skirt around obstacles in order to reach his objective. Rockefeller tends to frontal attack. Mr. Roosevelt engineered, in a time of domestic crisis, a vast revolution designed to bring the capitalistic system abruptly into line with modern social requirements. In a time of international crisis, Rockefeller has sought to define the problems that must be faced in the future and to encourage action today that will strengthen the nation and the free enterprise system in tomorrow's changing world.

It is now rather generally agreed that the greatest political phenomenon of our times is the rise to leadership of a man whose grandfather was reviled only half a century ago as an unconscionable, monopolistic ogre, an oppressor of widows, orphans and honest workingmen. Even more remarkable is the fact that the grandson should be described by AFL-CIO President George Meany as a dedicated, aggressive liberal and should be a guest of honor at the Urban League's awards dinner with two former collaborators, Jacob Potofsky of the Amalgamated Clothing Workers Union, and David Dubinsky of the International Ladies Garment Workers Union. "I am glad," Potofsky remarked in reference to past cooperation of the three men in civic and philanthropic work, "to see a reunion of that fine firm with that good old American name of Dubinsky, Potofsky and Rockefeller!"

Aboard the big airplane, climbing steadily up through darkening skies, the Governor of New York worked for a while on papers taken from his brief cases, signed a dozen letters and then, laying aside his horn-rimmed reading glasses, came over to sit beside the waiting interviewer. He was already a little rumpled. He was beginning to need a haircut. The luster was gone from his shoes. He dug a small bottle out of his pocket and shook out a vitamin pill. He takes them regularly and always has a supply of the newest cold pills on hand. He settled his five-foot-ten-inch frame comfortably back into the big chair but not to relax. Associates who have known him for twenty years will tell you they have never seen him really relaxed. Yet he can shed his worries like a coat to play golf (rather poorly) or to dance or to visit an art exhibition, and this gives him great powers of regeneration.

"Now, let's see," he said, tossing down the vitamin pill, "the last time we got together we were talking about how the President unexpectedly ran into Khrushchev in the corridor at the first summit meeting in Geneva. I only wish I'd made notes on that conversation! The President was great! Now what's on your mind today?"

"I thought we might go way back to when you were a boy, Governor. There are several points I'd like to clear up about vacations at Seal Harbor."

"Sure." He turned to look out at the cottony clouds through which the plane surged steadily southward. "I like to talk about the coast of Maine. . . ."

# ONE

# John D.'s Grandson

The island of Mount Desert lies hardly a long stone's throw off the coast of Maine between Penobscot Bay and Frenchman Bay, where the ragged and rocky New England shoreline is occasionally, but only occasionally, broken by small sandy beaches. Mount Desert is a twenty-mile-long ovoid island of green mountains and bright lakes and trout streams and it is almost split in two by a finger of water called Somes Sound. It has been inhabited since the 1760's by fishermen and their families who, during the last century, have been joined each summer by large numbers of "outsiders"—wealthy families on vacation from the big Eastern cities. Since the turn of the century, one of the summer families has been that of John Davison Rockefeller, Jr. The second son of Mr. Rockefeller, however, has never been an "outsider" on Mount Desert. He was born there.

Nelson Aldrich Rockefeller drew his first wailing breath at 12:10 P.M. on July 8, 1908, in the Sears cottage on Wayman Street in the fashionable but conservative resort town of Bar Harbor. The cottage was then owned by the Washington newspaper publisher Edward McLean and his wife, Evalyn, who had purchased it from J. Montgomery Sears and rented it to the Rockefellers for the summer. Mrs. Rockefeller was attended by Dr. Allen M. Thomas of New York. The baby weighed nine and a quarter pounds at birth and was named for his maternal grandfather, Senator Nelson W. Aldrich.

Mr. Rockefeller sent the news of Nelson's birth by telegram to the boy's other grandfather, John D. Rockefeller, Sr., who that day celebrated his sixty-ninth birthday in New York, and received back a happy word of congratulations. The year 1908, however, was not one of general rejoicing for the Rockefeller family or the officers of the Standard Oil Company, which the elder Rockefeller had built from scratch into one of the greatest business trusts in history and by means of which he had become the world's first billionaire. For some years, there had been a rising journalistic and political clamor against "the trusts"—railroad, steel, sugar, coal—and the Standard Oil Company had emerged in the public mind as the No. 1 example of the evils of monopoly. Political cartoonists such as Frederick B. Opper, newspaper columnists such as Finley Peter Dunne, reporters and authors such as Ida M. Tarbell, Lincoln Steffens and Upton Sinclair crusaded vigorously and effectively for federal action to curb unbridled big business and to protect the public and the working-men. Ambitious young politicians as well as older politicians with an ear to the ground made a career of fighting for reform and de-nouncing the Morgans, the Carnegies, the Armours and the Rocke-fellers as ruthless and piratical destroyers of free competition. Be-cause of his great personal wealth, Rockefeller probably was the best known and the most often flayed in speeches and newspapers. A typical illustration was an Opper cartoon of a great, apelike thug, labeled "Standard Oil Trust," kicking and stomping on a little fig-ure labeled "The Public," while the police looked the other way. A balloon coming from the thug's mouth said, "You ain't got no rights," and a jingle under the cartoon said:

> O is the Oil Trust, a modern Bill Sikes;
> He defies the police, and does just as he likes.

President Theodore Roosevelt made political hay by fighting the trusts in rather haphazard fashion, and at the time of Nelson

Rockefeller's birth the Standard Oil Company was in the midst of a massive legal battle against a dozen different federal and state attempts to break up Rockefeller's network of companies and sub-companies on the grounds that they were a monopoly in restraint of trade and in violation of the Sherman Antitrust Law. In August of that year newspaper front pages were crowded with stories of the appearance of the elder Rockefeller himself in court, where, "like a country gentleman regaling friends with some tale of the good old times," he attempted to show that the Standard Oil empire "had been built up by benevolent assimilation" of other companies. Rockefeller's definition of a trust, commented the New York *World*, was "a philanthropic institution created by the benevolent absorption of competitors to save them from ruin, combined with the human conservation and ingenious utilization of natural resources for the benefit of the people."

A year later, the government won its case and Standard Oil of New Jersey was ordered to divest itself of all subsidiaries. This was confirmed by the United States Supreme Court on May 15, 1911, and the Rockefeller high command began the work of splitting up a combination that had plants all over the country, owned 88,000 miles of pipe lines, processed 68,200,000 barrels of crude oil a year, sold almost 4,000,000 barrels of lubricants a year and owned a fleet of 78 steamships and 19 sailing vessels. The mere possession of such wealth in an era when radical labor leaders were calling on workers to organize and strike against sweatshop conditions in many industries was enough to make the Rockefeller name an epithet in many American households. But worse was to come. In 1913, some nine thousand coal miners went on strike in southern Colorado, demanding better hours and wages and union recognition. One of the largest companies involved was the Colorado Fuel and Iron Company, in which the Rockefellers were major stockholders. Although they knew little about operation of the company, Mr. Rockefeller, Jr., was a member of the board of directors, and he backed the company officers in their contention that the strike was all the fault of "outside agitators." The strike dragged on for months and was marked by violence that led to a Congressional investigation and the calling out of state militia. On

April 20 there was a pitched battle between militia and mine guards versus armed strikers in a miners' tent colony at Ludlow, near Walsenburg, Colorado. The tents were burned and some twenty-five strikers or their relatives were killed or wounded, including two women and eleven children who died of suffocation in a cave where they hid to escape the gunfire.

The Ludlow "massacre" aroused great public feeling all over the United States. Workers from other cities joined the strikers. Mines were wrecked and buildings looted. Workers held mass meetings in New York and staged hostile parades before the Rockefeller offices at 26 Broadway, shouting that John D. Rockefeller, Jr., ought to be shot down "like a dog." An apparent plot to bomb the Rockefeller offices and an attempt to demonstrate at the Rockefeller home at Tarrytown, N.Y., were thwarted, but popular feeling against the Rockefellers ran as high as ever in history against a prominent American industrial family, if not even higher. The Colorado strike violence was to have a great effect on the future attitude and actions of Mr. Rockefeller, Jr., who would devote himself to eliminating paternalism and installing progressive management in the companies under his influence. He would insist that management take responsibility for the social and economic conditions of the community of employees.

But, at the beginning of World War I, the Rockefeller name was anathema in labor and political circles and in countless American households. That year, Nelson Rockefeller was six years old and having trouble learning to eat and write and throw a ball with his right instead of his left hand.

II.

The Rockefeller children—Abby, John Davison 3rd, Nelson, Laurance, Winthrop and David—were not particularly aware at an early age of either the great wealth of the family or the controversy that had raged around the family name. This knowledge came to them gradually and naturally as they grew older and with knowledge came a burden of responsibility, which they regarded as very great. It fell largely on the eldest brother, John, who was quiet and serious, almost shy, and temperamentally most like his father. Responsibility rested lightly, if at all, on the shoulders of Nelson as a child and it would be difficult to imagine how he could have experienced a more carefree and normal boyhood.

The family lived, of course, as wealthy families were expected to live in the first decades of the century but by no means as extravagantly as some. There were three main bases of operation. First, there was a town house at No. 13 and, later, at No. 10 West Fifty-fourth Street near the mansion of the elder Rockefeller. The home of Mr. Rockefeller, Jr., was of nine stories, with an infirmary, a gymnasium, a playground and squash court, in addition to large living quarters for the staff. The drawing rooms, the library, the music room and the family suites gradually were filled with art treasures, including exquisite Persian rugs with silver and gold thread and Gobelin tapestries which Mr. Rockefeller collected as avidly as his wife picked up antique brass and Oriental objects of art and, later, modern paintings. In time, the collections grew to such size that the house next door, No. 12, was transformed into a kind of art gallery to accommodate the overflow.

The second family base was Pocantico Hills, a four-thousand-acre estate near Tarrytown, some thirty miles up the Hudson River from New York City, where Mr. Rockefeller had a house and where he supervised the building of a home for his father. In giving instructions to the architect, he said that his father wanted "a residence so simple that friends coming from no matter how humble an environment, would be impressed by the homelikeness of the house; while those who appreciated fine design and beautiful furnishings would say, 'How exquisite!' " He also purchased what experts believed to be an original or an early copy of a Praxiteles statue of Aphrodite for the new establishment, despite his father's concern that he was being overcharged and probably could not get his money back if he ever wanted to sell it. Eventually Pocantico Hills had driving and riding trails; a $500,000 playhouse with bowling alleys, swimming pool and squash court; and—much later—homes for four of the five Rockefeller boys.

Seal Harbor on Mount Desert Island became the third family residence for summer vacations. In 1910, when the Rockefellers moved into their own summer home there—The Eyrie, a huge, sprawling house atop a high hill overlooking the sea—no automobiles were permitted on the island. Bar Harbor was one of the most fashionable resorts on the New England coast. Seal Harbor was more isolated and quieter but with a good protected beach and a harbor almost enclosed by huge rocks and a slender finger of land. Mr. Rockefeller later built a large playhouse and kitchen in the woods behind the big house and a huge formal garden for Mrs. Rockefeller. Handsome Oriental tomb statues which Mrs. Rockefeller bought in Korea were placed beneath trees at one side of the garden, and other bronze and stone Buddhas were installed in quiet, peaceful nooks in the nearby woods in the manner of Japanese shrines. The playhouse had a bowling alley and a squash court and there were tennis courts nearby. Down the hill were stables for riding horses and for Mr. Rockefeller's driving horses and eventually the woods were laced with miles of roads that he built and over which the family rode or drove almost every day.

The Rockefeller family, however, did not spend all of the time at these three homes. As the children grew older, there were long trips through the Western states and journeys to Europe in addition to visits with Mr. Rockefeller, Sr., at Ormond Beach, Florida. Mrs. Rockefeller was able in a pleasant, undisturbed way to run several households at the same time and, on trips, each of the children was assigned certain duties, such as tending to luggage or polishing boots or buying tickets so that their journeys were organized like a small army on the move. Each child also had a specific allowance—usually starting at twenty-five cents a week—and each was expected to save 10 per cent, give 10 per cent to charity and keep an accurate account of every penny spent.

Nelson was frequently in trouble as a small boy not only because he was a poor bookkeeper but because he was perhaps the most serious disturber of the peace in the Rockefeller household. Mr. Rockefeller's mother and father were devoutly religious and in their home each day started with prayers before breakfast, a custom that was followed in the family of Mr. Rockefeller, Jr., and, later, in Nelson Rockefeller's

own home. At mealtime, discipline was effectively if not sternly enforced by Mr. Rockefeller and the children were expected to be on
time and to mind their manners. Nelson was most often tardy. He
also was restless at the table and he frequently felt called upon to
amuse his sister and brothers by clowning or making remarks that
they thought were excruciatingly funny. Such outbursts did not please
his father and occasionally he was sent from the table and very occasionally his father spanked him. Eventually, his seat at the table
was moved so that he was not close to certain of his brothers.

Mr. Rockefeller also was concerned because Nelson was naturally a
"southpaw" and used his left hand for almost everything. At that time,
parents were likely to regard left-handedness as unfortunate and
there was a widely-held theory that it could be easily corrected. Mr.
Rockefeller began correcting his son at an early age, instructing him to
shift his spoon or knife to his right hand. Nelson failed to respond.
After a rather long period of failure, Mr. Rockefeller appeared at the
table with a rubber band and a piece of string. The rubber band he put
around his son's left wrist. He attached one end of the string to the
rubber band and held the other end in his hand as he sat at the table.
When Nelson started to use his left hand in eating, his father tugged
gently on his end of the string, pulling the left hand away from the
knife or fork for which it was reaching.

In time, Nelson's left-handedness was partly overcome but not
without considerable childish confusion that might well have been
frowned on by child psychologists a generation later. As he grew up,
the boy became more or less ambidextrous. He did most things with
his right hand but he played tennis left-handed and he learned to write
—not very well—with either hand. He also developed a remarkable
inability to spell which would last a lifetime. This may have been due
in part to the fact that his mother was a mediocre speller or to his
own peculiar vision. For instance, in reading he frequently transposed
letters or figures; in other words, he would read the characters backward. If he saw the numerals 76, he might read them aloud as 67. This
made him a slow reader and would affect him all his life in a limited
way, making reading less easy than it might otherwise have been.

Laurance and Nelson, only two years apart in age, were a kind of partnership from very early childhood. They were always up to something and, owing both to age and temperament, Nelson usually was the leader. It was not, in childhood or later, a one-sided partnership, however, because Laurance was quick-witted and amusing, the kind of a boy who could deflate some of Nelson's grandiose ideas with a couple of penetrating words. "We led a delightful, happy life together," Nelson said long afterward. "He could always put the rapier right through me with a twist but he was amusing about it and I loved it."

When they were small and full of mischief, Nelson and Laurance slept in the same room, often to the dismay of their governess and other members of the household staff. They engaged in roughhouse games and pretended they were hunters in Africa or explorers in the Arctic when they were supposed to be studying their school books or to have turned out the lights and gone to bed. One of their favorite stunts after they had been told to go to sleep was to drag all the blankets and mattresses off their beds and build a tent or a cave or an igloo in which they crouched for protection against a blizzard or, perhaps, an Indian attack. There was a trunk between their beds and the boys secretly rigged it with wires and an electric light bulb so that they had a kind of electric burner on which they could heat a cup of chocolate after lights were out. Such activities brought frequent discovery and punishment—usually by a governess who opened the door, grabbed the first small boy she could reach, paddled him soundly and warned them both to get to sleep. Paddlings in no way deterred the mischief but, in order to share equally in the hardships of their partnership, Nelson and Laurance took turns sleeping in the bed nearest the hallway door so that the same one would not always be grabbed for the evening spanking.

All of the Rockefeller children had to earn their own extra spending money, of which they never felt they had quite enough. They planted and tended their own gardens at Pocantico. They raised rabbits, which they sold to laboratories. They pulled weeds at so much per dozen weeds. They practiced their music—a cello, in Nelson's case. But there was plenty of time for exercise and play and they made the most of it. Their father taught them to ice skate, although none became as accomplished as he, and took them for long walks in the woods, where he knew all of the trees and wild flowers and could tell interesting stories about them. Their mother read to them and taught them to play Numerica and organized gay picnics on summer days. They all had a modest amount of sports equipment such as roller skates and tennis racquets and bicycles and boats, but none ever showed any particular interest in the traditional American game of baseball.

Mr. and Mrs. Rockefeller devoted a great deal of time and thought to the problem of bringing up their children in a simple and healthy manner so that they would never feel that the family's great wealth set them apart from other boys and girls anywhere. In this, they were more than moderately successful. The children had no more spending money, and frequently less, than their companions, they conformed in dress to the youthful fancies of the day and they were encouraged to avoid any ostentatious display of wealth.[1] But it would be highly inaccurate to suggest that as they grew up the Rockefeller boys were no more privileged than the ordinary American boy. They had their own tennis courts and swimming pools and bowling alleys and horses and boats and canoes and, in their childhood, there was always a young man companion to watch over them and instruct them in games. Furthermore, they were encouraged to buy good equipment that would last. When Nelson wanted a radio during his high school days he made a formal agreement with a youthful electronics expert to build a five-tube set and install it at a cost not to exceed $150.

[1] Various legends have grown up in regard to the simple manner in which the Rockefeller children were reared. One delightful but false story is that the boys sailed in a small boat that was older and less expensive and slower than the boats of their companions. This prompted a youthful friend to ask them: "Why don't you ask your father to buy you a good boat like the other boys have?" To which one of the Rockefeller boys supposedly replied: "Who do you think we are —the Vanderbilts?" None of the Rockefellers has any idea how this myth originated and they are pretty tired of hearing it repeated but they have about given up hope that it will be forgotten. A possible explanation of the origin of the story will be found in my book *Those Rockefeller Brothers*.

When he became interested in photography he invested his allowance in the best foreign cameras and persuaded his father to build a fully-equipped darkroom so he could develop his own pictures.

The Rockefeller children, nevertheless, were taught a sound respect for money and its use, but they were never allowed to forget their father's attitude that the Rockefeller fortune was a responsibility and a trust and that it would be their duty to see that it was used to secure the widest possible benefits for humanity generally. "I suppose," one of the brothers remarked much later, "that all of us felt that responsibility was the only thing we had more of than our classmates."

Nelson was naturally inclined to feel at home in almost any company except, perhaps, that of Eastern society families whose sons went to Groton or St. Paul's. Nelson didn't go to an exclusive preparatory school, and the Rockefellers were not "in" society as it was represented on the newspaper society pages and in the Sunday rotogravure sections.

There were, of course, childish incidents when some boy on the school bus or at play might taunt a Rockefeller child by shouting: "Hello, Mr. Moneybags Rockefeller. How many yachts do you have today?" But Mrs. Rockefeller told her children to make a joke of such remarks by saying, "Oh, we have only sixteen yachts now but we're getting some more." And it wasn't often that the occasion for a retort arose, because the Rockefeller boys were determined to "belong" to the crowd in school or at play and they usually succeeded.

"I never in my life felt any conscious embarrassment or concern about the family name or the family's money," Nelson once remarked. "I never felt any different from other people—not even when I was with the Indians in the Andes Mountains. The only times I ever felt shy or uncomfortable was at certain society affairs when I didn't know the boys who were from the better prep schools. I didn't fit into their group."

III.

Mrs. Rockefeller kept a neat file of the letters which her children wrote to her when she had to be away from them and among these were occasional examples of their school work and other mementoes.

go amuse yourselves by building a play cabin.' It was after we were older that we had more elaborate things."

There were only occasional social affairs at Seal Harbor when the boys were small but on Sundays the whole family left the big hilltop house together and walked—the boys often reluctantly—down the hill to attend church services. In the evenings, Mr. Rockefeller frequently got everybody together for a musical hour. Sometimes the family orchestra took over with Mrs. Rockefeller at the piano, Mr. Rockefeller playing the violin, Nelson the cello and Winthrop the drums. At other times they would sing hymns, which the head of the family particularly enjoyed. Once, during Mrs. Rockefeller's absence, Nelson wrote her that

> we sang hymns tonight but luckily Pa had to go to Church so we had to stop at a quarter to eight.

About this time, Nelson and Laurance decided that the names their parents had given them were a bit "sissy" and that they would correct the matter by choosing their own names. Nelson decided to become "Dick" and Laurance chose "Bill." The "Dick" failed to stick with Nelson, but Laurance became "Bill" to practically the whole family and to close friends for the rest of his life.

At first with an older companion and later alone, Nelson and Laurance frequently went on overnight camping and fishing trips with sleeping bags and campfire cooking equipment. Sometimes they walked and sometimes they loaded a pony cart with supplies and wandered deep into the wooded mountains of the island. All of the boys learned to cook after a fashion and they often bragged that the meals they turned out over the campfire tasted as good as the food served at the Rockefeller table, a comparison that should be strongly discounted in Nelson's case because he always would eat almost anything that was placed before him and seldom paid any attention to what it happened to be.

There was a cave on the hillside below the Rockefeller house at Seal Harbor where Nelson and Laurance sometimes hid out and where they made a timid effort to learn to smoke cigarettes before deciding to accept their father's standing offer of $2,500 for not smoking before their twenty-first birthdays. (Nelson and David were the only winners of the prize.) But the two boys' greatest enjoyment at Seal Harbor was the woods behind the mansion where, before any roads were built, they could imagine themselves deep in Indian country and beset by many dangers. After seeing Western logging operations on one of their summer journeys, they decided to fell a little timber and build a log cabin of their own.

The plans on which they finally agreed represented no small-time operation. They marked out an eight-by-ten-foot floor plan for the cabin with a spot for an indoor fireplace. Then they began hacking down trees and trimming them and, when they had cleared a wide circular area, they hitched their ponies to the logs and dragged them to the site. When the cabin walls were up a few feet the boys rigged a set of pulleys and ropes so that the ponies could be used to lift the logs to the desired height and lower them gently into place. A door of split logs was hung and two windows were fashioned so that they could be closed and latched for defense against savage Indians. The fireplace was constructed so that it had an outside flue and the roof was shingled. A shed was built a short distance away for stabling the ponies. It was a good cabin, solid and rain-proof and the boys often cooked and slept there, and more than thirty years later Nelson would be able to poke around among the logs—now tumbled down—and point out that the foundation was still in place and that the latches were still on the crumbling windows. "It was a big project for us," he reminisced. "Even then we always had some big project going."

IV.

As much as Nelson loved the life at Seal Harbor, the broad, high hills of Pocantico were still home to him and would remain so. One day in 1921 he arrived eagerly at Tarrytown after being away for a few weeks and could hardly wait to see what had happened in his absence. From his grandfather's house, he ran across the lawn to see his rabbits and found seven young ones very hungry because their feeding dish had been turned over in one corner. He quickly put things to rights and then went to inspect his garden. There were purple pansies in a flower bed, there were fine cabbages in Winthrop's garden, the corn in John's garden was as high as his knee and some gourds that Nelson had planted were wildly climbing the flagpole. A breeze drifting across the hills scattered petals from a few white roses that were still in bloom. It was a beautiful day and, as usual, Nelson could hardly restrain his enthusiasm.

"Gee! I love this country," he yelled to an older friend who had accompanied him home. "I'd give three weeks at Seal Harbor any time for three days here at Pocantico!"

Later that summer, Nelson spent July in a boys' camp near Upper Saranac, New York, where he lived in a tent with five other thirteen-year-old boys and a camp monitor. If he was homesick, his letters —with the spelling corrected—didn't show it.

> I went fishing this morning and caught one fish.

> We are going on a trip to Fish pond today. Only ten boys are going, they are the ones that got the highest marks in tent inspection.

> We went on a 12 mile canoe trip with six carries. It was great fun. . . . I paddled all the way in the bow and carried one end of the 80 lb canoe on the carries. I was pretty tired. . . .

> I have charge of the cannon which they fire every morning and night when they up and down the flag. I clean, load and fire it. It is great fun.

Later the same year, when his parents were on a trip to Japan, his letters reflected a kind of all-out enthusiasm with which he habitually entered on whatever he was doing, even if it was going to dancing school.

> I have been going to dancing school with Jimmy. I like it very much. . . .

> I have been having a wonderful time. We have been playing marbles and croquet. Yesterday Aunt Lucy took John and I to the play (The First Year). It was great. Tomorrow she is going to take

John, Laurance and I to the movie (The Three Musketeers). It will be great. Everything is lovely here.

Some of his other letters in these years included the following:

Dear Ma and Pa,

. . . I had lots of fun at the opera . . . We had a box and it was great. I think it would have been better if they had sung in a language that you could understand but the costumes and acting was great. Last night I went to hear the Harvard Glee Club. . . . The singing was great and I would like to hear more of that kind of singing. . . . Laurance and I ploughed our garden with Toby and the plough only broke twice before we finished.

Dear Pa,

I want to thank you lots for the knife. It is a peach. . . . You don't know how handy it is to have one with your name on it. I am always losing them. . . . Laurance and I added up all the money you owe us and we figured that we would get about $15 each. You had better come back soon or we will put you in bankruptcy. [Mr. Rockefeller had urged the boys to take long walks for exercise and rewarded them at the rate of ten cents a mile in extra spending money.]

Although almost everything was "great" for Nelson in the mid-1920's, his school work was not so great. In 1923, he worried that he might be put back a grade because he had been too busy to keep up with the work, but he managed to scrape by. In 1924, Mr. Rockefeller was advised that Nelson's eleventh-grade work showed marks in French and in mathematics that could not be certified for college. "Nelson should work harder," the school principal added. Mr. Rockefeller took this advice to heart and the next day he handed his son a small book in which to write down every day just when and how long he had studied each subject. Later, looking over the book, he found that Nelson had recorded an average of two hours and fifteen minutes a day of study for five days a week. His grades, however, had not improved.

"It seems you're not devoting enough time to study," his father said.

"I guess you're right," Nelson replied. "Maybe I can do more studying in the periods at school when I don't have classes. That's an hour and a half more a day."

In addition, he agreed to his father's suggestion that he should not listen to the phonograph or the radio at all from Monday morning until after school on Friday. Mr. Rockefeller had no doubt that Nelson could improve his grades if he wanted to make the effort. "But," he added, "you go at things with too much of a rush and a dash. You're careless about the way you study but any time you want to put your mind to it you can do much better work without spending any more time at study than you do now."

Nelson put his mind to it and improved his marks in everything except Spanish, on which he had to do special work during the summer vacation. Even then he didn't get his grades up to college requirements and had to go to school half an hour early three days a week in an effort to catch up. As he labored through his senior year in 1925 these troubles prompted him to do some heavy thinking about college. John already was at Princeton University and it had been more or less assumed that Nelson also would go there. But the entrance requirements were stiffer than at some other colleges and there was no assurance that he would be eligible when the time came. His parents were in France during the fall term in 1925 and he wrote them several letters about his school work.

October 25, 1925: . . . I find the Math pretty hard but I go to the teacher afterwards when I don't understand. The physics isn't so very hard as yet but it takes a good deal of time. We have a peachy new English teacher and we are really doing some work there. The French is about the same as ever. I have been doing between four and five hours of home work every night. Up to now I have not gotten to bed much before eleven and usually later. But I don't think it is good for me to stay up so late so I am going to try and get more done in the afternoon. . . .

We came down from the country, that is Bill [Laurance] and I. It works much better. I have kept the Ford here and use it to go to school in. It is very convenient and saves a lot of time. We always go and come to school together, so you see it saves us forty cents a day on bus fares. I have had no accidents and not been even spoken to by a cop. Except the ones that are trying to sell tickets [to a benefit] in Yonkers.

X—— and I have been ever so good, we have not wasted one minute in school. In fact, I hardly see her any more. To make up, I have been to see her three times on Sunday. She is still as sweet as ever, but I promise you I am not letting it interfere with my studies in the least bit! So you needn't worry at all. . . .

Ted and Tad and I are going to see the Princeton-Harvard game. . . . It will be great to see Johnny again. . . . I went to see "Sunny" [a musical show] Friday night. . . . That is the first time that I have been out since school started. . . . It is more fun, driving around in the Ford, especially in heavy traffic. I pretend I am a taxi driver and have a great time. But of course I am very careful so it is perfectly safe. . . . Of course, we all miss you both terribly. . . . I am just beginning to realize what wonderful parents I have. With all the love in the world, I am,

Your devoted son,<br>Nellie

November 7, 1925: . . . I am still having to do a good deal of work . . . but I guess I will live through it. I seem to be getting on pretty well at present. I guess the affair between X—— and me is about over. . . . We have not fallen out or anything of the kind . . . and we are just as good friends as ever but that's all. . . . I am pretty well booked up already for the Christmas vacation . . . and I also have received four or five Deb. coming-out invitations. I have accepted nearly all of them so far.

I have been thinking very strongly of going to Dartmouth instead of Princeton. Dr. Caldwell [at Lincoln School] is strongly in favor of this and so are the other teachers in school. I really think that it is a better all around college and that I would get more out of it. What do you all think about it? I got the fur coat this afternoon. Oh, it is a peach.

November 21, 1925: . . . I had a talk with Dr. Caldwell and Mr. Finley; and we decided that the first thing to do was to drop the Spanish. This means that I will not be able to go to Princeton but I think it is for the best. . . . By stopping the Spanish I am able to walk in the morning, which is great because I needed the exercise badly.

. . . You said that the French cars had snappy things on their radiator caps. Well, if you would like to bring me something in that line I'd love to have one . . . it will have to be something that is long and flat and not too high. Something like a bird or a dog running.

Oh, Pa, I want to know if you would mind if I learned to drive the Dodge with William along. There is no hurry but I thought that it would be just as well if I knew how to drive it. In case any change in cars should be made next summer!!

With heaps of love,<br>Nell

There was more to Nelson's choice of Dartmouth than his problem of high school credits. Mr. Rockefeller was a friend of Dr. Ernest Martin Hopkins, the Dartmouth president, and Nelson had met and admired him. Of Hopkins, Mr. Rockefeller once said: "If I were a young man trying to decide what college to go to, I would find out what college Dr. Hopkins was president of and go there." But when Nelson discussed the college problem with him, Mr. Rockefeller declined to specify.

"You can get a good education at many colleges," he said. "If I pick one for you, the responsibility is on me. If you pick your own college, it's your responsibility."

Nelson picked Dartmouth, partly because of Dr. Hopkins, partly because it was small and democratic in campus affairs and partly because he wanted to get away from the many outside activities that would be sure to distract him if he remained in the New York City area. There had been a great many distractions in his senior year at Lincoln School. He had discovered girls and he found that he enjoyed parties and dancing immensely and, despite his rather strict upbringing, there was ample evidence that at seventeen he was strongly attracted to the gay crowd of youngsters from wealthy families that flitted from party to party en route to the excitement of bootleg gin and speakeasies. Many young men and women among his acquaintances would become active participants in the escapades of the Roaring Twenties and, as an acquaintance once remarked to Mr. Rockefeller, "anybody with your money and five sons has a right to expect at least four black sheep in the family."

There was, however, a strongly religious attitude in the Rockefeller family and a persistent sense of responsibility, and in the latter part of his senior year Nelson got down to hard work at his books and completed high school in reasonably good scholastic standing. He was pleased when he was accepted for matriculation at Dartmouth. The town of Hanover, New Hampshire, seemed far out in the backwoods, far away from New York's bustle and excitement and a likely place to do some hard work. That, he decided, was what he was looking for.

# Education

When Nelson Rockefeller arrived at Dartmouth College in the autumn of 1926 he was eighteen years old, a stocky and broad-shouldered boy with a heavy shock of curly brown hair that usually tumbled over his forehead and big hands that always seemed to be in his way. Like most of the six hundred or more other freshmen, he was a youthful combination of superficial self-confidence, brashness, naïveté and uncertainty but he had had a big summer and he kept telling himself that now he was going to settle down and prepare himself for a useful life.

His summer had ranged from Seal Harbor to Long Island to France and it included several experiences that he related in letters to his parents in rather revealing fashion. After a weekend at the eastern end of Long Island with two young friends, Ted Martin and Tad Bullock, he had boarded the S. S. *Aquitania* for Europe and promptly wrote home in an effort to forestall the possibly unhappy results of a motoring incident.

Aboard S.S. Aquitania
June 20, 1926

Dear Ma and Pa,
 . . . When we were driving back [from the end of Long Island] we were coming along on a peachy straight concrete road with nobody

29

in sight. I opened up the cut-out and stepped on it. Way down the road ahead there was a car parked. We came roaring along and when I got near I opened up a couple of whistles, and we sped by. Well, the trouble lay in that there was a cop on the other side of that car. Ted having already assured me there were no cops on that part of the Island. Well, you can imagine what happened after that. Naturally, I got a ticket. After he was all through writing it out, I called him over and told him I was sorry but I couldn't come to court as I was sailing. He said that was all right that Ted could go in my place. Then I told him that I didn't want it to go in in my name as the papers would be liable to get hold of it. He said it had to go down in the book but he thought that if Ted came around and saw him before the trial he would be able to fix it up by putting Ted's name in instead of mine. He asked if I was trying to hide my arrest from my father and I said no, I would tell you. . . . We parted friendly. He was a nice fellow!

The next letter was written after he and his brother John had arrived in France to make a bicycle tour. They visited some picturesque and interesting places but

> . . . Havre was far less attractive and much more commercial. Everybody rushed about, making a lot of noise which I don't think is very becoming to the French. They get all excited. . . . I bought some lovely etchings of Rouen. . . . They cost about fifty francs and Johnny thought it was a horrible waste of money but I finally got him to pay for them (he is treasurer at present). I think they are quite a find. We are both crazy about Mount Saint Michel . . . oh, it was great. . . . Everywhere we've been we've found nothing but nice people. . . .

And a later letter, July 11, 1926, from the Grand Hôtel de France (Blois):

> . . . You know a very sad thing happened on my birthday. We were at Tours at the time and . . . we happened to be taking an all day bicycle tour of the chateaus. . . . We went on all day enjoying the sights, all the while oblivious of that all important fact. And to tell you the truth, it was not until about six, just before we got home, that Johnny happened to think of it. To celebrate the occasion, we

went to a cafe-movie house, where we spent half the night drinking
lemonade and watching Pola Negri in an American movie. (It
wasn't so hot; in fact, afterwards, we wished we had gone to bed.
But it was fun as an experience.)

There were two other developments worthy of mention after
Nelson returned from Europe. Mrs. Rockefeller did considerable worrying about the kind of friends her son would choose at college. She
talked the problem over with Mrs. Mary M. Billings French, with
whom she served on the board of the Y.W.C.A., and discovered that
Mrs. French's son, John, also was going to be a freshman at Dartmouth. In no time at all, they decided that it would be a good thing
if their sons were roommates at college. It is unlikely that anything
worse could happen to a college freshman than to have his mother
pick his roommate, but the two women decided at least to give it a
try by getting the boys together, and one day late in the summer the
Frenches paid a visit to the Rockefellers at Pocantico Hills. John
was a slight, quiet boy with light hair and a shy smile. He had been
a star student in high school and he was as much of an introvert as
Nelson was an extrovert. Yet, they seemed to get along all right at
their first meeting, probably because John seemed deceptively timid
and Nelson was always aggressively determined to make anybody and
everybody feel at home. Their mothers were pleased and it was
arranged that they would room together at Hanover. This, as it turned
out, was one of the best things that ever happened to Nelson. During
four years at college, the two boys would have their quarrels and
their periods of mutual resentment for one reason or another but,
to a great extent, they complemented each other almost perfectly.
John was quiet and inclined to spend too much time alone; Nelson
was always on the go and trying to do more things than one boy
could handle. John was a brilliant student and, fortunately, this
aroused not so much Nelson's envy as his intensely competitive
spirit. "He was a tremendous influence," Nelson said many years later.
"He was brilliant but I was damned if I was going to let him take
me. So I worked."

Before leaving for Hanover, Nelson had a long talk with his father

and assured him that he intended to make the most of college. He
also asked him for advice.

"Do you think it would be all right if I call on Dr. Hopkins when
I get to Hanover?"

"I'm not sure I would do that," his father replied. "Don't you
think it might seem like an intrusion?"

Nelson nodded but he was obviously disappointed.

"Well," his father went on, "now that I think it over perhaps it
would be all right because I know it would be to pay your respects
to Dr. Hopkins, whom you like."

So, when he arrived in Hanover, Nelson started his college career
the way he liked to start any new enterprise—by getting in touch
with the head man. But the next day he quickly discovered that he
was just another freshman on the Dartmouth campus.

## II.

The freshmen matriculated and fixed up their rooms on the first
day at Hanover. Nelson, without his mother's assistance, had already
arranged to get together at college with Sheldon Stark, whom he had
known at the Lincoln School, and Randolph Martin, and the three
of them moved their belongings into two dormitory rooms where
John French joined them for the first semester. (Thereafter Nelson
and John were together in their own rooms.) Mrs. Rockefeller had
shipped furnishings for Nelson's room to Hanover but the bed was
too big and he had to send it back to be cut down to size.

"But hurry," he wrote his mother, "because at present I am using
a $6 mattress that I got for temporary use. We have all four desks in
our room and it looks pretty business like. Not much in the other
room yet."

The second day, the sophomores arrived and the freshmen were
put in their place. They had to wear little green caps. Nelson was
summoned to help move sophomore trunks to sophomore rooms.
He was sent on errands and he was ordered to shine shoes and beat
rugs. The pressure of hazing didn't let up all day, and by the time

he and his roommates went around to Ma Smalley's boardinghouse for supper they were exhausted and wondering whether college life was really worth while. They were still more doubtful when they returned to their dormitory rooms, only to be aroused at nine o'clock by sophomore shouts of "Class of '30 out—'30 out!" Then they had to file down to the large hall of the dormitory where upperclassmen were congregated. The thirty freshmen in the dormitory were ordered to line up and answer questions and perform silly stunts. Those who were slow were whacked across the bottom with large wooden paddles. They were heckled and ridiculed and generally given a rough time, not being released until after midnight. The hazing went on for three days and nights, getting rougher all the time. On Friday there was a freshman-sophomore football "rush" or general brawl in which three freshmen were knocked cold. "I remember Nelson pushing and shoving," a friend said later. "His shirt had been torn off his back, but he was laughing like crazy and having the time of his life." That night the hazing was worse than ever, particularly after several sophomores got hold of some bootleg liquor. The rough treatment and especially the rough language shocked Nelson.

> . . . I never in my life heard such swearing and such language [he wrote later]. . . . Five freshmen got knocked out that night, one fellow from our dorm. . . . He was a peachy sport about it. . . . Saturday we all had to dress up. Our dorm was given a pair of socks, a triangular piece of cloth, a baby's bonnet and a rattle, per freshman. Besides this we were allowed to wear our underclothes. Luckily, it was warm, for we had to wear this costume, if you could call it that, all day. After the football game, which Dartmouth won 59 to 0, all hazing was over and we all came home and went to bed. I've never been so tired in all my life. I hadn't had six hours for the last three days. . . . I've been to church twice today [Sunday]. It certainly seemed good to get back into such a peaceful atmosphere. Well, despite all the paddling, etc. we've gotten for the past week, we've enjoyed it.

Nelson quickly got into the Dartmouth routine and the Dartmouth uniform of unpressed corduroy knickers or pants and green sweater or sweatshirt. He was as sloppy as anybody on the campus and far more exuberant than most about everything except such extracurricular activities as Saturday-night trips to Lebanon for illegal beer. He didn't drink—"I just never felt that I needed a drink to have a good time"—and he didn't smoke. He enjoyed such social occasions as there were during the school year and he spent a lot of time making friends, particularly with boys who were far from home. There were two Japanese freshmen, for example, to whom he introduced himself and with whom he became friendly, and there were several boys who were working their way through college among his particular group of friends. But, even as a freshman, he had a remarkable knack for being honest and direct in such friendships and avoiding condescension.

> I recently returned from a visit to Dartmouth College where my son is a student [a mid-Western man wrote to Mr. Rockefeller]. . . . I feel I should express to you the high opinion I formed of the young man [Nelson] from my recent observations of him and also express to you an appreciation which I think every father who has a son in Dartmouth owes to you because of the modest manner in which Nelson lives at the school. I know that it has had a beneficial effect on my boy and has made the burden of sending him to Dartmouth considerably lighter.

"He was," one classmate, Pete Calloway, said many years later, "an honest-to-God Christian, thoughtful of others and completely without prejudice. Another boy and I lived too far away to go home at Christmastime, for instance, and when Nelson heard that we were going to be in a cheap hotel in New York during vacation he invited us to have Christmas dinner with his family. I thought that was something when you consider what a personal family affair Christmas dinner usually is. It was quite an experience for us. All of the Rockefeller family was there and they treated us as if we were members of the family. After dinner, Mrs. Rockefeller took us up to the top floor to see her wonderful collection of Japanese prints, and later she took us to the theater. At college, Nelson may have been the worst-dressed boy on the campus. At least, he was certainly casual. He didn't like 'show,' and the fact that the family had money just didn't enter into his friendships at Dartmouth. He felt at home with everybody and everybody felt at home with him."

This apparently was less of an overstatement than might seem likely at first glance, although there were at least a few students who didn't like the Rockefeller heir or his ways. He was defeated at one time when he ran for a class office and at least one boy changed his place at table at Ma Smalley's boardinghouse because he didn't like Nelson's manners. But for the most part he made friends easily and widely. He did not have to make any special effort to be liked and in one class election he polled a record vote for vice-president.

"Making friends was no problem for him psychologically," one student remarked. "On the other hand, I don't believe he had many really intimate friends. He helped or tried to help several students who were having a difficult time financially but he may have instinctively tried to avoid intimate friendships because of the possibility that someone would impose on the family name or money."

Nelson wrote to his parents after a couple of months at college that he had "met some awfully nice fellows already. But I'm sort of going slowly at first so as not to make any mistakes. Anyhow, I don't have much chance to go visiting." His days were crowded because he needed a lot of time for study and, later, because he was on many committees or involved in strenuous campus activities. He crawled out of bed at 7 A.M. and had breakfast, sometimes cold cereal with cream and a glass of milk because he could keep such food in his room. He made his own bed and straightened up his own room and vacuumed the carpet. "The janitor made such a mess of things that I told him to keep out." He studied from 8 to 10 A.M. and then attended classes until mid-afternoon, when he went to practice with the soccer team on which he eventually became a regular. After supper he studied until about 9 P.M., when he and his roommate took a break to eat some cake or candy or whatever Mrs. Rockefeller may have sent him by mail. Sometimes another boy or two might drop by his room and there would be half an hour of talk, or perhaps he and John French would chat for a while before going back to their books, but none of his classmates recalls him as a regular at dormitory bull sessions. When he did take part in such talk fests, he was likely to discuss religion or ethics or human relationships. "He always seemed to have minority people—the downtrodden—on his mind," one classmate summed up. "But he wasn't a great talker and he didn't seem to think that he had the answers to all the world's problems as some of us did. He was more of a doer than a heavy thinker."

Nelson had a phonograph and a stack of records in his room but he did not play them often and, in fact, showed no great interest in music until much later, when he became enamored of jazz bands. "But he enjoyed dancing," a classmate recalls, "and at such parties as we had Nelson usually tried to dance with every girl there before the evening ended." His college allowance was a modest $1,500, out of which he was supposed to pay almost all his college expenses. He was also supposed to keep accurate accounts of his receipts and expenditures and to check them over with his father at regular intervals. Because of his tendency to look at numbers in reverse, he often inscribed the wrong figures and his accounts were sometimes in a hopeless tangle that distressed Mr. Rockefeller. "Pa has a completely orderly mind," Nelson once explained. "Mine was somewhat disorderly in that respect." As a result, he was frequently broke and had to borrow money from John French or others to go to the movies or to patronize the campus sandwich wagon. Once he decided to pick up some extra cash by waiting on table at the boardinghouse but quickly gave up the idea when someone pointed out that he might be taking work away from a boy who really needed the money. He had no automobile at school, although many students did, and during his first year he observed his father's suggestion that he should not go on the college football trips, in which large numbers of students participated. When the Dartmouth team played Yale, for example, the campus was almost deserted for the weekend and Nelson entertained himself by going for a long walk in the woods, where he picked up four bright red and yellow autumn leaves to enclose in a letter to his mother with a wish that she could see the beauty of the countryside. He also missed the Harvard game, but one of President Hopkins' assistants showed up with an automobile and a hamper of food and took Nelson and several other boys to a hunting cabin in the woods, where they ate and had a snowball fight. "I don't know when I've had such a good time. And I think it did us all a world of good."

He devoted an increasing amount of time to campus affairs. He was one of six freshmen appointed to run the class "Informals"—a kind of social meeting once a week under supervision of the Student Council—and he was also on the Chapel Committee.

> I have been very fortunate [he wrote his parents in reference to the Chapel Committee]. It is our duty to criticize the service and make suggestions to improve it . . . in conjunction with the faculty committee. . . .
>
> By some mishap, I was appointed chairman of the Informals Committee, so that now I am responsible for the speaker and entertainment for our Wednesday night class gatherings. . . . I've learned two things from this work. First, I've lost my feeling of incompetency, of not being able to handle a job without relying on someone else. In other words, if something has to be done . . . I feel that I'm fully capable of doing it and will know or have some idea of how to go about it without an inward fear. And, secondly, I'm losing my fear of standing up before a crowd and saying what I've got to say, for I have to preside. . . .
>
> I went over . . . to the White Church [on the corner of the campus] to see if I could get a job there and, as luck would have it, one of the [Sunday school] teachers is going to have to leave his class, so I will take his place. I wanted a permanent job, so I'm very well satisfied.

At the White Church, he had a regular class of eight- to ten-year-old girls. He enjoyed these Sunday-morning sessions and frequently wrote to his mother about his experiences as a teacher. His class was well behaved except for two youngsters who insisted on talking and giggling. He finally gave up hoping to get them interested and had them sit at one side of the room so they would not disturb the class. At the end of the term, he wrote his parents that "I shall miss my little girls very much. I wish I had been able to do more for them."

When he went to Dartmouth, Nelson had a decidedly unfavorable view of college fraternities. French was inclined to agree with him and in the spring of 1927 they composed a letter criticizing the fraternity "rushing" system because it interfered with scholastic pursuits.

> Johnny and I wrote a vox pop [letter to the school paper] today on the question of fraternity rushing. If it is printed I will send it to you. You see, we don't have time to fool around with the fraternities yet; and we get about seven invitations every Sunday for open house. Then, too, the boys are all the time coming around to our rooms. . . .
> I'm going out in the woods now with Johnny to hunt for wild flowers and moss [for window boxes they had put up in their room]. The flower boxes are coming along fine . . . they're something new for a dormitory room and there's lots of talk . . . but I really think most everybody sort of envies them, although they kind of hate to admit it. . . .
> All the freshmen rules were taken off . . . and we don't have to wear little caps any longer and can walk on the grass. . . .

Another letter in April said that Nelson had become very much interested in photography and had joined the photography club. He was taking pictures of a lacrosse game with Yale and a baseball game with Boston College which were being played on adjacent fields one Saturday when he met his physics professor.

> We sat down on the top of the grandstand where we could see both the games—one on each side of the stand. Before long the President came walking along, so we hailed him and he came up and joined us. And for the next two hours we three had a most enjoyable time—eating peanuts, telling stories and watching the games. A very worthwhile afternoon!!

The antifraternity article written by Nelson and John French was published and caused considerable comment, but Nelson wrote that "nobody was sore about it; most of them said we just didn't understand the rushing system." By this time—mid-April—the two boys were accepting invitations to various fraternity houses and beginning to get a different view of the system.

... I suppose we ought to go to some of the open houses although I do find them an awful waste of time. The callers are still as numerous as ever. Fifteen fellows came around Thursday night and not all at once either. I don't know what it will be like when rushing starts officially. It certainly is hard on your studies . . . but I guess there is nothing to be done about it.

And a few days later:

Now that I am getting to know some of the boys I quite enjoy going to the open houses. They always ask Johnny and me together, which makes it still more enjoyable.

On May 24:

Last night the Phi Gamma Deltas gave a feed at one of the Outing Club cabins and asked about 15 freshmen. I went and had a great time. We played baseball before supper and then after supper we sat around and sang songs and I finally walked home in the moonlight with Gerry Swope and another boy. I got to know a lot of very nice fellows and I think the "feed" was a good idea—only it must be rather expensive for the fraternity. Tonight I am going to the following fraternities—Alpha Delta Phi, Psi Upsilon and Sigma Alpha. I'm really getting to know an awful lot of fellows going around this way and if it didn't take up so much time it would be great. . . . I do enjoy everything so much up here.

A few days later, when Nelson heard that his brother Laurance had decided to go to Princeton, he expressed doubt that it was a wise decision and indicated that Dartmouth might be a better choice.

I certainly like the friendly attitude up here [as compared to a big school like Princeton]. Why, by now I think Johnny and I know—to speak to—all of what are known as the Big Men on campus.

Nelson and John French eventually became members of Psi Upsilon, but they never lived at the fraternity house. In their senior year, they lived in the house of the senior society Casque and Gauntlet, to which both belonged, and slept in a long row of beds in the society dormitory—a room that was reputed to be the coldest spot in Hanover.

Nelson's first college year did nothing to establish his reputation as a scholar but it did a great deal to establish him as a busy and well-liked man around the campus. "He has two particular qualities," President Hopkins commented at the end of the year. "One, his fearlessness in expressing convictions to which he has come after serious thought, and the other, his willingness to revise his opinion on the submission of new evidence or the acquiring of new acquaintance-ship with the facts. . . . A man becomes a priceless member of the college who shows the disposition and the capacity to think things out himself. . . . It is a great gratification to me that Nelson is so definitely one of this sort."

III.

It was rather remarkable that in his last three years of college Nelson added a certain degree of scholastic attainment to his record, despite the fact that his campus activities steadily increased. His freshman year had suggested that he wasn't going to be able to get out of the rut into which he had fallen in high school.

October, 1926—As for physics . . . the prof is great. . . . As soon as we get well started, I'm going around to see him some evening. You see, my idea has been to get to know the teachers as soon as possible. . . . I felt I would get more out of the courses if there was more of a personal relationship between the teacher and I. . . . I have figured out I will need to do about 36 hours of studying [a week] which means 6 hours every day. . . .

November, 1926—Had lunch at Dr. Hopkins and dinner with a professor's family.

January, 1927—Got a C in French—first time I haven't been at the bottom of the class, so I feel pretty good. . . . Since Christmas vacation . . . I've not been as interested in study. . . . I don't seem to care . . . have no fear of exams. . . . It is really very interesting for me to watch and see the funny way my feelings have been acting of late.

When he returned to school in the autumn of 1927, however, he began to show the benefits of association with John French. He still was busy with soccer—"please be a little careful, not too reckless in the games . . . remember you will need your teeth and nose and legs again," his mother urged—and other nonscholastic activities and, as vice-president of the sophomore class, he took a leading role in a memorable campus brawl with the freshmen the following spring. The battle grew out of defiance by the freshmen of the rules imposed on them by upperclassmen. A freshman flag was run up as a sign of revolt. Sophomores tried to take it down. There were numerous fist fights and some of the freshmen class officers were "kidnaped" and tied up. At one point, a group of freshmen attempted to storm a sophomore dormitory which Nelson and a group of classmates were defending. Nelson got a black eye in the first clash but he managed to get hold of a fire hose, which he dragged to the door of the dormitory and turned on the freshmen, holding them off until reinforcements arrived. Later, the undergraduate governing body decided to settle the class dispute by staging an organized fight on the campus. A long rope was stretched in the center of the campus and the freshmen lined up on one side. The sophomores lined up on the other, with the class vice-president in the van. A cannon was fired and the two classes fought to carry the rope to specified goals. For the most part, the rope was forgotten and the classes fought each other for an hour with the freshmen getting the best of it until the Hanover city police arrived to put an end to the brawl. The fighting was good for news stories in the big city newspapers and the Boston *Herald* carried a headline saying:

JOHN D., JR., SON
MAULED IN FIGHT

Plays Heroic Part as Freshmen Best Sophomores
at Dartmouth

Many in Encounter
Knocked into Coma

Nelson apparently feared this publicity might cause his father distress and promptly wrote him, explaining the circumstances. His father, however, was more pleased than annoyed and replied that his son must have experienced a lot of fun when he got hold of that firehose.

Campus brawls, however, didn't mean Nelson was neglecting his books. He had learned how to concentrate and to make far better use of his natural abilities. "Nelson didn't learn easily or quickly," John French once remarked, "but he was conscientious and persistent. He studied every evening and studied hard. He didn't let anything interrupt him." Basically, what happened was that Nelson couldn't stand to be shown up by French, who easily was elected to Phi Beta Kappa in his junior year. He worked because he was competing with his roommate but the result was highly satisfactory—two A's and three B's at the end of the semester, which put him in the highest three per cent of his class.

His father wired him that he was "bursting with pride" at the good marks and his mother wrote:

> I really and truly nearly shed tears of joy when Papa read me President Hopkins' letter telling us of your good marks. Of course, I have always realized that you had a good mind but I feared (a little) that you might never or at least for some time know what you could do with it. . . . Dear boy, your life, if it is to be really useful, consecrated and successful will need all the brains, all the courage, all the wisdom and all the patience that you have in you and when you use wisely all that is in you, thus more will be given you. . . . I am sure that you have the power but it must be harnessed to steadiness and a desire for perfection.

It would be erroneous to suggest that Nelson suddenly learned to be patient or orderly or to concentrate his abilities along a given line. But he had learned that when he could bring himself to work hard and systematically he could achieve his goal. It was a lesson he would frequently forget in the future but he would always come back to it when the chips were down. He continued to keep his scholastic record up at college, and eventually earned a Phi Beta Kappa key.

"When John French heard that I'd made Phi Beta Kappa," Nelson recalled later, "he said that if a plugger like me could make it he was going to throw away his Phi Beta Kappa key. He later denied saying it, but I remember it very clearly."

In his junior year, Nelson was more active in Psi Upsilon, he was a regular on the soccer team, he was editor of the college publication *Pictorial* (for which he took many photographic studies himself), he still conducted his Sunday-school class, he held several campus offices and he was in Green Key—an honorary society whose members were chosen by election. "I was very lucky," he wrote home, "and came out ahead." Despite all these and other activities, his grades held up and in October of 1928 he was notified by the head of the economics department that he was eligible for the honors group. "I went around to see him and he convinced me that the honors group was the thing—consequently I'm going into it. . . . It means a little bit more work, but a lot more to be gotten out of the course."

As a member of the honors group, he decided that he should cut down drastically on his outside activities and he resigned from everything except the *Pictorial* and the Outing Club. "I'm feeling more and more strongly," he told his parents, "that outside activities are a waste of time and that if one wants to get much of anything out of college, he had better devote his time to studies and the more cultural aspects of life."

I'm thankful to say that at last I've had the chance to start on a reconstruction program for my work [he wrote his parents on November 14, 1928].

. . . The economics honors work is turning out to be very interesting. . . . After Thanksgiving, we each take any business we want and make a complete survey of it and then apply the economic principles we have been studying. Of course, I have chosen the Standard Oil Company for my study.

I think it will be extremely interesting as I am ashamed to say that I know comparatively little about it. I was thinking the other day that Grandfather has never mentioned the Company to us, nor has he ever told us anything about his stupendous work in organizing the Company and leading it for so many years. In our work, and as time goes by, we will continually be hearing and learning about the Standard Oil Company but always from outside sources. It seems to me, therefore, that if it could be possibly arranged in some way to get Grandfather to tell us sometime maybe a little about his experiences, that it would be invaluable to all of us. And I can't emphasize this point too strongly. It would be an outstanding and unforgettable experience in our lives, I am sure. If you would consider this, and maybe take it up with Grandfather—if you thought it worth while— I certainly would appreciate it. . . . It would be perfect if he could possibly do it this vacation as I will at that time just be launching on a study of the Company, and then, too, Grandfather will not be back with us for a long time after that.

Mr. Rockefeller replied that he was sure that his father would be willing to talk to Nelson about the Standard Oil Company. He also arranged to send him the manuscript of a history of the life of John D. Rockefeller, Sr., which was written by a former employee who had had many long talks with the founder of the company. This was a very flattering account of the elder Rockefeller's career and one that was never published, but it delighted Nelson and threw him into one of his "all-out" moods.

. . . I don't know when anything has interested me more than this study [of the Standard Oil Company]—it really was thrilling! For the first time I felt that I really knew Grandfather a little—got a glimpse into the power and grandeur of his life. The night I finished reading the . . . biography, I wanted to write Grandfather and tell him what I had never realized before. But after several weak attempts at expressing my feelings I gave it up. For the first time, I realized the significance of his life and its influence for good on this earth and I was just left speechless. . . .

I sincerely feel that I got more out of reading that book than I did out of any other course last semester. . . . Among other things it brought out the importance and value of money. And I was able to

see as never before the reason and true significance of keeping accounts as you have always asked us to do. As I thought over the
principles behind the mechanics of keeping accounts it dawned upon
me that I have up to now merely been obeying the letter of the law,
as it were, and not the spirit, and that I have been missing the whole
point. Therefore, I have been sailing under false colors, as it were,
and as much as I appreciate your very generous bonus of $100.00 I
don't feel I can accept it—at least not until I have attained the real
goal and not merely an artificial one. Therefore, with many thanks,
I am returning it by enclosing a check for $100.

Nelson never did get to talk to his grandfather about the Standard
Oil Company, possibly because the old man just didn't want to
discuss the past, but he wrote a forty-five-page thesis on the company
and got an A on it in Economics II. The thesis examined the methods and the reasons behind the creation of the Standard Oil
monopoly by amalgamation of many small companies, and it looked
into the problem of free competition—largely from the viewpoint of
an efficient monopolist. No historian will ever mistake the thesis
for an objective history nor will any reader learn the unpleasant
facts of ruthless business competition, but a few excerpts are interesting as reflections of Nelson's thinking at the time.

> Mr. Rockefeller, with his abhorrence of waste and his accurate
> methods of accounting, always knew to a penny the state of the
> business and saw to it that every drop of oil, every piece of machinery
> and every man in the enterprise was doing full service. . . . These
> men [the executives of the company] showed from the beginning a
> quicker insight into new conditions and a readier flexibility in ad-
> justing themselves to meet new problems than most of their rivals.
> . . . From the very start, Mr. Rockefeller saw he was going to need
> lots of ready money and in many instances at short notice. And as
> he himself says, he wore holes in the knees of his trousers begging
> for money from the banks. . . . They all worked hard, often getting
> to the office at six-thirty and staying until nine at night. When there
> was no work in the office to be done, Mr. Rockefeller used to go out
> and work in the refinery wherever a hand was needed. His life long
> policy towards his workers was to expect one hundred per cent of

faithful effort from them, and in return he gave fair play and a wage at least as high as, usually higher than, the prevailing market rates. . . . When a fire broke out in the refineries, as they often did in the early days, everybody in the firm turned out to help fight it. While the fire was still burning, Mr. Rockefeller could be seen with paper and pencil, making plans for the rebuilding. . . . No time was ever lost. You may wonder why so much time has been devoted to such seemingly unimportant details. But it is these little things on the inside of the Company which, when put together, mount up so far, that have always been overlooked by people who study the Standard Oil. . . .

. . . it might be well to mention a very important point and one that has never been understood by the public—namely the reason for Mr. Rockefeller's silence all through the history of the Standard Oil Company in the face of the bitterest attack and slander. There are two main reasons: 1. That the accusations were false and therefore would fall of their own weight when time had revealed the truth. 2. That if any public explanation of the real reasons for the great and quick success of the Company were attempted it might have been made so full and explicit that it would necessarily invite other capitalists to come into the business and do likewise. Then, too . . . a genius for silence was born in [Mr. Rockefeller]. . . . The inevitable result of the policy of silence was the creation of a myth that the company undermined or oppressed or crushed out competitors—a hardy fiction which has diminished but slowly under the impact of fact. . . .

[The thesis then discussed the ruinous competition in the oil industry and said Mr. Rockefeller's idea was to combine for the protection of all and that the Standard Oil Company assumed all the risks at a time when it was evident that the larger number of competitors could not continue.]

Those who didn't wish to come in could go on just as before. They were not forced to sell out their business under threats of being crushed out, nor were any of them coerced into selling. But, as Mr. Rockefeller himself says, "We left them to the mercy of time. They could not hope to compete with us." . . . Many cases were reported . . . in which the smaller companies were treated unmercifully. Nearly all of these have been reviewed since and in every one the facts prove unquestionably that these companies were treated with extreme fairness and in many cases with generosity. This is a very broad statement to make, but I have the facts to back it up. . . .

[The thesis then discussed Standard Oil arrangements for rebates from the railroads and other business practices which were justified as being accepted at the time, and it suggested that "the exigencies of politics required that the Republican party after the election of 1904 should display a spirit of reform" that led to prosecution of the monopolists.]

The Standard is often said to have gained its monopoly power through local price discrimination, bogus independents and espionage. These charges were all proven to be false, except in a few rare instances throughout the country, in 1906 when the Company was up before the federal courts. . . . Grandfather once said that in the old days that if a man would slip on a banana peel and fall down, he'd jump up and turn around and curse the Standard Oil Company. . . .

By the means of their monopoly power, the Standard Oil Company stabilized the producing as well the refining business. It had been a fluctuating, haphazard business under a reign of cut-throat competition. . . . Mr. Rockefeller said that at no time did the Standard Oil Company lose money, even under the worst conditions. . . . The highest percentage of earnings to net assets in any year was in 1903 when the percentage was a little over thirty per cent and the highest percentage of dividends paid was in the year 1900, when the dividends were nearly 25 per cent of the net assets. Now, there is no doubt that this was much more than a fair return on their investment. And, of course, these large earnings came only through high prices which in their turn were made possible by the monopolistic position of the Standard Oil Company. . . . If things had developed without the Standard monopoly, prices would probably have been somewhat lower, but the profits would probably have been proportionately much lower and the industry most likely would not have developed nearly as fast. The Standard took in profits that would have otherwise gone to waste—that is, of course, not wholly true but I think it is to a large extent. . . . It is fair to judge that the Standard monopoly did restrict to a considerable degree the proper allocation of capital. It is a questionable matter whether the benefits of the Standard monopoly offset the resulting high price and improper allocation of capital.

Probably they don't.

Mr. Rockefeller, Jr., read the thesis and told his son that he had "a fine, breezy, charming style" and that he had done very creditable work. Mr. Rockefeller, Sr., never read it.

IV.

Throughout his first three years in college, Nelson gave the impression that he was determined not to miss anything that went on and his parents frequently warned him to be careful of his health.

"Don't forget the milk; sleep as much as you can," his mother wrote him many times. Once she remarked that he looked thin when she visited him at Hanover and said that she was sending more food by mail. She worried about his health after Nelson joined most of the student body in digging out victims of a serious flood near White River Junction in November of 1927, and the next fall she wrote him that she was "glad to know that you are going to bed early and taking better care of yourself."

His plan to get to bed early apparently was short-lived because he wrote her in December of 1928 that "this is the 52nd letter I've written since I got back [from Thanksgiving vacation] . . . and I still have quite a way to go. I planned to do nothing but work when I got back and I've done everything but. This afternoon I had six meetings of various committees and organizations and I have three tomorrow afternoon. I'm trying to back out of things as much as possible. I've definitely decided to quit soccer next fall."

In this period, Nelson was struggling at intervals to face up to life and decide what he was going to do about his career. As with everything, he was inclined to approach the problem directly and energetically, a little as if he were playing soccer and needed only to concentrate on driving the ball between the goal posts. He wasn't very sure, unhappily, of where the goal posts were, and he kept casting around for guidance. In the summer of 1928, he again had gone to Europe, where he lived for a while with a large French family at Le Mont-Dore and met numerous European youngsters with whom he played tennis and went on automobile trips. One night on such a trip they were unable to get hotel accommodations and had to sleep "in a hay loft in a tiny village. In the morning we stripped to the waist and washed and shaved at the town fountain. All the peasants stood around and watched us as if they had never seen any one wash before." The trip showed him a new side of life and made him eager to know more.

> Some people have to learn by experience and I'm afraid I'm one of them [he wrote his parents later]. Maybe the summer after next we [William Alton and Nelson] will go on sort of a bumming trip and follow the seasonal day laborers in the West from one harvest to another. I'm very anxious to get the day laborer's point of view if I can before I start work. It seems to me that it would be very valuable to know what kind of a life they lead and to go from one place to another trying to get a job and experience some of the hardships that are so common. . . . It would make me appreciate far more the wonderful opportunity with which I have been blessed —it is so easy to take all the comforts of life which have so plentifully come to me more or less for granted. . . .

In regard to his business career, Nelson seemed to feel that his ambitions might be stymied if he went into his father's office or attended only to family affairs. His father wrote once:

> In the college atmosphere where the point of view and environment is so different from that in which you have been brought up, I don't wonder that it is easy to lose track at times of the family point of view. On the whole, however, the family point of view is a pretty safe foundation to work on, even if the structure which you may rear thereon is somewhat different from those which others have built.

In the summer of 1929, young Rockefeller brought up the problem again.

Another thing that has been taking up my thoughts of late is the question of what I'll do when I graduate. Frankly, I don't relish the idea of going into some business—not that I don't think I could make a go of it—but there is nothing very appealing, challenging about it. Just to work my way up in a business that another man has built, stepping from the shoes of one to those of another, making a few minor changes here and there and then, finally, perhaps at the age of sixty, getting to the top where I would have real control for a few years. No, that isn't my idea of living a real life. . . .

His son's impatience, his urge to move rapidly and on his own did not disturb Mr. Rockefeller, Jr., unduly. In his letters and his conversations, he called Nelson's attention to the opportunities which leadership in a large enterprise offered for developing friendly relations between employer and employee, for creating good working and living conditions, for introducing fair and adequate wages as well as for taking the lead in turning out a product of high quality at reasonable prices. Seeing that such a vision of business leadership interested Nelson, he reminded him that more and more younger men were coming into leadership of large American industries, so that there would be no need to wait until he was sixty to make his influence strongly felt.

You will know [he pointed out on one occasion], that, while I shall be glad if you boys find your life work in some of the manifold lines which your father and grandfather have been working in, so long as you earn your living in some worthwhile occupation, where there is opportunity for real service, I shall be satisfied. The decision of where that shall be can only be made by each individual. . . . Time helps to solve so many problems and make clear so many paths. Fortunately, there is no haste . . . and I feel sure that as the days and months go by you will get added light.

When Nelson was home on vacations, Mr. Rockefeller frequently invited his interest in various family affairs, asked him to attend board meetings to talk with his associates or spend an afternoon going over plans for some enterprise. "The thought of having you commence to get in touch with these problems, to which I have given so much time and thought," he said, "gives me the greatest pleasure.

I am sure you will find them immensely interesting and absorbing."

Although Nelson took most things in stride, he occasionally suffered remorse because he felt that he took life too lightly. In the spring of 1929 his concentration on having a good time caused his mother to write him a letter of reprimand. In his reply, as usual, he went overboard in dramatically denouncing himself for acts that could not have been very serious, but which he managed to magnify into heinous crimes.

> Dear Ma,
>
> I have just received your letter and coming as it has along with several other things it has been a great lesson to me. All of a sudden, like the lifting of a heavy fog, I realize for the first time how unutterably selfish and thoughtless I have been getting to be. It stands out in bold relief and glares me in the face—I don't see how I could have kept on the way I've been acting. My own interests have been the only ones which I have taken into consideration and I have plunged on wildly, disregarding everything and everybody. . . .
>
> . . . What can I do now? I'd like to hide from everything, back out of all the complications I'm in, none of them serious, but all the results of my selfishness. But to run from them would add cowardice to my selfishness. To apologize does no good. I spend half my time saying I'm sorry and I'm going right ahead and doing the same or a worse thing. To think you and Pa have gone on uncomplainingly— both of you with 100 times the number of responsibilities that I have—and purely to add to my own amusement and convenience I've left the arrangement of details and asked you both to do things for me that I have no right to ask anyone to do—much less you two who have done everything for me. Both of you have been so unselfish, patient, thoughtful and kind. . . . From this very minute, I will lead a new life . . . that will not be centered around myself. . . . I shall try in a small measure to make up for the discomfort I have caused you both in the past. God alone knows how humble I feel.
>
> Your thoughtless son,
> Nelson

Any parents might have been justifiably alarmed by such a letter but, knowing Nelson, the Rockefellers doubtless took it calmly.

In his senior year, Nelson was made a senior fellow and President Hopkins advised Mr. Rockefeller that it was a deserved honor. He wrote that Nelson may have been "a little handicapped by his name" during his college career but

> I think unusual importance should be attached to the fact that Nelson has won for himself an esteem and an affection which has carried him through to prominent undergraduate position by election of his fellows and has now won him the special recommendation of the committee to assist me in picking senior fellows. The common remark of the undergraduates, in their own vernacular, has been: "Nelson rates it and ought to have it." . . . I have been delighted to see Nelson's steady progress, his spirit of indefatigable industry, and the balance and sanity of his judgment which commands increasingly the respect of all with whom he comes into contact. He is not a docile type, and he has that added power and that increased potentiality which attach to men who arrive at their eventual beliefs by questioning along the way as to whether one or another belief is valid. He embodies in his own person the attitude and the spirit which we are trying to inculcate into the college as a whole. . . . Nelson is a fine boy and greatly respected and liked by all of us.

The fellowship freed Nelson from the routine classroom work, gave him wide choice of the subjects he studied and had a rather marked effect on his future because it encouraged his interest in intellectual and aesthetic achievement as contrasted to the direct action approach which had dominated his life. Nobody should get an erroneous impression from this that he slowed down his pace or retreated to an ivory tower, because he would always be dominated by a desire for the active approach, the direct attack on problems. But, perhaps for the first time, he began to see that it was necessary not just to plug away at something but to look around at the world in which he lived and try to figure out what he wanted from it or what he would like to do about it. This idea was such a revelation to him that he wrote an article for the June, 1930, issue of the *Dartmouth Alumni Magazine* in a generous effort to share his knowledge with others. The article, amazingly, was entitled: "The Use of Leisure."

. . . In his [the student's] freshman year, everything is new. . . .
The whole year is spent in orienting himself to this strange new
world. . . . The next year a decided reaction usually sets in. The
earnest, wondering-eyed freshman goes through some strange meta-
morphosis during the summer, and comes back to college . . . a
blustering would-be man of the world. . . .

At the end of the year every sophomore must decide to what subject he wants to devote the major part of his junior and senior
years. . . . I chose economics as being most likely to be useful to me
in business. In fact, I had picked the great majority of my courses
with a view to preparing myself for a better understanding of the
problems in everyday life, present and future.

The idea of taking some courses in order to make the most of
my leisure had never entered my head. I had felt no such need for
most of my spare time was taken up with outside activities. . . .
There had been no time to delve into the many subjects that
fascinated me, no time to sit and mull over things with other fellows;
in fact, I am ashamed to say that I hadn't even stopped to think
where I was headed.

Then at the end of the year, by a stroke of great good fortune,
I received a fellowship. . . . So I decided to give up my regular major,
keep on with the outside activities, study music and explore in the
fields of architecture, painting and sculpture; subjects that I had
neglected up to then. . . . With this program I have not been tied
down to a regular unbending routine, and have been able to spend
time on the extra-curricular activities when needed. Of these, I spent
most of my time with the Arts, an organization with unlimited
possibilities of promoting interest in the various arts among the
undergraduates but one which had dropped into disrepute several
years ago as it had come into the hands of a group of light-footed
tea drinkers, at least so rumor has it. However, it was revived last
year, and due to the ability and perserverance of this year's board of
governors, with whom I had the privilege of working, the Arts came
back into its own on campus stronger than ever. . . .

Now some may wonder why a year spent in this way is more
worthwhile than one spent in the ordinary manner. Every man that
graduates from college must work at least eight hours a day, five
and a half days a week from next summer on—that is, if he ever

wants to amount to anything. And, of course, the really ambitious ones will work for much longer hours than that. However, these men are going to have a little free time on their hands from the first, and as time goes by they will have more and more, until they finally retire. The big question is, to what use will they put this time? Movies, cards, golf and gossip are all very popular forms of diversion but, when carried to an extreme, they have a decidedly narrowing influence on the individual. . . . What is the cause? Well, while in college he [the individual] is forced by popular opinion to spend what spare time he has either in extra-curricular activities or in being a good fellow with the boys. And neither of these pursuits—worthy as they may be—are very conducive to an intelligent use of leisure. . . . If a man . . . is going to have to keep his nose to the wheel for twenty or thirty years after he graduates, would it not be of infinite value to him if he could spend his last year at college totally free?

And, if you will . . . pardon the personal reference, this is exactly what I have had the privilege of doing this year. With the result that my whole attitude toward education has changed. It is no longer the old game of just doing enough work to pass the exams and get good marks. There has been no one to check up by giving me a quiz on pages 315 to 375 inclusive. I have been working for the personal joy and satisfaction derived from it. . . . I don't claim to have sprouted wings or to be any kind of an authority . . . but I have developed a growing enthusiasm and appreciation that will stay with me. . . . And to my mind colleges in the future will have to lay greater stress on training students how to use [their] freedom, for it isn't something that can be picked up after graduation. . . . I have discovered the key to the door that opens out into a field of interest totally unrelated to the material side of life. And it is now up to me to unlock this door and explore the ground lying beyond.

The broad ideas expressed in this little essay had a marked effect on the author. He did develop a real interest in art and for a while he toyed with the idea of becoming an architect. In his last year in college he and Walter Chrysler, Jr., planned to establish in New York a quarterly called *The Fine Arts Magazine*, which was to publish new and experimental poetry, prose, plays and photographs, but it died a-borning. On the other hand, Nelson took charge of The Arts organization at Dartmouth and made it exceedingly popular. For example, he started a music library of recordings in a room where students could come to listen. He also organized an outstanding program that brought such figures as Thornton Wilder, Bertrand Russell, Edna St. Vincent Millay, Harry Emerson Fosdick, Carl Sandburg and Vachel Lindsay to lecture at Dartmouth. This was the way Nelson liked to pursue the muses.

> Carl Sandburg spent Friday and Saturday here, speaking Friday night [he wrote his parents in February, 1930]. I stayed with him practically the whole time he was here and had a most intensely interesting time. He really is a very delightful person and very well informed. . . .

And on another occasion:

> I have spent most of the last two days with Vachael Lindsay, who was up here under the auspices of The Arts to recite his poetry. . . . He was charming and interesting. . . . He asked me to come and stay with him.

As the time for college graduation drew near, Nelson's enthusiasm for doing things in a big way showed up in a letter to his mother:

> . . . It is the custom here at the [fraternity] house of all getting together after exams for a few days at a cabin or somewhere. I thought that if you would approve and it would be convenient that I would ask the fellows to come down to the country [Pocantico Hills] for three or four days . . . around the eighth of June. . . . There would be absolutely no drinking and no girls. . . . We could get a few extra cots and put them upstairs outside of Johnny's and my rooms. There are twenty-one fellows in all and they are a very nice bunch. . . .

The thought of an invasion by twenty-one college boys, even if they were a very nice bunch, horrified even the Rockefellers and they tactfully switched their second son's plans to a resort hotel by promising to foot the bill up to a reasonable amount.

Nelson's graduation *cum laude* was good for several feature stories in the big city newspapers, including one that said he was one of the active sponsors of a student campaign to popularize shorts for warm weather wear on the campus. It added:

> His [Nelson's] four years at college have been marked by an economy that would be a credit to a student of very modest means. It is well known among the students that his monthly allowance has been just enough to cover his college expenses. While the majority of students have automobiles of some description . . . young Rockefeller's family allowed him to have a car only in his senior year. And that car was a cheap one, three years old.
>
> "Rocky" or "Nell," as he is known on the campus, has lived in one of the cheapest of the Dartmouth clubs and has always avoided the more expensive social events. . . . Even his clothes have been inexpensive, and those he wore on hikes were considerably the worse for wear. . . .
>
> Young Rockefeller occasionally has been visited by his father, who always stayed at the modest Inn, where rooms with meals cost but $6 a day, and he has come in an automobile which was no match in resplendence for the cars of other visiting parents.

# THREE

# Marriage and Travel

Superficially, at least, the family atmosphere in which the third generation of extremely wealthy Rockefellers grew up was nearly ideal. Mr. and Mrs. Rockefeller, Jr., were wise and moderate and devoted, and determined to give their children the opportunity to develop into normal, healthy individuals who would know their own minds and enjoy useful lives. The five brothers were encouraged to be interested in each other, they fought and quarreled no more than might have been expected and they were strongly inclined to present a united front to the world whenever necessary. Yet there were, of course, problems.

Mr. Rockefeller, Jr., was sensitive, repressed, retiring and so modest that his wife sometimes complained. He was patient in all things and acted only after thoughtful consideration. Nelson was aggressive, noisy, exuberant, careless—a complete extrovert. Mr. Rockefeller, Jr., was an only son, intensely devoted to his own father, for whom he had the utmost respect and admiration. Nelson, on the other hand, was the second of five sons and he grew up with the knowledge that his brother John would bear the brunt of family responsibility. Nelson was strongly competitive and he was reaching out from an early age in an effort to assert his own personality and to find his own place. No matter how much he loved his elder brother—and they were congenial companions—it was not in Nelson's nature to be second man on any totem pole.

As a result, Mr. Rockefeller, Jr., was at times perplexed and apprehensive about his second son. He wished that Nelson had greater patience and stability, that he had more interest—and was more accurate—in keeping accounts and that he showed promise of developing toward him a more formal relationship, such as he had experienced with his own father. He also was somewhat awed by the very close, completely free and easy, relations between Nelson and his mother, who had a remarkable ability to create a feeling of companionship with her children at any age. Mr. Rockefeller was thoughtful and tireless as a father, but he could not unbend and sometimes he could not understand youthful whims. Nor could he understand the frank, uninhibited talk—of popular music, of current fads, of escapades—in which Nelson and his mother reveled. Occasionally, he said frankly that he was horrified by their conversations.

But if Nelson was not particularly close to his father in companionship as a child, he was strongly aware of his father's constant (even if not easily expressed) love and he was very much influenced by his father's high moral character. The bloody strike against Colorado Fuel & Iron Company, in which he was pictured as the principal villain, had been both a revelation and a shock to Mr. Rockefeller, Jr., and it caused him to change his whole approach to problems of labor and of human relations. With the help of W. L. Mackenzie King, later Premier of Canada, he developed what was then an enlightened program for labor-management relations and, against some strong capitalistic opposition, promoted it effectively not only in companies where the Rockefeller interests were great but as a general policy.

> I think it cannot be too clearly seen that this is a period of transition in which Organized Labor is bound to come in for an ever increasing measure of recognition [he wrote in 1919]. The path

of wisdom on the part of managements seems to me to be that of bringing about the necessary adjustments in the most natural way and the one least liable to lead to friction.

Nelson could not avoid being strongly influenced by the family background—the stern devotion to the Baptist Church, the firm insistence on honesty, tolerance and fair play, the determination to lead not just an ethical but a useful life, the tireless effort to expend hundreds of millions of dollars wisely in a vast philanthropic program—all, possibly, an unconscious kind of penance for the manner in which the family fortune was founded in a less social-minded era. Mr. Rockefeller, Jr., provided an example of a man who had the courage to stand for and promote what he believed was right, regardless of the consequences. It was an attitude that Nelson would follow in his own career, and occasionally the consequences would be highly discomforting.

## II.

Mr. and Mrs. Rockefeller, Jr., grew up in an era when letter writing was one of the social graces and both wrote frequently to their children when the family was separated. Even when they were all in the same city—often when Nelson and his father were working in the same offices—they put into writing their thoughts on subjects that had been discussed and that they considered important. The Rockefeller children were persistent letter writers, too, but by no means as skilled. In 1928, after Nelson had visited Versailles and Rheims and inspected the postwar restoration work that was made possible largely through contributions by Mr. Rockefeller, he wrote his father that

> it makes me feel proud. I only hope that I shall grow up and live a life that will be worthy of the family name. I'm sure Johnny will because he already thinks and acts exactly like you, Pa. I see the likeness . . . more clearly every day. But as for myself—well, I'm a lot different and I don't think the same way. But I hope that despite this, I'll come out on top, as it were.

Mr. Rockefeller may have sometimes had doubts as to just where his son would come out but he expressed them only indirectly, as when he wrote to Nelson on his nineteenth birthday.

. . . It hardly seems possible that our little curly headed boy of yesterday is nineteen tomorrow, so . . . splendid a man, of whom we are very proud and of whom we have the highest hopes. What a change has come over you in the last two years. Always friendly, loveable, high-minded, it used to be almost impossible for you to apply yourself to any task or to adopt method in your work. Nor could you see the value of the daily task, nor the importance of doing it faithfully and well whether interested in it or not. Now you are a much harder task master over yourself than anyone else ever was. You have come to see the value of method, of planning your work and the importance of doing it to the best of your ability each day. Each year that passes makes me more grateful for you boys and more confident of the useful future that lies before you. . . . I am glad you wrote me so frankly and fully about your further camera bill. My chief regret was that my attitude in our several talks . . . was apparently such as to make you hesitate to tell me what you wrote. Of course, I was disappointed at your financial condition as it developed. But far more do I prize and cherish your confidence, and I cannot forgive myself when my attitude has even seemed to be such as to cause you to hesitate to talk with me freely about anything on your mind. . . . Forgive me for letting my temporary disappointment so show in my manner as to chill you and hold you aloof.

Now that you have so fully made up your mind to conduct your finances on a sound and business like basis, I know you will carry out your purpose and I will gladly do all I can to help you.

Good night, dear boy, God bless and keep you and make you a power for good in the world, is my earnest prayer.

Lovingly,

Father

And a few months later:

. . . Let me express the hope that in the spirit of the strenuous life you are living [at Dartmouth], you are not forgetting to write down your receipts and disbursements, so that your accounts will be in good shape when next we look them over.

And much later, in January of 1929:

> . . . it was a great satisfaction to me to have you bring your accounts up to date at the end of the year so completely and all by yourself. In contrast with past years, the year 1928 stands out as a red letter year in every way from your financial point of view. . . . I feel sure that some day you will see the value [of keeping accounts]. . . . Be sure to get regular exercise. . . . Work of any kind is always much easier and much better done when one is physically fit.

Mr. Rockefeller repeatedly emphasized to his son that he alone could make the decisions that would lead to his living a happy and useful life, but he usually added that "you do not know how happy it makes me to have you take up with me any subject that you want to discuss. There is always a solution, and we can always find it together if we approach matters both of us with open minds." On another occasion, he wrote to Nelson that he could not

> tell you how happy the latter part of your letter . . . made Mama and me. To know that you are so contented at Dartmouth . . . gives us happiness. . . . Parents need encouragement and appreciation quite as much as children—perhaps they are more grateful for it even than children. . . . It is our earnest desire . . . to help you in giving you the opportunity for the finest, most stimulating and uplifting contacts; to be ready always, when you ask for it, to give you the benefit of any experience which we have had—but to leave to you always the decision in matters which affect your own life—that that decision will be based on a knowledge of all the facts in the case, in so far as they are available, and that it will always be inspired by the finest idealism, we are happily and gratefully conscious.

Occasionally, he also offered some indirect suggestions, as when Nelson had stayed late at a dance on Sunday morning.

> . . . I do not . . . say that it is wrong . . . but there are certain things which we relegate to the six days of the week and do not do

on Sunday. . . . I have no wish or desire to force my perhaps old-fashioned view of the subject upon you. I would, however, like to have you think it through fully and frankly and . . . reach a conclusion as to what position is best and proper for you. . . . Whatever conclusion you arrive at . . . will not be questioned.

Nelson replied that there were times when it was difficult to avoid staying at a dance after Saturday midnight, and his father responded:

. . . You are quite right in feeling that there is no particular difference between one minute before twelve and one minute after. I agree with you that the vital question is the effect on one's own Sunday, both as regards how it is spent and how one feels. . . . Please do not feel that you are bound to me in any way by what you have said. I shall regard it merely as an expression of your feeling that, all things being equal, Sunday morning is a poor time to stay out very late. There may and doubtless will be exceptions.

Mr. Rockefeller was gratified in November of 1928 when Nelson wrote that he had been very much interested in a speech which his father had made on the fundamentals of religion, an address which had attracted considerable attention.

"Some time I should like to sit down with you, with the manuscript before us, and discuss any points about which you are not clear [he wrote his son]. Such a discussion would be very helpful to me, for in this address I sought to formulate my own thoughts on religion in its simple and elemental terms. . . . Isn't Mr. Hoover's election splendid?"

The attitude that Mr. Rockefeller encouraged in his sons in regard to money was important, and slightly involved. Nobody could accuse the family of being "soft" in regard to money matters. They were suspiciously on guard against a world that had countless schemes to relieve them of part of the burden of wealth either by private or philanthropic ventures. Yet the brothers always knew that the mere accumulation of money was not their problem; that money merely represented a tool with which they could work and that they would be judged in life by what they built with the tools at their command. Mr. Rockefeller, Jr., never let them forget that the important thing was the way they used their money. On one occasion he sent Nelson a note saying he thought he would be interested in an enclosed quotation because "we are all of us engaged in the business of giving money away." The quotation from Aristotle said:

> Things which admit of use may be used either well or badly. . . . Anybody can give or spend money but to give the right amount of it at the right time and for the right cause and in the right way, that is not what anybody can do, nor is it easy. That is the reason why it is rare and laudable and noble to do well.

At home, Nelson had been driving a Dodge that was getting along in years but in the spring of 1928, with the connivance of Laurance, he began a campaign for a newer vehicle. They tried to approach the subject indirectly so that their father would suggest that the old Dodge should be replaced. Mr. Rockefeller was not deceived but he said he would think about it, providing the boys strictly observed the fifteen-mile-an-hour speed limit he had established at Pocantico Hills. Once the subject had been opened, Nelson made his big pitch in a long and stilted but ingenious letter from Dartmouth in which he sought to please his father by his serious consideration of the question of a car but also to make sure that he got the sporty number he wanted rather than a more serviceable vehicle which his father had suggested.

May 8, 1928

Dear Pa,

First, I would like to express my appreciation of your attitude on the car question. It has been one of great generosity and desire to cooperate to the fullest extent. Due to your open mindedness and your desire to do the best thing, I'm sure we will always arrive at the best solution of problems—a solution that will be equally satisfactory to both of us.

As to the immediate car question—having a car up here would be nice, I'll admit, but as we brought out in our talk there are several objections and unfavorable precedents that might arise from it. The alternative of having a new car—which of course would belong to you as the other cars have—and of being able to hire a car at college when I really need one, is more than a generous one. I had been thinking of a new car, but as I said before you had already been so generous that I didn't feel I had any right to bring it up. But when you suggested it I was overjoyed. [Mr. Rockefeller replied tartly that it was Laurance, not he, who had suggested it.]

A Buick will be an ideal car, I'm sure, and it is exactly what I had been thinking of. Now as to the question of a roadster or a five passenger touring car. I received your letter and I'm sure I understand how you feel. I've given the matter careful consideration during the past three days—even dreamed about it—and I have talked to fellows who have Buick roadsters & 5 passenger touring cars.

At first, I thought it would seem more practical to get the 5 passenger car for all around utility. And this fact would hold true if it were not for the fact that I think we have here somewhat of a special case. While I am using the car between Pocantico & New York and around the city, it is rare that I ever use the back except for baggage due to the fact that Laurance & John both have cars, as well as the family cars driven by the men. Then the only other time I use the car is motoring to and from Maine, and while I'm up there. As to the former, I've never motored up or down with more than one other. Then, when you stop to think, practically every family on the island has at least one car which the younger members drive. When we take some one with us, it is nearly always for the pleasure of their company rather than the necessity of the ride. Going to dances and things—whether raining or not—it is rare that any of the cars are full. Usually there are not more than two or three in any car. I can remember occasions when I have on rainy nights had a full car, but that was rather from preference than necessity.

Therefore, after thinking the situation over pretty carefully, I really have come to the conclusion that I would really rather have the roadster—that is, if you don't object. I can't imagine anything more ideal that that black Buick we saw. But if you would rather get the five passenger car I would be tickled to death to have it. My honest opinion is though that the roadster would fill the ticket by far the best—taking all things into consideration.

If you do decide to buy either, and you don't know how I'd appreciate either, I'd be all the more grateful if you could get it by the 14th of June, so that I could have it for those couple of weeks before going on the trip.

I'm sorry to have written such a long letter, but wanted you to know just exactly how I felt. I can assure you, whatever happens, I'll be happy. Laurance knows just what I would want in either event, so I'll trust him for details.

Lots of love & thanks,

Nell

For one reason or another—possibly because he was simply overcome by the unrestrained flow of words from Nelson's pen—Mr. Rockefeller bought his son a black Buick roadster with a red stripe around the body and six red wire wheels. He specified that it should not be taken to Dartmouth, although he said Nelson could hire a car at college when he really needed it. Nelson replied excitedly that, although he hadn't yet seen the car,

you don't know how much pleasure I've already received from just imagining about it. I've taken you all out for rides at least a dozen times; I've imagined the way I'll put the lights and horn on it. I've even gone so far as to try to draw futuristic designs for the radiator cap. People must think I'm crazy because every Buick I see I rush up and examine. . . . There's one thing I've thought of . . . I really hate to ask you. . . . Could I have two mirrors put on the wheels that are on the sides of the car? . . . I'd be glad to pay for them myself only I really can't afford it at present.

Nelson's bursts of enthusiasm and his disorderliness distressed Mr. Rockefeller, who labored to get his second son to adapt himself to a more sedate and measured pace. On one occasion his father offered to help him pass his English tests by sending back to him all of his letters with the misspelled words underlined so he could look them up in the dictionary. Nelson declined this offer but made a countersuggestion.

I know there are various words I can't spell [he said]. I could stop and look them up in the dictionary but that would be wasting a lot of time, so instead of looking them up I'll just underline the words that I'm uncertain about and you'll know that, if necessary, I could take the time to look them up.

This must have seemed an odd approach to the problem, especially when Mr. Rockefeller looked over the results. Nelson had underlined a dozen words in the letter, most of which were spelled correctly. But he had completely ignored almost as many that were incorrectly spelled. For a good many years, Mr. Rockefeller patiently and quietly persisted in his endeavor to help his son into more orderly habits.

> You have great admiration for your Grandfather Rockefeller [he wrote Nelson]. Remember that one of the qualities that made him great, and that not infrequently made him successful over other people, was his ability to wait and to be patient to a degree that was almost superhuman. Waiting is often hard work, much harder than working and doing, but not infrequently it is the quickest and most effective way to accomplish the desired end and it is the goal that the wise man keeps his eye on.

In time, some of his father's advice rubbed off on Nelson. In time, too, Mr. Rockefeller's concern as to Nelson's volatility was allayed, and he would write that his "cup was running over with happiness" and pride in his son. But, as he grew older, Nelson would continue to challenge his father's conservative, traditional attitudes and to urge Mr. Rockefeller to actions that were more dramatic and more advanced than he might ordinarily have favored. Nelson frequently pushed his father to give him greater authority in family affairs, and sometimes he got what he wanted. Mr. Rockefeller was, however, a man who preferred to move cautiously rather than enthusiastically. Relations with his son had not always been smooth and his campaign to slow down Nelson's tempo would never be very effective. Father and son were temperamentally far apart.

### III.

Nelson's relationship with his Grandfather Rockefeller was erratic but important if for no other reason than that he was the genius behind the family fortune, the man so often pictured as a piratical monopolist miraculously transformed into a God-fearing philanthropist who gave away five hundred million dollars for the benefit of humanity. This publicly split personality might have had more psychological impact on the grandsons of Mr. Rockefeller, Sr., but for the great gulf of years that separated their generations. When Nelson was a small child, his grandfather was already more than seventy years old and retired from all business affairs, and the popular image of the elder Rockefeller had been softened by the press agentry of Ivy Lee. There were no more angry newspaper headlines, the bitterness of congressional investigations was forgotten and the newspapers were happy to publish photographs of an aging philanthropist gently swinging a golf club on his private links or handing out bright new dimes as souvenirs.

Yet, Nelson's earliest memories were not much affected by this latter-day public personality either. He knew his grandfather as a relaxed and pleasant elderly man with a ready smile and quick, bird-like eyes in a face of yellowed parchment. But, most important of all, his very earliest impression of the old man was that he was a great wit, a humorist to be compared with Will Rogers. There is no accurate record to show the quality of Mr. Rockefeller's humor, but his grandsons not infrequently dined at his home on Sunday, and Nelson remembers that he often stood at the head of the table, trailing a spotlessly white napkin in his thin fingers and talking so entertainingly that everybody, including small children, were entranced. Often his stories were deadpan accounts of some sad circumstance into which an acquaintance had fallen, and occasionally he would lift the napkin to wipe an imaginary tear from his eye. But the stories always ended up with an unexpected twist that made it all a huge joke and sent the children into screams of laughter. They loved the stories even when they had heard them before and, for as long as he lived, they would enjoy visiting their grandfather's home.

The elder Rockefeller was not all jokes, however. He often found time to listen gravely to his grandchildren's problems. He cautioned Nelson—with only partial success—not to burden himself with details of business. And he occasionally wrote pleasant little letters, as when Nelson had sent him a gift in 1923.

. . . The maple sugar you sent was very acceptable, and we all thank you for it. We thank you because maple sugar is so good and sweet

and everybody likes it; but more because you were so thoughtful and
kind as to remember us away down here in Florida, where we do
not make maple sugar, and we will try and get even with you some
day for all your kindness to us.

Lovingly,<br>Grandfather

As Nelson was growing up, he became aware of his grandfather's
role in American industry but he was not particularly interested until
he wrote his thesis on the Standard Oil Company. Thereafter, he
took advantage of his not very frequent contacts with Mr. Rockefeller,
Sr., to talk to him about business affairs and to seek his advice, which
was not often given except in very general terms. Or his grandfather
would listen patiently to his ideas and then cool him off with a
remark that "it is all very interesting, but what do the figures show?
It's the figures that count."

   ... It seems funny to think that today is Grandfather's 90th birthday
   and my 21st birthday [Nelson wrote to his parents on July 8th,
   1929].... The 90 makes my 21 seem mighty small and insignificant,
   just like a little sapling standing by a mighty fir. But the sapling still
   has time to grow and develop and someday it might itself turn into
   a tree of some merit. Who knows?

And later he wrote that "I played golf with Grandfather last
Saturday and on Columbus day. I have had a chance recently to get
to know him better than ever before and every time I see him my
admiration grows deeper. He certainly is an extraordinary man."
By the time Nelson had graduated to the world of business, his
grandfather, although far removed from workaday affairs, still liked
to hear about what was going on. After the noontime meal he would
sometimes retire to his favorite Morris chair, lower the back to a
semireclining position, spread a white handkerchief over his face
and ask Nelson to sit beside him and talk about his work. Sometimes
he would comment but most of the time he listened until he dozed
off.

   We went to Grandfather's for lunch today [Nelson wrote his
   father in 1932]. Afterwards he took me aside and we had a little talk

for half an hour or so. He certainly is an extraordinary man, about the finest I know. There are few people that I really admire as being all-round successes, but he leads the list. His point of view and outlook on life are so perfectly grand. And what a sense of humor!

Mr. Rockefeller, Jr., was pleased by the letter and told his son that "nothing could give me greater satisfaction than does the fact that you are beginning to understand and appreciate Grandfather." Mrs. Rockefeller also was interested and remarked that she wanted Nelson to know more about the career of his Grandfather Aldrich. Then she added:

> which leads me to the point that I want to make, which is that I hope you boys will . . . not only know what he [your father] is doing but will understand the motives and principles that underlie his actions. I think that your father's high-mindedness and absolute honesty are very rare and I am counting upon this becoming a family tradition.

IV.

Mrs. Rockefeller may well have been the most direct single influence on Nelson as he grew to manhood. She was the daughter of a strong, self-made man who had started life on a Rhode Island farm, completed his education with one year at East Greenwich Academy, worked for a wholesale grocer's firm, moved into Providence city government offices and to the House of Representatives in Washington. In 1881, when he was forty, he was elected to the United States Senate and in the next three decades became the able and iron-handed Republican leader of the chamber, powerful enough to defy President Taft by raising tariff rates in 1909. He was a man with varied and enthusiastic interests—in art and literature and politics. He enjoyed life and encouraged his children to have a good time, to learn to sail, to visit art museums, to travel in Europe. He even encouraged his daughters to buy new dresses, as long as they chose bright and gay colors. He didn't worry much if they couldn't spell— and Abby Aldrich was weak in that department—so long as they developed their minds and had good taste. Abby thought he was wonderful and was greatly influenced by his attitudes.

As Mrs. John D. Rockefeller, Jr., Abby made no attempt to disguise the fact that her outlook and her training were quite different from those of her husband, but to a great extent they complemented and balanced each other in harmonious fashion. Where her husband was strait-laced, careful and retiring, Mrs. Rockefeller was full of enthusiasms, outspoken, witty and at ease in any company whether it was high society in New York, politicians in Washington or *avant garde* artists in Paris. Her charm was such that it was long remembered by almost everyone who came into contact with her even briefly, and her life was almost completely devoted to her husband and children. "Your father," she once wrote to one of her children, "is so wonderfully thoughtful himself and so considerate of all the people with whom he comes in contact that I am sure he must occasionally find the rest of us somewhat difficult. Perhaps there is a little bit too much Aldrich in us and not enough Rockefeller!"

There was certainly plenty of Aldrich in Nelson. He was filled with the Aldrich zest for life, the endless quest for new and exciting experiences and the love of people, of crowds and of political adventures. In personality he was, perhaps more than anyone else in the family, like his mother, and they had similar tastes and interests.

Mr. Rockefeller's health was not good and he and his wife frequently went to Hot Springs, West Virginia, to rest. In April of 1920, Nelson wrote to his mother that he had been to see the circus and that "I am sending you a little sachet that I made this morning without the help of anyone." A few days later, he informed her that he and Laurance had been paid $13.20 for eight rabbits that they sold to the Rockefeller Institute laboratories. The next summer, Nelson's rabbits died and his mother wrote him:

> This is a letter of condolence. I have just learned of your great loss and I am most truly sympathetic. To think of those dear little rabbits all dying is too sad. . . . Mothers and babies are very sensitive things, they have to be taken great care of or accidents will happen. Perhaps it was too cold for the babies or it may have been unwise

to move the mother just before they were born. I know how disappointed you must be.

I saw a lovely little police dog today. I am dying to buy him but Papa hasn't taken kindly to the idea yet.

Mrs. Rockefeller's letters were more seriously concerned with her son's attitude as he grew older.

... You must have lost a lot of school work, which will mean some good stiff studying for the rest of this year [she wrote in February of 1923, from Ormond Beach, Florida]. If you can only train yourself now to concentrate and to stop fooling except in play time, you will do yourself an endless service for which you will be thankful the rest of your life. . . . Remember you are the one that has to live most with yourself, and the more you exercise your mind the better time you will have and the more you develop your imagination the greater success you will be. I am eager that you shall be much above the ordinary in character and achievement. The world needs fine men. There is great work waiting to be done. I want you to train yourself to meet any opportunity the future may hold in store for you. Learn to use your brains now before it is too late. . . . Don't throw this letter in the waste paper basket, thinking that it is a lecture. Just think that your mother, who loves you very much indeed, wants you to put your best into life and get the best out of it.

From your devoted,

Mother

Again, Mrs. Rockefeller wrote that she hoped Nelson was being kind to the younger children. She remarked that "if any one should ask me if there was anything in the world making me unhappy" she should have to say that she didn't feel that her sons were always fair and kind to each other. "Think it over," she added, "and see if you do not agree with me." But, almost always, the letters exchanged by Nelson and his mother were a reflection of their common interests and were full of expressions of deep affection. About Christmastime, in 1927, Nelson sent her as a present a college fraternity pin.

Dear Ma,

A word of explanation about the pin. Each member of the fraternity is allowed one regular sized pin and one smaller "sister" pin, as it is called. I am giving you the latter; I don't expect you will be able to wear it much, but keep it as a symbol of the love that comes with it.

Your devoted son,<br>Nelson

And again he wrote in 1928:

> . . . at present I don't see any girl that I know that I could ever love enough to marry. I suppose I'll meet one some day. Mum, if only you were a girl that would solve the problem. But then, of course, I'd be without the best mother in the world.

The feeling was mutual and, on Nelson's twenty-first birthday, his mother wrote him that perhaps

> she was expected to give . . . advice, but I don't feel just that way. I feel that one of the best things that ever happened to me was having you for a son. I love being your mother and having you old enough to be a friend and companion. I am trying to take care of myself so that I can live many years to see the fine things that I know you are all going to do.

Mrs. Rockefeller was inclined to give her son advice in small things—she was happy he was using the vacuum cleaner in his room at Dartmouth "because you can . . . study better in an atmosphere free of dust"—and to protect him in financial matters— "A notice came from the bank that you had overdrawn . . . and I had Miss Kelly deposit $10 for you. . . . I haven't mentioned it to Papa, thinking that it was better for you to do so, and also because I know that it would disappoint and grieve him." This was an attitude that would continue until her death and, many years later, she wrote to Nelson: "I can't tell you how grateful I am to you for your telephone messages. I hope you telephone from the office and get it put on the bill there for I am sure your dear father would be shocked if I started telephoning freely to you, which I have a great desire to do."

Mrs. Rockefeller devoted a great deal of time to arousing the interest of her children in poetry, art, literature and music. "I am glad that you have put in music [in college courses]," she wrote to Nelson. "I feel as if we as a family miss a great deal by leaving music out of our lives and I feel as if it were my fault because Papa is really very musical and knows lots about it." And later: "I am enclosing the [book] of poems. . . . I feel as if the Rockefeller family should cultivate their poetic side, and I am beginning myself." Despite his love of dancing, Nelson never exhibited any musical talents but he did develop an interest in art. His mother had been one of the sponsors of the earliest introduction of modern French painting in New York and, when Nelson was at Dartmouth, he began studying art in a kind of dogged, do-or-die manner. Soon he was all enthusiasm.

January 2, 1928

Dear Ma,

You don't know how much I enjoyed our two trips to Mr. Davies and the visit to the Down Town Galleries. I feel as if I had been introduced to a new world of beauty, and for the first time I think I have really been able to appreciate and understand pictures, even though only a little bit. I hope to continue this when I am in New York and maybe do a tiny bit of collecting myself. I feel that was the outstanding event of my vacation.

His mother replied that

it would be a great joy to me if you did find that you had a real love for and interest in beautiful things. We could have such good times going about together and if you start to cultivate your taste and eye so young, you ought to be very good at it by the time you can afford to collect much. . . . It is very sweet to me to hear what you say about your Mother and very comforting, too, because so often I feel that I fail to be what I should like to be for your sake, but my love for you, dear, is very deep and you can always count on it.

Nelson told his mother that he was "enjoying the course in landscape gardening more than I can say—sometimes I wish I had majored in Art, but I guess the economics will be of more value. I do love some of those other things, though. . . ." And, in 1928, Mrs. Rockefeller wrote him she was having a luncheon for seventeen art critics who "will see the . . . pictures that I have gotten together in my gallery. . . . My mind is also full of ideas for a new Museum of Modern Art for New York. I have great hopes for it. Wouldn't it be splendid if it would be ready for you to be interested in when you get back to New York to live."[1]

In his junior year at Dartmouth, Nelson felt that he was becoming rather expert. "In psychology the other day," a letter to his mother said,

> we were given a book of 125 masterpieces of all periods and countries. There were two copies of each painting—one the original and the other was the original only mutilated in some way. For example, a tree was moved or an arm held differently. . . . We were supposed to pick out the original in each case. I'm glad to say, Mum, that your training has had its effect. I hate to say so myself, but I not only had the highest per cent right by far . . . but I ranked in the exceptional group of all those who have taken the test throughout the country. I wouldn't have mentioned this but I thought that you deserved all the credit and therefore should be told that your efforts had not been in vain. I think perhaps I'm beginning to acquire some of your good taste.

The next year, he wrote that he had "been doing quite a bit of oil painting and sketching. . . . The last time we met for sketching, we had a man pose in the nude. He was a real model and could hold a position. . . . I really think I'm getting something out of all this." But when Nelson talked about becoming an architect, his mother was not inclined to encourage him. "I am glad if you feel absolutely sure," she wrote, but

> there are lots of things to think over. There are so many fine things that it is possible for you to do and so many things that seem necessary for some one to do. I am terribly eager that the high standard of citizenship set by your father shall be maintained by you boys. It seems as if all of you would have to join in the battle for righteousness in all walks of life, business, church, professions and private life,

[1] Mrs. Rockefeller was largely responsible for the founding of the Museum of Modern Art in New York, which stands on the site of the Rockefeller homes. Mr. Rockefeller was the largest single contributor to the museum (more than $5,000,000) and Nelson eventually became president.

no small or easy job. This has always been the dream of my life, but of course each of you will have to work out your own salvation and, as we trust you, so we can have faith in your futures.

Nelson soon gave up the idea of becoming an architect—"I felt I couldn't justify it," he said later—but he pursued his interest in art with a kind of relentless determination to learn and to understand everything. In the spring of 1930, he described to his mother a day that, upon reflection, seems incredible.

> Just back from a wonderful visit to Boston. We saw Fritz Lieber and his company of Shakespearian players put on Othello . . . and King Lear. They were both great. . . . Yesterday I spent the most interesting kind of a day possible. In the morning I went to the Boston Art Museum and spent several hours in the American wing. . . . Then I visited the Egyptian and Greek wings for an hour or so. Before lunch I stopped at the Boston Library to see the Sargent paintings. In the afternoon, I went out to Cambridge . . . and we made a thorough tour of the Fogg museum. It was great. . . . Then we stopped in at the Harvard Library to look it over and see Sargent's two murals. . . . And finally we went to visit the exhibition of Modern Mexican painters shown by the Harvard Modern Art Society. I met the fellows who were running it and enjoyed both the exhibition and the sponsors. I had a minute when I got back to Boston, so I dropped into the Doll and Richards Galleries to see an exhibition of O'Hara's water colors. . . . He uses lovely fresh colors. Tomorrow afternoon I'm going out to a little community with the Episcopal minister here in Hanover. I'm going to give a little talk and show some slides.

Oddly enough, this direct—and superhuman—approach to art worked out well for Nelson. He became reasonably expert in matters of modern art or, if not expert, enthusiastic, and his contribution to the development of art in the Americas was considerable. He never was able, however, to convince his father that abstract or nonobjective art meant much. As late as 1950, Mr. Rockefeller told Nelson that he really didn't have time to read the publications that were being sent to him by the Museum of Modern Art and that, unless his son objected, he would like to have them discontinued. And when Nelson proposed that his father should sit for the Italian sculptor, Marini, whose work was extremely modern, Mr. Rockefeller replied:

> As much as I hate not to do anything that any one of you children ask me to do, I just would not be happy to go down into posterity or even to be represented in any of your homes in the manner shown by the photographs [of Marini's work], which I am returning herewith. I think, on further thought, that you will agree that that manner is so foreign to me in every way that it would be an anomaly to have me portrayed in it. Pray forgive this declination and try me again sometime on something easier.

On the other hand, Mr. Rockefeller appreciated beauty and was quick to acknowledge an artistic success. When, in the 1940's, Nelson was building his own home at Seal Harbor, his father was quite critical of the plans which architect Wallace Harrison had drawn for a modern structure on a thin point of land adjacent to the harbor. But after he had seen the house, he wrote his son:

> As you well know, I have spoken often with some skepticism in regard to your house which in design and construction is so foreign to anything my staid mind could conceive that I had grave doubtfulness as to how successful it would be. In view of this attitude on my part I hope you realized how completely captivated I was by the place and how abjectly I apologized for my skepticism. . . . It is beautiful in its location and the marvelous views which it commands.

A spirit of open-mindedness and tolerance was emphasized time and again in Nelson's communications with his parents, particularly in regard to prejudice for reasons of race, creed or color. The Rockefeller attitude was ably summed up in a letter that Mrs. Rockefeller once wrote to John, Nelson and Laurance.

> For a long time I have had very much on my mind and heart a certain subject. I meant to bring it up at prayers and then later have it for a question to be discussed at a family council. . . .
> Out of my experience and observation has grown the earnest conviction that one of the greatest causes of evil in the world is race hatred or race prejudice; in other words, the feeling of dislike that a

person or a nation has against another person or nation without just cause, an unreasoning aversion is another way to express it. The two peoples or races who suffer most from this treatment are the Jews and the Negroes; but some people "hate" the Italians, who in turn hate the Jugoslavs, who hate the Austrians, who hate the Czecho-Slovaks and so it goes endlessly.

You boys are still young. No group of people has ever done you a personal injury; you have no inherited dislikes. I want to make an appeal to your sense of fair play and to beseech you to begin your lives as young men by giving the other fellow, be he Jew or Negro or of whatever race, a fair chance and a square deal.

It is to the disgrace of America that horrible lynchings and race riots frequently occur in our midst. The social ostracism of the Jew is less brutal, and yet it often causes cruel injustice and must engender in the Jews a smouldering fire of resentment.

Put yourselves in the place of an honest, poor man who happens to belong to one of the so-called "despised" races. Think of having no friendly hand held out to you, no kindly look, no pleasant, encouraging word spoken to you. What I would like you always to do is what I try humbly to do myself; that is, never to say or to do anything which would wound the feelings or the self-respect of any human being, and to give special consideration to all who are in any way repressed. This is what your father does naturally from the fineness of his nature and the kindness of his heart.

I long to have our family stand firmly for what is best and highest in life. It isn't always easy, but it is worth while.

Your Mother

Mrs. Rockefeller, a member of the family once said, "put ideas into Nelson's head and he has always tried to live by them."

v.

"Nelson didn't have any steady girl during his first three years in college," a Dartmouth classmate said. "He was playing the field with an open mind." This seemed to be fairly well confirmed during Nelson's trip to Europe in the summer of 1928 when he wrote home about meeting numerous attractive girls, including one who "really is a peach—full of fun, nice looking, very intelligent and has a great deal of *savoir faire*. . . . It has really made the trip across a great deal more interesting; in fact, very delightful." There were other girls mentioned in his letters, too; so many that his mother wrote him: "I don't know much about all these girls that you have been seeing in Paris. I comfort myself with the thought that there is safety in numbers."

The numbers increased as Nelson prolonged his visit with his Aunt Lucy Aldrich in Paris, attending luncheons, teas, dinners and meeting a Belgian princess, a viscount and an American girl whom he took to Montmartre to see the street dancing on July 14. "We had a wonderful time . . . there certainly were some interesting sights and people to watch. . . . I think this is going to be the most profitable summer I ever spent." After he had returned to college he saw the American girl again and wrote his mother that she was "just as nice as before and I am very fond of her. . . . I think it was extremely good for me that I met her. It sort of broadened me out a little more as far as girls are concerned."

Nelson's broadening out in regard to feminine companionship put quite a strain on his relations with Laurance at one point. The younger boy viewed girls with a jaundiced eye and remarked that he couldn't think whether it would be worse to flunk his high school examinations or to see Nelson get engaged to some dame. He quickly got over this attitude, however. Brother John, on the other hand, watched Nelson's schoolboy romancing with something of awe. On one occasion he borrowed Nelson's automobile at Tarrytown to do a little courting of his own at Vassar. "I didn't know the road," he told Nelson later, "but I just turned your car loose on the highway and it headed for the nearest girl's college, you have it so well trained."

All of the talk about Nelson's fickleness, however, was something of a smoke cloud, because one girl's name kept bobbing up from the time he was out of high school. She was Mary Todhunter Clark of Philadelphia, whose family usually spent the summer at Northeast Harbor on Mount Desert Island. Nelson had a Ford touring car at

Seal Harbor, a vehicle richly endowed with tootling whistles and horns and spotlights and odd gadgets, and he was always driving it over to Northeast to see the Clark gang, which consisted of six brothers and their sister, Tod. As the families became better acquainted over the years, Nelson's expeditions were more often to see Tod than her brothers. He invited her to Dartmouth social affairs and usually reported that "we had a good time. She is always full of good fun and never dull." Mrs. Rockefeller asked Tod to an Easter vacation house party at Pocantico in 1928 and Mr. Rockefeller, who always called her Mary, told Nelson that she was "an exceptionally fine girl, so bright, so clever . . . and withal such a fine spirit."

Then, in January, 1929, Mr. and Mrs. Rockefeller and David made a long trip to Egypt and they invited Miss Clark to accompany them. Nelson was delighted but a little worried. Also in the party were a man and his son, B——, who was about Miss Clark's age. Jealousy invaded Nelson's thoughts.

> I'm crazy to hear about your trip [he wrote his parents before they had even reached Paris]. What is happening and what are you doing . . . ? I do so want to know how you all like Tod and whether she has been all you expected as a travelling companion, which I know she has and probably a lot more. I've been a little worried about B——, but I'm counting on Dave.

There was a week of suspense but then he received word from his mother that "Mary has been a great success" and that B—— came on board with influenza, "then was inoculated for typhoid, had a temperature of 104 and now has sinus trouble." This should have reassured the jealous suitor but Nelson's imagination was working at top speed. He wrote his mother again, describing the qualities he admired in Miss Clark and saying that he had tested his feelings for her by making friends with other girls to see whether he could "get to like them better." He couldn't. He wanted his mother to tell him all she thought about Miss Clark. "Well," he concluded, "enough said. . . . Probably Tod's engaged to that young B—— by now anyhow. But we'll hope not!"

That spring Nelson invited another girl to the Dartmouth house party, but he warned his parents not to

> think I'm forgetting Tod or have fallen for Y———. Well, I have fallen for Y——— in a sense but it doesn't effect my love for Tod in the least bit. I think I'm too young to only know and like one girl, so I periodically fall for some one—about once a year—but always giving them to understand how I feel toward Tod.

This experimental program didn't work very well and in the summer of 1929 it fell apart completely when Nelson and Laurance were on a trip to the Arctic aboard the famous International Grenfell Association sailing ship. The trip itself was worthy of note in addition to its effect on Nelson's romance. Sir Wilfred T. Grenfell was a noted missionary doctor among the Eskimos but he was getting along in years and his health was failing in 1929. As a result, the voyage irked Nelson because it was poorly managed and at first he had to waste a great deal of time sitting around on deck doing nothing. To make it worse, the ship's cook fell ill and the two Rockefeller boys spent most of the voyage in the galley washing dishes, emptying garbage and cooking for fourteen crew members.

> Dr. Grenfell [Nelson wrote when they were off Newfoundland] is a remarkable man and a very devout Christian but he certainly needs to take a few lessons from an efficiency expert. . . . The natives up here are even worse. They just sit around and go fishing when the spirit moves them. . . . Why, if any of them were half way ambitious he could make some money. But I suppose there is no use getting excited about it. Perhaps they get more out of life that way than we do rushing around. . . . Anyway, it's a great experience.

It was still more of an "experience" after Dr. Grenfell left the ship on its homeward voyage and Laurance suffered an appendicitis attack while they were fog-bound off the Bay of Islands. Nelson was worried about Laurance and he feared that they would miss the twice-a-week train they were supposed to take to Maine. He vainly tried to persuade the officer in command to proceed through the fog. The officer refused.

"Look," Nelson argued, "we know that there is a cliff straight ahead of us and you can get a foghorn echo off the cliff so that we will know when we get close to it. Then you can take a straight line—fog or no fog—into the harbor. This is an emergency!"

The officer rejected the whole idea.

"Then I'll do it," Nelson said in desperation.

"I'll take no responsibility," the officer snapped.

"Okay, I'll take the responsibility."

They made sail and crept through the fog toward the cliff. Oddly enough, it all worked out just as Nelson had predicted—"It really was a pretty simple matter," he explained later—and they made their train on schedule. By that time, Laurance was better and it was some time before he had his appendix out.

But, to get back to Miss Clark, the dragging days and nights on the sailing ship gave Nelson a chance to do a lot of heavy thinking, and on July 8—his twenty-first birthday—he wrote to his mother:

> You know, I'm beginning to think that I really am in love with Tod, whatever being in love means. I can shake it off for a while now and then, but it always comes back and I've never been able to develop a real affection and an admiration that is as all inclusive for anyone else. She is the only girl that I know who measures up anywhere nearly to the standards set by you, Mum. But don't get worried. I'm not going to run into anything in a headstrong way. . . .

That final sentence was far off the mark. No sooner had he gotten back for his senior year at Dartmouth than he was "really and truly desperately in love" and, despite his parents' urging that they wait, he and Miss Clark became engaged that autumn. Mr. Rockefeller was very much upset, not because of Miss Clark, whom he admired, but because his son had not consulted his parents before taking such an important step while still in college. For some weeks, Nelson had a rough time of it and he obviously was not at all sure how the crisis was going to be solved. In the end, Mrs. Rockefeller was the peacemaker.

Nelson was grateful for her efforts.

Dear Mum,

I can't tell you how much both Tod and I appreciate the cooperative attitude you have taken. . . . At first, all we thought of was the
fact that we both loved each other desperately and that we wanted
to get married some day—our thoughts didn't get any further than
that. And ever since we've been realizing that it wasn't as simple
as one would think. We both feel very badly that Pa feels the way
he does, but really we didn't mean to try and put one over on him
or go counter to his wishes. . . . Tod is such a marvellous girl, and
I really am terribly lucky. . . .

Mr. Rockefeller relented under gentle pressure from his wife and
gave the couple his blessing in November.

. . . I still am thrilling over Pa's wonderful letter [Nelson wrote his
mother on November 23, 1929], but, Mum, I shall always feel that
if it wasn't for you things wouldn't be the way they are now. However, that only goes to make me more grateful. You know, I honestly
think that I am the luckiest person in the world. To have you and
Pa for parents and Tod for fiancee . . . is really more than one person deserves. But I guess the thing for me to do is to see if I can't
make myself worthy of them all.

That winter, Mr. Rockefeller spent many hours selecting a pearl
necklace as a wedding present for Miss Clark. It was, Mrs. Rockefeller
reported, "perfectly beautiful" and all was well in the Rockefeller
family. In February, the engaged couple went to Florida and called
on Mr. Rockefeller, Sr., who played a round of golf with Miss Clark.
On June 23, 1930, immediately after Nelson was graduated from
Dartmouth, they were married at Bala-Cynwyd, a fashionable suburb
of Philadelphia. The wedding, which was attended by fifteen hundred
invited guests, was described in the *New York Times.*

Mr. and Mrs. John D. Rockefeller, Jr., the first members of either
of the immediate families to arrive, entered the church at 4:15. The
bridegroom a few minutes later made his entrance by the parish
house door almost unnoticed. Leaping from an automobile, he ran
up the steps, tossed his top hat into the hands of the waiting sexton,
William Armstrong, and slapped him on the shoulder. "The best o'

Four portraits from the family album of Nelson Rockefeller in the costumes that he wore for special occasions from babyhood to college.

The children of Mr. and Mrs. John D. Rockefeller, Jr.: Abby, John 3rd, Nelson, Laurance, Winthrop and David.

When Nelson (right, with cello) was a youngster, a small fry "orchestra" often gathered at the Rockefeller home in New York City, and occasionally Mr. Rockefeller, Jr., joined the violin section for a performance. At far left is the third Rockefeller son, Laurance, who played the piano. Nelson gave up the cello when the strings snapped during one of his solo performances.

Rockefeller (left) on the Dartmouth campus fence with members of the senior executive committee, 1930. To his left are, Nelson McGinnis, executive vice president of the Erie Railroad, Francis Horn, president of Rhode Island University; Milton Emerich, a Chicago brokerage firm official; Edward Jeremiah, a hockey coach at Dartmouth; J. W. Wiggins, an attorney; and L. L. Gallaway, advertising director of *Sports Illustrated*.

The Rockefellers and Charles A. Lindbergh in the black Buick sports car (with wire wheels and red trimmings) that Nelson ingeniously persuaded his father to buy when he was a junior at college.

Nelson Rockefeller and his bride, the former Mary Todhunter Clark, leaving the church in suburban Philadelphia in 1930.

The honeymooning Rockefellers in Japan, 1930.

The honeymooners (and friends) aboard an elephant in Indo-China, 1931.

In 1932, Rockefeller (center) attended the opening of Radio City Music Hall with Colonel Arthur Woods and Mrs. Raymond Hood.

As a young man just out of college, Rockefeller vainly tried to interest New York City Mayor Fiorello La Guardia in building a city opera and art center adjacent to Rockefeller Center.

Four generations: John D. Rockefeller, Sr., Nelson Rockefeller, John D. Rockefeller, Jr., and Nelson's first son, Rodman.

Nelson Rockefeller's mother, Abby Aldrich Rockefeller, with her grandson Rodman.

The children of Governor and Mrs. Nelson Rockefeller, in the early 1940's. Left to right, the twins, Michael and Mary, Ann, Steven (who carried his little suitcase everywhere) and Rodman.

luck, sir," the sexton faltered, and received a smiling "Thank you" from the Rockefeller heir.

There were ten bridesmaids in droopy lace hats almost as big as parasols and ten ushers in cutaways and with carnations in their buttonholes. Among them were the groom's three eldest brothers. It was a notable occasion in Philadelphia society, not exactly because a Rockefeller heir was getting married but because the bride was a member of a Main Line family.

This distinction was made perfectly clear a decade later when Philadelphians chuckled over a story, possibly apocryphal, concerning Nelson's appointment to an important governmental post in Washington. When the appointment was announced, a crusty Philadelphia socialite paused in perusal of his newspaper at the Union League Club to point out the front-page story to a companion.

"This fellow here—Nelson Rockefeller," he said in a doubtful tone. "Isn't he that New York boy who married into the Clark family?"

# FOUR

# Beginning Business at the Top

Mr. and Mrs. Nelson Rockefeller started their honeymoon at Seal Harbor, where they could swim and sail a boat and be practically alone except for twenty-four servants and a housekeeper in the Rockefeller summer home. They continued the honeymoon for almost a year on a trip around the world, which was a wedding present from Rockefeller's father. The young couple, however, did not look upon their journey as entirely a pleasure trip. They arranged a heavy schedule of meetings with foreign representatives of the Chase National Bank, the Standard Oil Company, the Rockefeller Foundation and various missionary establishments which the family supported. They also were armed with impressive letters of introduction to many foreign personages. Both Rockefeller and his bride industriously studied books—such as *The Growth and Development of China*—about each of the countries they were to visit. "We had the opportunity," Rockefeller noted later, "to get quite a feel of each country and the impact of United States groups on the people and their attitude toward us."

From the time that Robert Gumbel, of the Rockefeller office, saw them off with an armful of flowers at the railroad station in New York, the young couple were not much alone. They not only met old friends along the way and made new friends but they were greeted and often shepherded around by representatives of the oil company, the American Express, the Pennsylvania Railroad, the Matson steamship line and others at almost every stop. In Honolulu, in July, 1930, the Governor "gave us a tea to which he asked two hundred persons . . . a weekend party with the President of the Senate and his family . . . a big native feast . . . with hula dancers" and a visit to a leper colony which was a "very interesting but depressing experience. . . . Everybody we met couldn't have been nicer."

Japan was geisha girls and fishing with cormorants by torchlight under a full moon, temples and shopping, luncheon with the French ambassador and dinners with university leaders. At Mukden, late in September, Rockefeller was "sickened by the bound feet of the women" and in Korea he felt the people were sullen under Japanese rule. Peking, in October, was "fascinating" and filled with gay friends of Aunt Lucy Aldrich, including a noted Chinese philosopher whose name Rockefeller could not spell. Hong Kong was perfect but Canton was hot and sticky. There was a typhoon en route to Manila, where they danced until 3 A.M. before catching the boat for the Dutch East Indies. "We're taking things more easy now."

Java, Sumatra and Bali—the latter was "a bit flat"—flashed by, then Bangkok for Christmas, with four to six or seven events (Siamese dancing at Madame Songkla's, Pasteur Institute snake farm, white elephants and Grand Palace, Wat Phra Kaeo) on the schedule every day. They finally rebelled and tried to avoid oil company and other chaperons. "We haven't even had a meal alone for over a month. . . . We'd been making an effort to be nice to people for so long that we were just dying for a rest and a chance to be by ourselves. . . . We were at the end of our rope." One Standard Oil company executive was insulted but he insisted he was responsible for their safety and went with them on a jungle trip which "was too beautiful to describe."

The couple's trunks were delayed en route to Bangkok and they had to borrow clothes to wear to a royal palace reception on the birthday of the Queen, who was ill and couldn't attend. A crowd of some fifteen hundred persons stood in the royal gardens—"it was all very formal and hot" and Rockefeller's shirt melted—until the King came along and "told us how much his country was indebted to Pa and Grandfather. It was all very interesting and a lot of fun once but I certainly wouldn't care for much of that kind of stuff." In February, they were in India, making a pack-horse trip into the Himalayan Mountains near the borders of Tibet.

> . . . The Governor wired his aide-de-camp in Darjeeling—a charming Tibettan gentleman, Mr. Laden La—and we went to a Tibettan house for tea. . . . The son's bride of eighteen was all dressed up [in native costume]. Mr. Laden La fixed up our pack trip and gave us a pass to get over into Nepal. He also lent Mary his fur coat. We had the most marvelous views nearly all of the time of the snow-capped mountains . . . especially at sun rise and sun set. Mount Kinchinyanga (27,000 feet) was just across the valley for the whole trip. From Mount Landakfu (12,000 feet high) . . . to whose summit we went—we got a perfect view of Mount Everest (28,000 feet) and the third highest mountain—I've forgotten its name—which is 26,000 feet. We went to bed and got up with the sun and were out riding all day, with the result that we had a wonderful rest.

Rockefeller was impressed at many points on his trip by the unhappy personal relations existing at that time between Europeans and Americans and the peoples of the Far East. In Japan, for example, he saw a boy named Fujiyama (later killed in World War II) who had been in his class at Dartmouth, where he belonged to a good fraternity and was popular on the campus and at social affairs. After eight years in America, Fujiyama returned to Japan and a sudden awakening to racial prejudice. He could not take part in the activities of Europeans or Americans in Japan; he was not invited to their parties; he could not make dates with the girls or appear on the premises of any of the foreign clubs. He couldn't even play golf with a foreigner. He was bitter about Westerners when he talked to Rockefeller and particularly about Western diplomats, most of whom remained aloof from contact with any Japanese except high government officials.

In Burma, the Rockefellers made a boat trip up the Irrawaddy River with a group of wealthy and titled Europeans. Also on board were native schoolteachers, but the Europeans would not mix with them and made comments in their hearing that embarrassed Rockefeller. The aristocrats also looked down on the captain of the boat, who was continually trying to build himself up with them by describing how "worthless" the Burmese crew was, how he made them take off their shoes when they came in his office and how he enforced stern discipline. Then at Bhamo, Rockefeller wrote later, "we were walking on shore when one of the crew ran to tell us to turn back because there was plague in the village. . . . It was a very decent thing for him to do and represented the thoughtfulness and graciousness that we found among the nationals in most places." In India, Rockefeller felt the people were friendly toward Americans but not toward the British. Even the Indians who had been educated in England were bitter because when they returned home they could not get any of the better jobs.

> We also were impressed by the obvious fact that the British considered us as colonials. We were traveling with letters of introduction from Prime Minister Sir Ramsay MacDonald and stayed in various government houses. Yet it was obviously distasteful to all those below the Governor himself, particularly the young foreign office people, to have to be nice to young Americans. They couldn't see why we were there and made it clear to us. . . . All of these things left a very strong impression and one which we felt boded little good for future relations [of the West] with those countries. It was evident we were not handling ourselves as a people abroad in a way that developed confidence or respect.

Almost the only bright spot that Rockefeller observed in this respect was at Bangkok, where the new American minister was a Philadelphian and eager to learn about the country. Among other things, he invited a great crowd of Bangkok children to a Christmas party on the embassy grounds, where American ice cream was served and motion pictures were shown. "This unheard-of contact with the masses," Rockefeller remarked, "turned out to be a great success as a good-will gesture. But the first secretary of the embassy was horrified. He had never heard of such a thing. The sight of the striped-pants young man gingerly picking his way through the seething mass of ice-cream-happy children was a memorable one, indeed."

A high point of the honeymoon journey came in March when they visited Delhi for the inauguration of the new Indian capital. They had called on the famous Indian poet and author, Sir Rabindranath Tagore—he spoke "very pleasantly of his visit" with Mr. and Mrs. Rockefeller, Jr.—and had walked on the banks of the Ganges—"the temples were not very lovely but life on the banks of the Ganges is perfectly fascinating." They had visited the Taj Mahal, which "really is all it's supposed to be," and they had been snubbed in their efforts to get an invitation to visit the Maharajah of Kapurthala. Then word came that a couple with whom they had traveled part of the time, Mr. and Mrs. George E. Vincent, had managed to get rooms for them at Delhi despite the crush of visitors at the inaugural celebration.

> We've just had a charming week in Delhi with Mary and Nelson assisting in inaugurating the somewhat grandiose capital at New Delhi [Mr. Vincent later wrote to Mrs. Rockefeller]. At a dinner at the Viceroy's—a small affair of only 86 guests—Mary sat by the Viceroy with whom it was evident she got on famously. We dubbed her "Princess Mary" after this recognition of nation and family! The young people were going strong with undiminished enthusiasm.

Among other things, they went hunting with the Viceroy's hounds, which chased jackals instead of foxes. Rockefeller spotted one jackal as they were getting on their horses but it escaped to its hole and they didn't see another in three hours of hunting. Mrs. Rockefeller's horse fell but, as her husband pointed out, "the ground was soft. . . . I must say I wouldn't have [gone hunting] if it hadn't been for Tod, who was crazy to go, but as it turned out it was lots of fun."

The part of the visit that most impressed Rockefeller, however, was a meeting with the Mahatma Gandhi, the wizened little man who preached passive resistance to British rule and who, in time, would be the hero of India's independence struggle. While the Rockefellers had been hunting as guests of the Viceroy, Gandhi had been in jail because of his seditious activities as leader of the Congress party. But the British at last had been forced to undertake negotiations looking toward independence, and the Mahatma was released while the Rockefellers were at Ahmedabad visiting the family of a rich Indian mill owner, Mr. Sarabhai, an advisor to Gandhi. Mr. Sarabhai went to Delhi to see the Mahatma and that evening he telephoned that the negotiations seemed to be near collapse. He told his family to come immediately to Delhi because Gandhi might be returned to jail.

They invited us to come along. Mrs. Sarabhai got her eight children and four or five friends and we all took the one o'clock train to Delhi. We arrived the next day at noon. We created quite a stir on the way as it seems the English don't exactly travel in company with Indians. Something like our colored situation—and, of course, we ate with them in the diner. They couldn't have been nicer and most interesting to talk to, all of them, even though a bit radical.

Well, Mr. Sarabhai asked us to come and stay with his friend in Delhi but we thought that fourteen guests was enough and went to the hotel. That afternoon we all went to the house where Gandhi was staying. It was guarded by volunteer soldiers in green. Mr. Gandhi was having his day of silence, but he doesn't mind seeing people.

After a short wait, the Rockefellers were ushered through the house and to the back porch which overlooked the river. Sitting in the courtyard and operating a spinning wheel was the thin-legged little man with bald head and gold-rimmed glasses whose fame had spread around the world. He wore a white dhoti and there was a bottle of milk on the ground beside him. There were many Congress leaders and disciples in the courtyard, including Mrs. Sarojini Naidu, a noted poetess, and Miss Madeleine Slade, the daughter of a British admiral who had devoted her life to Gandhi's work. The Rockefellers were presented to Gandhi, who nodded but did not speak. After they had expressed the hope of talking to him later, he wrote a note: "Come back tomorrow. I'll talk to you."

> The next morning when we came to see him all the Congress leaders were there, so we only spoke to him for a minute or so, then he asked us to accompany him the following morning on his daily walk. That day at lunch, Mr. Sarabhai had arranged for us to meet all the Congress leaders. Needless to say, it was a most interesting meal. The night before we had been to dinner with Mr. Sarabhai and some twenty Indians at one of their houses. All of them were most pleasant and very intelligent.
>
> The next morning we were at Mr. Gandhi's house at ten to seven. Upon our arrival we found that he had not gotten back from the Viceroy's until two A.M. and that then he had had a conference with the Congress Working Committee until the morning prayers at four A.M. But it wasn't long before he sent out word to find out if we were there. He came out looking pretty tired, but very cheerful.

They drove out to an old Mogul fort on the edge of the city, a spot where Gandhi liked to walk. It was a dark morning, with heavy rain clouds in the sky, and there were distant echoes of thunder from a storm that was receding.

"We have finally come to an agreement with the Viceroy," Gandhi said with great satisfaction. "There will be one more conference later today to arrange all the details."

The rain clouds were breaking up with the coming of morning, and bright sunlight shone on the dark faces and the white costumes of the Indian leaders. Rockefeller felt he was watching a fateful moment in history from a ringside seat. Gandhi talked about the negotiations, saying that the Indian people could never reach fulfillment of their destiny within the British Empire. He praised Lord Halifax as a fine man and said that he had been so elated by the outcome of his talks with the Viceroy that he had slept only forty-five minutes.

> We . . . walked with him for about fifteen minutes, asked him some questions and then left him with the Working Committee. . . . He is a remarkable man—terribly nice, too.

II.

When they returned to New York in late April of 1931, Rockefeller and his wife established themselves in an apartment on East Sixty-seventh Street (they later moved to a triplex apartment on Fifth Avenue) and in a house at Pocantico which Mr. Rockefeller, Jr., had remodeled for them. "We spent all morning at our new apartment choosing colors for the various rooms," Rockefeller wrote his father on July 22. "We picked a perfectly swell pink . . . for the walls with a slightly darker shade for the woodwork. It is going to be a very snappy apartment."

There were, however, more important problems to face than the color of the woodwork. Rockefeller had to start his career—the idea of not having a career never occurred to him—and in that department things were not so "perfectly swell." He had started wrestling with the problem when he was still in college, telling himself that he had to make his own mark in the world. Mr. Rockefeller, Jr., seemed to feel that it was best for his son to find his own way. He may have believed that the trip around the world on which Nelson talked with many business executives would increase his interest in a business career within the family background. It didn't. What interested the young man most on the journey was his contact with peoples, his observation of the work of American missionaries (of whom he strongly approved because of their knowledge of the peoples among whom they lived) and of American diplomats (of whom he often disapproved because they did not know the peoples). And he was not at all impressed by the attitude of Western businessmen in the Far East.

> . . . I'm sorry to say that seeing and hearing so much about . . . business doesn't make me very keen to go into it [he wrote his father on December 15, 1930, from Sumatra]. It seems to squeeze all other interests out of the men's lives that are in it. In fact, I've spent hours and hours thinking over what is really the best thing for me to do. As yet, I've come to no conclusions.

In the summer of 1931, however, Rockefeller did go into the family office at 26 Broadway in an effort "to be of some small assistance" to his father along lines that were not in conflict with the work of his brother John, who had started a career in association with his father soon after he was graduated from Princeton. Some of the work was of little interest to Nelson and his secondary role further dimmed his enthusiasm, although occasionally he became excited about some of the projects. The plan of Mr. Rockefeller, Jr., to turn the Palisades —the towering cliffs along the west bank of the Hudson River—into a park, for example, was very much to his liking. "It is perfectly thrilling up there," he wrote to his father. "I had not dreamed it was half as lovely. I am very anxious to go up with you sometime." And his father kept assuring him that "it is nice to feel you are on hand to do anything that comes up and I shall not hesitate to turn to you if the occasion offers."

The arrangement, nevertheless, was not a happy one. Young Rockefeller chafed under the orderly, conservative operation of the office and he occasionally disagreed with his father. Typical, perhaps, was the question in 1932 of whether he should become a trustee of New York's Metropolitan Museum of Art, one of many problems that he discussed with his father both verbally and in written interoffice letters.

> After considerable discussion with various people and a good deal of careful thought on my part, I have decided to accept Mr. Coffin's invitation to become a trustee of Metropolitan Museum. In accepting this position, I realize that I am taking the responsibility upon myself against your better judgment. It is an added responsibility which will take some of my time and I realize it is wiser to wait until I have been down here [in the office] two or three years before making major decisions of this kind. However, I feel that the advantages which this opportunity offers are of sufficient importance to outweigh the above mentioned objections. . . . My feeling is that when such an opportunity comes up one should not procrastinate too long. . . . My justification for spending the time which I do in this work [such as the museum] is that I feel that the aesthetic side of a person's life is almost as important as his spiritual development

or his physical well being. And finally, as I said before, I feel that
the contacts which such a position offers are not to be disregarded.
I am sorry to go against your feelings in this matter but I hope you
can see my point of view.

Affectionately,
Nelson

Late in 1931, Rockefeller and two other young businessmen,
Fenton Turck, who had been a vice president of American Radiator
Company, and Webster Todd, son of a director of Rockefeller Center,
joined in an unusual business enterprise. Rockefeller was particularly
interested because it offered him a chance to do something on his
own without breaking entirely away from his father's office. The three
men formed a firm called Turck & Co. into which each put a few
thousand dollars for rental of an office and operating expenses.

The idea behind the business, which was Turck's, was that they
would act as intermediaries in arranging deals between various companies on a reciprocal basis. For example, they might locate a real-
estate firm called X—— that had office space for rent and a manufacturing firm called Y—— that had elevators for sale but needed
expanded office space. They would negotiate a contract whereby the
real-estate firm would buy elevators for their new building from Y——
and Y—— would take office space in an X—— building. For this
service, Turck & Co. would receive a fee. Sometimes there might be
three or more businesses involved in a triple-play deal that would be
mutually beneficial. Rockefeller consulted his father before going into
the firm and Mr. Rockefeller, Jr., felt that it was wise to encourage the
venture rather than oppose it because his son seemed to be happiest
when creating something for himself. John D. Rockefeller, Sr., also
was consulted by Rockefeller and Turck and quickly understood the
plan and gave it his blessing.

At the time, Mr. Rockefeller, Jr., was deep in the work of building
Rockefeller Center, the great complex of skyscrapers that was to rise
in the heart of New York City between Fifth and Sixth avenues and
to become a world-famous tourist attraction because of its gardens and
plazas and theaters and shops. Obviously, Rockefeller's connections

with the center, with the Chase National Bank, with the oil companies and other businesses was an advantage to Turck and Co.

"Nelson felt the company was an opportunity to be on his own," an employee of the firm commented. "He never played up the family prestige or family connections but, of course, the name was there and it was important to the firm. Nelson wanted something that would make him work at top speed. He wasn't easily discouraged. He was able to shift his tactics to meet changing situations and, if one thing didn't work, he was quick to say: 'Okay, let's try it another way.' It seemed to me that perhaps people first listened to him because of his name but they quickly realized that he was doing things on his own."

The business prospered for more than a year. Then Rockefeller bought out his partners, who were rather reluctant to sell, and changed the firm's name to Special Work, Inc., which was devoted mainly to renting space in Rockefeller Center on a commission basis, the same as various other individuals and real-estate firms. In all, Rockefeller was an aggressive renting agent and managed to contract for some 300,000 of the center's total of 5,500,000 square feet of space at a time when the country was deep in the great economic depression of the early 1930's. He also came in for some severe criticism by other real-estate operators because of deals that were made to entice tenants to the center. Some prospective tenants were offered below-market rates for a specified period and others were told that their unexpired leases would be taken over if they moved at once to the new quarters. Considerable bitterness developed and, in 1934, August Heckscher, whose building had lost some important tenants, sued the board of directors of Rockefeller Center for $10,-000,000, charging unfair competition and coercion of tenants. Papers were served on the directors, who included John D. 3rd and Nelson, but the suit was dropped before coming to trial. Rockefeller persistently maintained that the center's rental methods were both legal and ethical as well as customary practice in New York.

III.

Young Rockefeller was just as enthusiastic about establishing his home as he was about getting started in business. Even before they were married, he and Miss Clark had spent many days touring the highways and back roads of New England, searching for antique furniture for their cottage on the Pocantico Hills estate. Rockefeller became something of an expert on grandfather clocks and Cape Cod rocking chairs and on one occasion even bought the floorboards out of a farmer's attic to use as paneling.

Rockefeller also had a prominent hand later in decorating the Fifth Avenue apartment. He persuaded Henri Matisse to do (for a sizable fee) a mural for the fireplace wall of the living room and, in time, his collection of modern French and American paintings adorned the walls of every room in the apartment. His private collection of painting and sculpture, incidentally, includes virtually all of the well-known artists—Picasso, Dufy, Klee, van Gogh, Kiyunobu, Noguchi, Marini—and quite a few others that nobody ever heard of but whose work happened to please him.

Mary Todhunter Clark Rockefeller, however, was the home builder. She came from a very large, wealthy family and knew how to adjust to almost anything except the idea that anybody named Rockefeller was fair game for newspaper reporters. In time, she learned to adjust to that circumstance, too, but even then she would never agree that reporters had been within their constitutional rights when they lurked behind bushes and tried to crash their way into the church at her wedding.

She had grown up outside Philadelphia on an estate that was part of a grant by King George III to her maternal forebears from Wales. Her grandfather, George B. Roberts, had been president of the Pennsylvania Railroad and a whole host of relatives with many children lived in the neighborhood. Her father was an investment banker, Edward White Clark, and the Clark clan, too, was thickly scattered over the adjacent countryside so that she was accustomed to being among many relatives and friends. Her childhood was pleasant and carefree against a background of complete security and unity within the big family circle. On Christmas Day, for example, Mary Clark always went to a midday meal at the home of a member of the Roberts family, where perhaps twenty or more relatives would be present. And for dinner that evening she would sit down at the home of her father's brother, where there might be as many as sixty relatives at the table—so many, in fact, that her uncle built a special dining hall for such occasions.

Mary Clark went to Foxcroft School in Virginia, where she greatly improved in horseback riding but would have flunked French except for the fact that she learned so little about the language that the faculty refused to permit her to take the examination for fear the result would lower the scholastic average of the institution. That year several other girls from Foxcroft were going to finishing school in Paris, but Mary and her cousin, Miss Eleanor Clark, were not interested in finishing school. They went to Paris, however, and lived for a year in the home of a widow, Madame Louise Baudry, who had five daughters. The two American girls lived in one room of the fifth-floor apartment (no elevator) and ate their meals at the family table, where they couldn't understand a word for weeks. Eleanor was studying piano and practiced five hours a day on an upright in their room. Mary sat in the same room and, with marvelous power of concentration, studied French literature so successfully that she was the only one of half a dozen American girls in her class at the Sorbonne who passed the course. (The friendship with the Baudrys, incidentally, continued, and many years later three of Mary Clark Rockefeller's children lived for a while with two of the Baudry girls, who, by then, had families of their own.)

When she married Nelson Rockefeller, Mary Clark was a tall, slender brown-haired girl with a quick, orderly mind of her own. She was candid and outspoken among her friends and she had a kind of tart, penetrating wit that made her both entertaining and companionable. It wasn't always easy for her to adjust to being a Rockefeller, not only because the name attracted publicity but because she had to accept the discipline that the Rockefeller family had always imposed on themselves. Nevertheless, the close family ties, the clan atmosphere were familiar to her and she fitted smoothly into Pocantico Hills and into the Sunday gatherings at the elder Rockefellers' dinner table. She managed, too, to remain out of the public eye for years, even when she was traveling everywhere with her husband.

The Rockefellers' first child, Rodman Clark, was born in 1932 and Ann Clark—all of their children have Clark for a middle name— was born in 1934. Rockefeller took parenthood with utmost serious- ness and, on one occasion, gave his mother a lecture on how she should behave toward little Roddy. "I took it very meekly," his mother re- marked later, reflecting that she had had some experience in bring- ing up children, "but it amused me greatly."

Mary Rockefeller's interests, however, were not limited to her family. She was a good gardener and she was interested in music and literature. She participated eventually in many civic endeavors, rang- ing from the Defense Advisory Committee on Women in the Services to the Garden Club of America; and she belonged to numerous organizations, ranging from the English-Speaking Union to the Ladies Aid Society of the Union Church of Pocantico Hills. But, actually, she devoted most of her civic efforts to the Bellevue School of Nursing in New York City.

"When she first became a member of the Board of Managers in 1932, she was young and shy and didn't want to speak up," an as- sociate at the Bellevue School commented. "But she was always tremendously interested and she devoted so much of her time to the school throughout the years. She is a very real person and, after she resigned as president of the board, we missed her very much."

IV.

For the first couple of years of his business career, Rockefeller was dividing his time between his father's office and his own affairs with more and more of his time devoted to Special Work, Inc. But in the summer of 1933 he decided that he was making a mistake and, perhaps, neglecting family responsibilities. On July 3, he put his thoughts into a letter which was delivered to the adjacent office of his father.

Dear Father,

As you know, I am continually in a state of flux as far as my ideas and theories are concerned and I realize that this has made things rather difficult for you in the past, for which I am very sorry. Perhaps I may be oscillating back and forth but at least I like to think of myself as making steady progress. Now it happens that at the present time I have just emerged into a new period with an entirely new line-up as far as certain of my ideas are concerned.

I went into Special Work, Inc., because I felt lost and beyond my depth in the work of this office. Special Work gave me a chance to do things on a smaller scale—where if I made mistakes it didn't make so much difference as the responsibility rested squarely on my shoulders. There is no question but that this work has been of the greatest possible value to me and I have confidence where before I was groping fearfully in the dark. However, I have come to see things more clearly in their true proportions and now realize that the activities of Special Work, Inc., are not all important. Furthermore, I am beginning to see more clearly the importance and even international significance of some of the things that take place in this office. . . . Up to now my background has been too limited to fully appreciate some of these things.

The purpose of this letter is to tell you that Special Work is running smoothly now and will require very little of my time in the future. Therefore, I hope that I will be able to be of distinctly more assistance to you. . . . For the immediate future, my plan is to become more familiar with all phases of your . . . interests. . . . Of course, if there are special problems which I can handle or help you with I will be only too glad to do what I can.

To summarize, I might say that I simply want you to know by this letter that I am back in the fold again as far as my interests are concerned and that from now on my one desire will be to be of as much help to you as I possibly can with my limited experience. I can assure you that I will spare nothing toward this end, for, although not very apparent, our appreciation for all you have done is un-limited.

Affectionately,

Nelson

Mr. Rockefeller, Jr., was gratified that his second son had made his decision entirely on his own. He replied that he was sure that "the experience you have gained in your own business has been of great value . . . and helped fit you to be increasingly useful in the larger affairs of our office." Later that year, he complimented his son on his handling of office matters from time to time and on "the evidence of the keen interest you have taken" in family affairs. He also occasionally wrote an interoffice memorandum of a more critical nature, as when he noticed in the accounts of David, who was still in college, an item of $100 that had been given to him by Nelson to help pay his expenses on a trip to Florida to see his Grandfather Rockefeller.

> . . . While this was most kind of you, I am wondering whether it was wise. As you, of course, must know, it was not because of the cost involved that I did not pay the expenses of David's trip to Ormond, but because of a principle, having to do with the wise use of money which his desire to make this trip south raised. Whether I was right or wrong . . . is perhaps aside from the point, for I obviously did what I thought was right. Your gift, made on a generous impulse, vitiated to that extent the lesson which I was trying to help David learn.
>
> . . . Let me say in closing that I appreciated fully the generosity of your impulse and have written this letter only to raise the query as to whether it is wise for you to have acted upon it without first having ascertained the purpose which led me to take the position I did.

The family affairs covered so much ground that young Rockefeller was active in a dozen different enterprises in these years, including the execution of a program for selling some eighty parcels of family property in Ohio, building a block of modernistic apartment houses and starting a company of his own to sell hand-painted postcards for a quarter a card. He also was widely but incorrectly credited with influencing his father to issue a notable statement favoring repeal of the prohibition laws in the United States. As the story was told, young Rockefeller persuaded his father that prohibition was a failure by taking him on a two-block tour of midtown speakeasies and then pointing out that all of them were on Rockefeller-owned property. The fact was that Mr. Rockefeller, Jr., issued his statement in 1932 only after consultation with a number of noted authorities, including George W. Wickersham, who was head of a commission investigating the problem of prohibition and gangsterism. "I couldn't have taken him on a speakeasy tour," his second son said later, "because I didn't know how to find a speakeasy in those days."

In 1934, Rockefeller broadened his knowledge of family affairs by going to work for the Chase National Bank, including a spell in London and Paris. He accompanied his uncle Winthrop Aldrich, president of the bank, on a busy tour of the United States to discuss depression problems with bankers and businessmen in all of the large cities—a trip that featured so many luncheons and dinners and informal get-togethers that even Rockefeller reported he was near exhaustion by the time they left San Francisco. Some months later he was in Paris and London, giving luncheons for Standard Oil executives and entertaining Chase National Bank officials at dinners; playing tennis with relatives of the Royal Family and going for a ride with a man whose name he couldn't remember but whose coach-and-four had just won all prizes in a national competition. He didn't become enthusiastic about banking but in Paris he spotted a new French automobile that fascinated him, a sleek black number with a long and graceful snout. When he returned to the United States he asked Edsel Ford, a neighbor at Seal Harbor during summer months, about the car and discovered that Ford also had seen and been impressed by the French design, and had ordered one of the cars for himself.

"Could you get just a body sent over for me and mount it on a Ford chassis?" Rockefeller asked.

Ford didn't see why not and had the job done in 1935. The result was so satisfactory that it became the basis of the Lincoln Continental design later produced by the Ford Company. Rockefeller was delighted with his hybrid car, so much so that he was still driving it a quarter of a century later on Mount Desert Island.

Rockefeller had been a director of Rockefeller Center almost from the time he finished college, but he began devoting a major part of his time to the huge real-estate operation in the mid-1930's as the first buildings were being completed. In those days of severe economic depression the $125,000,000 skyscraper development not only was losing money at the rate of around $4,000,000 a year but was burdened with a mortgage for $40,000,000 that Mr. Rockefeller, Jr., had negotiated to complete the construction. At first, in addition to his interest in Special Work, Inc., Rockefeller was mainly concerned with promotion stunts to build up interest in the Center. He had an easygoing charm, one reporter wrote, "that made him the logical man, as the Center's various buildings were completed, to open bunny gardens in the Sunken Plaza, dedicate wisteria exhibits and skating rinks, present certificates and gold buttons to outstanding construction workers, and so on. On these occasions he made graceful little speeches with the manner of a particularly articulate and successful basketball coach." He also pleased his father, who wrote him that he was "both proud and happy to have been so well represented . . . by you" at a center ceremony.

The young man doubtless needed praise because earlier he had gotten the center into one of its worst public relations muddles by arranging for the famous Mexican artist Diego Rivera to do a mural in the lobby of the main office building, 30 Rockefeller Plaza. The deal with Rivera was started in 1932 when he was regarded as one of the world's foremost muralists and when his powerful Mexican style had attracted the attention of young Rockefeller and his mother. There were protracted negotiations in which Rockefeller agreed with Rivera's desire to use color rather than sepia in his painting.

"I have gone into this question with Mr. [Raymond] Hood and Mr. [Wallace] Harrison [the architects] and they are quite agreeable, in fact, very enthusiastic . . . about using some color," Rockefeller wrote the artist on October 13, 1932. "May I take this opportunity to again tell you how much my mother and I appreciate your spirit in doing this mural under the existing circumstances."

By November, Rivera had presented his sketch for the mural,

which was approved, and had written for Mrs. Rockefeller a synopsis of the painting which he said he hoped to do as a fresco. "I believe," he added, "that actually the place of this fresco is truly a magnificent place in itself, and also in the whole world being given the importance . . . and passing events of the building in which it finds itself. . . . Permit me to thank you now for this wonderful opportunity . . . added to all the good things for which I owe you already in aiding my work."

By May, 1933, the artist was far along on the work—a painting sixty-three feet long and seventeen feet high, dominating the lobby of the building. A great deal of publicity, helped along by the Center's public relations staff, attended his efforts, and about a hundred tickets a day were issued to artists, students and others who came to watch him work. But as the painting progressed, the directors of Rockefeller Center became alarmed. Instead of following the sketch and synopsis that he had presented, Rivera was putting on the wall a picture with far-reaching political implications. On May 4, 1933, Rockefeller wrote to Rivera:

> While I was in the . . . building at Rockefeller Center yesterday viewing the progress of your thrilling mural, I noticed that in the most recent portion of the painting you had included a portrait of Lenin. The piece is beautifully painted but it seems to me that his portrait appearing in this mural might very seriously offend a great many people. If it were in a private house, it would be one thing but this mural is in a public building and the situation is therefore quite different. As much as I dislike to do so, I am afraid we must ask you to substitute the face of some unknown man where Lenin's face now appears.
>
> You know how enthusiastic I am about the work which you have been doing and that to date we have in no way restricted you in either subject or treatment. I am sure you will understand our feelings in this situation and we will greatly appreciate your making the suggested substitution.

Rockefeller frequently has remarked that he is an incurable optimist about almost everything and he more or less proved it by expressing confidence that Rivera would pay any attention to the opinions of his capitalist employers. The artist not only ignored the request but began working at an intensified pace and introducing all kinds of unexpected ideas into his painting. In vivid colors, he imbedded in the wet plaster scenes of poison gas warfare, huge germs of infectious hereditary social diseases, so placed that they were related to a civilization that revolved around night clubs and bridge parties, a massed attack by soldiers spraying liquid fire and backed by airplanes and tanks, a Communist demonstration on Wall Street with plug-ugly mounted police swinging clubs at workers bearing such slogans as "We want work, not charity—down with imperialistic wars." Almost the only really pleasant part of the mural was a group of students and folk dancers wearing peasant headdress beneath a red flag that indicated the scene was in Soviet Russia.

It seems unlikely that Rivera and his political mentors ever believed that the mural would become a part of the décor of the seventy-story capitalistic office building, but the circumstances offered a wonderful opportunity to use the artist for propaganda purposes. Rockefeller talked to Rivera in his most charming manner and came away feeling that things might be worked out satisfactorily, but that proved to be another illusion. On May 9, Hugh S. Robertson, executive manager of the center, wrote a formal letter to Rivera stating that the plan for the mural approved by the center had given "not the slightest intimation either in the description or in the sketch that you would include in the mural any portrait or any subject matter of a controversial nature. . . . We cannot but feel that you have taken advantage of the situation to do things that were never contemplated . . . [and] that there should be no hesitation on your part to make such changes as are necessary to conform . . . to the understanding we had with you." Rivera went right on painting as he pleased until the next night at 9 P.M. when a messenger climbed up the scaffold and asked him to come to Robertson's office on an upper floor. Rockefeller was not there, having been conveniently sent out of town on another mission, but Robertson told Rivera that their contract had not been observed, gave him a check that completed full payment of $21,500 and asked him to retire from the scene. The artist did, but only after a vulgar and contemptuous gesture directed at Robertson and the capitalistic system in general.

Even before Rivera could leave the building, a Communist parade of demonstrators formed in the street carrying signs that said: "Workers protest against attempt to destroy Rivera's fresco" and "Save Rivera's art." They caused enough confusion to require police to intervene and to capture front-page headlines in the newspapers next day. The mural was covered with canvas. Rockefeller did not want to see it destroyed and he secured the center's consent to have it removed and installed in the Museum of Modern Art, where he believed a fee of twenty-five cents could be charged viewers to cover the expense of installation. This plan collapsed, however, when it proved impossible to remove the mural and, one Saturday midnight in February, 1934, workmen began chipping the painting from the plaster wall. The destruction of Rivera's work was good for more newspaper headlines and many letters of protest to the Rockefellers, such as one saying: "Your family achieved a little measure of immortal fame—as destroyer of one fine example of the only vital art which the Western World has produced in five hundred years."

It was typical of Rockefeller that he held no resentment against Rivera, although the artist wouldn't speak to him for years. Eventually, they again became friends. Robertson lost no time in hiring another artist, José Maria Sert, to fill in the yawning space in the lobby of the building with a sepia mural featuring such characters as Abe Lincoln and Thomas A. Edison.

By 1937, Rockefeller had worked his way up in the center organization to become executive vice-president, and was taking an active role in handling major problems. He touched off a reorganization of the center's executive staff that eliminated several highly paid jobs and led to his assumption of the duties of president in May of 1938. Later, when he and his four brothers owned the center, he served as chairman of the board and as president at various intervals. Among other things, he initiated a labor relations program that eliminated the original company union setup at the center and recognized nine

American Federation of Labor unions. The center has never had a strike except one brief wildcat affair during the war. Rockefeller also had a hand in establishing an employee pension program for members of the center staff, the first such plan offered all employees of a major firm in the field of building ownership and management. He later installed a scholarship program for children of employees of the center and the Radio City Music Hall, with two full-time college scholarships each year and five annual scholarships for children of employees interested in medical, educational, welfare and technical careers.

During World War II, when there was a great shortage of office space, Rockefeller Center broke out of the red on an operating basis and a few years later began making a profit after depreciation on an operating basis. By 1959, it had boosted its total gross income to $27,500,000 and had long since lifted the mortgage on the old homestead. It had also started a new phase of expansion with the construction of a forty-eight story Time & Life office building.

Rockefeller's labors in the creation of the center represented more than just a desire for commercial success. New York City, with its mighty spires and noisy traffic and surging crowds, has always fascinated him and his pride in his hometown is limitless. Every so often, he has to go for a walk just to look at the skycrapers from different angles or catch a new vista down a crowded street. And on such jaunts, particularly around Rockefeller Center, he's pretty sure to stop a couple of times, point out a particular view to his walking companion and exclaim: "Look! That's New York—isn't it wonderful?"

v.

Rockefeller's life during the 1930's was by no means confined to the world of commerce. In that decade, his interest in art expanded rapidly and in several directions. As a trustee of the Metropolitan Museum of Art, he had little room to exercise his talents or his energy because that institution was run in a highly conservative fashion by the iron hand of its president, George Blumenthal. Rockefeller looked elsewhere. At one time, he interested New York Mayor Fiorello La Guardia in a plan to enlarge Rockefeller Center northward by building a municipal theater, an opera house and a new home for the Museum of Modern Art. When La Guardia gave up the idea, Rockefeller turned to promotion of the Museum of Modern Art, which his mother had helped found and which had elected him a trustee in 1932 and treasurer in 1935.

Rockefeller was largely responsible for sparking a campaign that raised $2,000,000 for a new home for the museum. The unusual modern building was ready in 1939, when Rockefeller was elected president to succeed A. Conger Goodyear, one of the founders. Geoffrey T. Hellman reported in *The New Yorker*:

> Rockefeller's elevation to this fashionable aesthetic post coincided with the moving of the Museum . . . to a spectacular building of its own. The opening was marked by a fifteen-minute congratulatory address by President Roosevelt on a national hookup and by a speech by Rockefeller, in which . . . he rather pointedly failed . . . either to mention that [the museum] had already been in existence for ten years or to allude to the part which Mr. Goodyear and others had played in founding it and in building it up. "It sounded as though the Museum had just opened that night," a member of the audience later reported. "It came as quite a surprise to the staff."

The Museum of Modern Art under Rockefeller's guidance operated with considerable fanfare and attracted large audiences to its special exhibitions of modern American and European painting. Rockefeller pressed a policy that favored the showing of Latin American painting and sculpture, much to the satisfaction of Rockefeller and our neighbors to the south but without creating any great impression on the world of art. Nevertheless, the museum became one of the big attractions in New York and its membership rose from 3,500 when Rockefeller became president to 25,000 in 1959. Rockefeller served as president at two different periods and later became chairman of the board. He has watched over the museum like a nervous parent, contributed heavily to its development and, when fire broke out there in 1958, he rushed from his office, donned a fireman's protective suit and dashed into the smoke-filled building to help rescue endangered masterpieces.

The museum has carried on a vigorous educational program and has circulated its exhibitions throughout the United States in educational and nonprofit institutions. In 1952, a five-year grant from the Rockefeller Brothers Fund provided $125,000 to develop a program of cultural exchange of the visual arts with other countries. After successful exhibitions in Brazil, Japan, Paris and elsewhere the program was taken over permanently by the museum's International Council, with the aid of contributions from interested groups and individuals.

The Museum of Primitive Art, which was found by Rockefeller in 1954, is devoted to collecting and exhibiting the "artistic achievements of the indigenous civilizations of the Americas, Africa and Oceania, and of the early phases of the more developed civilizations of Asia and Europe." The nucleus of the collection was pieces of primitive sculpture which Rockefeller had collected for himself but to this were later added many masks, ritual vessels, ornaments and figures, so that it became perhaps the most comprehensive collection of its kind in the world.

Although his pursuit of excellence in modern art took up a great deal of Rockefeller's spare time during the 1930's, he managed to work into his schedule a reasonable amount of tennis, riding, golf and swimming and a few big-game hunting trips in Alaska and Texas. In 1939, with three friends and a guide, he flew in an amphibian plane to a remote lake in Alaska to hunt bear. The party didn't have much luck for a couple of days but on the third day Rockefeller and the guide spotted a kodiak and a grizzly bear in mountainous territory and maneuvered themselves into position for a shot. Rather excitedly, Rockefeller fired and the kodiak bear fell. The other bear lumbered away and the hunter leaped up to take a look at his prey.

"Shoot again!" the guide yelled, but Rockefeller was so nervous that his second standing shot missed the mark and the bear charged him. The Indian guide dropped to one knee and shot the animal dead but it was so close that he was shaking with fear when he stood up.

Later, on the same trip, Rockefeller and the guide pursued two mountain goats up a ridge some four hundred feet high and very narrow. The goats crossed a narrow ledge that dropped off into sheer cliff and the guide followed them. Rockefeller got to the ledge, looked down and suffered a severe attack of vertigo. For five minutes he couldn't move, and then he was able only to give up the chase and back slowly down from the ledge. Although he had never before been bothered by heights, the experience had a kind of traumatic effect on him and he has suffered from vertigo ever since.

On a much later occasion, Rockefeller was brushed by near-tragedy while sailing off Greece, but it was a trip on which he had had a premonition of disaster. With two other couples, the Rockefellers had chartered a yawl for an expedition among the Greek islands. Before they arrived in Athens prior to embarking, Rockefeller began worrying about equipment, particularly life preservers.

"We'll get some of those pull-cord life jackets," he told his wife.

"Why bother?" she replied. "The boat will be fully equipped."

"I suppose so," he said, "but it keeps popping up in my mind that we should get some. I've been thinking about it for days."

He raised the subject again before they got on the boat, but nobody else in the party was concerned and, although Rockefeller grumbled, nothing was done. He was still worried as they put out to sea and immediately made an inspection which showed that there were no life jackets aboard and no life preservers except air cushions. Looking further, he found the boat had only one dinghy, which would carry five persons, and one air mattress, which might support four. There were nine persons aboard, six passengers and three crewmen.

He was taking a nap after lunch when the floorboards in his cabin blew up. Gas had accumulated around the Diesel engine and a spark had ignited it and started a fire in the engine pit. Immediately, there was danger that the fuel supply would be ignited and explode.

"I simply had been expecting it," Rockefeller said later. "I knew something of the sort was going to happen."

The crew got nowhere by throwing water on the flames around the engine. Rockefeller got the dinghy and air mattress over the side despite heavy seas, linking the mattress to the dinghy by a line so it could be towed. He found the medicine case that he always carries on trips and treated one of the passengers, Mrs. Lawrence Roberts, who had been badly burned on the legs and face. The yawl was ten miles at sea and the waves were so rough that the chances of rowing to shore in an overloaded dinghy were not favorable. They were about ready to try it, however, when a young boy in the crew boldly grabbed a piece of canvas, jumped down into the engine pit and smothered the flames. "I think," Rockefeller remarked, "that he really saved our lives."

Mrs. Roberts was in a state of shock and they made sail immediately for the nearest island. It was uninhabited. That night they hove to. The next morning the wind dropped and they were stranded for eight hours. Mrs. Roberts was in great pain by that time and, when evening brought a fresh wind, they made sail in the darkness. Rockefeller took the wheel and, despite a near-miss on a cliff, reached port at night and got Mrs. Roberts to a doctor.

## VI.

Rockefeller crowded a lot of experience into his first few years as a businessman but he still wasn't sure of just where he was headed. The presidency of Rockefeller Center, the presidency of the Museum of Modern Art, membership on the boards of various business and philanthropic enterprises might seem enough of a career for one man. But for Rockefeller it was no more than a restless beginning; it had been too easy and it had been too much the result of his inherited position. For several years, he had been in close contact with a group of men who liked to take a broad, almost philosophical look at what was happening in their country and in the world. Their horizons were not limited by the impressive skyline of Rockefeller Center or of Wall Street. They were trying to look ahead, to weigh the danger of war in Europe, to know what was in store for the nation's economy and for the political development of the world community. Just as at Dartmouth he had discovered, with some surprise, that there was more to college than passing examinations and kicking a soccer ball, Rockefeller now found that there was more to a career than building a skyscraper or negotiating a wage agreement with a labor union. He was still a man with a keen yearning for action but he began to acquire a sense of direction and an ability to look forward toward a broad horizon. He could not, perhaps, see very far or very clearly but he was learning how to look.

In the late 1930's, when the Nazi regime in Germany was creating turmoil in Europe, he accepted an invitation to deliver the commencement address at the University of New Hampshire. He began by saying that he probably was expected to hand out a lot of advice and to paint a rosy future for the young men and women who were now going out to face a world that was torn by tremendous economic chaos and faced with a grave threat of a great war.

"But I can't do it," he went on. "I feel it is only realistic to say that all those rosy promises of golden opportunity for college youth are strictly the bunk. I want to tell you that the honeymoon is over, and that when you leave the sheltered campus of this great educational institution you will be stepping out into the cold gray dawn of reality.

"The responsibility of the world of tomorrow is on your shoulders. . . . I believe that the solution of these problems lies very much in your hands and mine. It is up to this generation to restore peace and order."

# South American Enthusiasms

It was springtime when Nelson Rockefeller fell in love again—this time with a lush, green tropical countryside or perhaps it would be more accurate to say with the whole continent of South America. On a bright, sunny day in April of 1937 he stood in the bow of a ninety-foot boat steaming on the Orinoco River in eastern Venezuela and studied in wide-eyed wonder the swamps and jungles that slid into view on either bank. Everything fascinated him. That night, listening to the weird noises in the jungle blackness, Rockefeller poured out his enthusiasm and delight in a hastily scrawled letter to his parents.

> We have been coming down the most beautiful tropical river all day in the Standard Oil Company's yacht. We spent the last two days visiting the oil fields in the interior of eastern Venezuela in the company's planes and then went on the boat last night. . . . This is low swampy country, a dense overhanging growth which changes character from time to time. The trees are full of monkeys and birds of all descriptions and colors, big and small. There are alligators on the banks . . . every once in a while you see a big turtle, fast asleep on top of the water. But most interesting of all are the Indians. They

111

live in little palm leaf huts along the river, wear practically no clothes and paddle around in hollowed out logs. They spend their time getting bark from which is made tannic acid and fishing. . . . The pelicans do a much better job of the latter.

I really think we have learned more in the last week than ever before in such a short time. . . . We met the President and all the members of his cabinet at two parties and called on the Governors of four states, plus talking at great length to many men in the Standard Oil Company and others. . . . Unless something unforeseen happens it looks as if this would turn out to be one of the soundest . . . countries in the world—and there's certainly plenty of oil here.

In a way, the trip was one of the turning points in Rockefeller's life. His background and his training already were carrying him in the direction of certain broad social and humanitarian objectives. But he was young, his viewpoint was confused and uncertain and his immediate course was vague until he saw at first hand the problems and the potentialities of Latin America's underdeveloped economy. This vast and often backward part of the world, rich in natural resources, represented to him not an abstract sociological problem such as those he had wrestled with in his father's office but a concrete, understandable opportunity for direct action. He could see problems and feel the challenge: the kind of challenge he had been seeking.

The love affair with Latin America did not develop easily or spontaneously. As a boy, Rockefeller had felt no affinity toward the peoples south of the border and even had such serious trouble with the Spanish language that he dropped it from his school work.

More than a decade passed before he discovered that dropping Spanish had been a mistake but then, with his customary enthusiasm, he plunged into an intensive Berlitz School course so that he could learn to speak the language. This change in attitude grew out of the fact that, in 1935, he had made a substantial investment in Creole Petroleum Company, the Venezuelan subsidiary of Standard Oil of New Jersey, and had become a minority stockholder representative on the board of directors. Eager to see for himself what was going on, he arranged to tour South America two years later with his wife and a party that included Eleanor Clark, Joseph Rovensky of the Chase National Bank, Jay Crane of the Standard Oil Company, and Winthrop Rockefeller. The party was carefully briefed in advance as to economic and social and political conditions in each of the countries they would visit during their three-month tour, and they drew up a list of important business, banking and government personalities with whom they would talk.

This was a well-planned business tour but, oddly enough, when Rockefeller got back home his sharpest memories were of things outside the normal sphere of business and banking. In addition to his delight in the back country of Venezuela, he had been impressed by meeting Dr. Albert A. Giesecke, former president of the University of Cuzco in Peru, a man who could talk with great authority on the pre-Columbian history of South America. Rockefeller was fascinated by this first glimpse of the ancient culture and traditions of the continent. Through Dr. Giesecke, he met a noted archaeologist, Dr. Julio César Tello, who had been director of the Archaeological Museum and also a member of the Peruvian Senate. Dr. Tello had found and excavated more than one hundred mummy bundles in the desert tombs at Paracas. The mummies were wrapped in layers of materials that had been woven before 800 A.D. and they represented an important historical treasure if they could be preserved. But there had been a change of government recently in Peru and as a result Dr. Tello had lost his seat in the Senate as well as his job as director of the museum. He told Rockefeller that now the government refused to give him the necessary funds to continue the work of opening the bundles and treating the woven material so that it would not be ruined by exposure to air and moisture.

The reason for the refusal was of particular interest to Rockefeller: the government leaders were predominantly of Spanish descent and they looked on Indian culture as inferior. This was enough to spur the young American businessman to indignant action. When he called on the President, he brashly brought up the problem of the mummy bundles, expressed the opinion that they were a national treasure and added that, as a trustee of the Metropolitan Museum of Art in New York, he was working on plans for developing closer ties between museums in New York and in South America.

"It is my intention," he said, "to provide the money necessary to unwrap the mummy bundles and dry out the materials, providing the Peruvian government will make provision for permanent maintenance of the collection." This offer of North American aid so impressed the government officials that they agreed to maintain the collection and, in time, Dr. Tello got back his job as director of the museum.

Like his mother, Rockefeller is a tireless collector of *objets d'art,* but his interests are so broad that he has no special field and sometimes very little discrimination. He is just as likely to stumble on and buy a prettily painted wooden horse from an ancient carousel—as he did early one morning on New York's East Side—as he is to pick up a rare piece of carved jade in Hong Kong. In Peru, he hired a tri-motored Ford airplane and, with his wife, his brother and Eleanor Clark, flew to the ancient Inca city of Cuzco, which is more than eleven thousand feet above sea level. In order to reach that altitude, before taking off the pilot of the plane removed most of the seats and other heavy equipment that could be spared. At Cuzco, Rockefeller was fascinated by the colorful native woolen textile market and dashed around excitedly, buying armloads of blankets and serapes. When the party returned to the plane, the pilot shook his head in despair.

"With that weight," he sighed, "we may never make it over the mountains."

Rockefeller optimistically predicted that they would make it and after a few more protests they took off and wobbled safely over the peaks on the return trip.

On another occasion, a companion who was familiar with Rockefeller's inability to resist buying odd souvenirs flew ahead of him to a South American city where the airport was overrun by salesmen of native handicraft, most of it bad. One vendor offered him a particularly hideous traveling bag, festooned with alligator claws and other odd trappings. "No," he said, "I won't buy the thing but I'll bet you sell it before the day is over." He went on to his hotel to wait and, a couple of hours later, he was not at all surprised when Rockefeller arrived proudly carrying the amazing alligator bag.

A second important impression that Rockefeller brought back from his trip around South America was that there was an incredible lack of sympathy and understanding between Latin America and the United States. The Latin Americans were culturally and economically oriented toward Europe. They had little knowledge of the United States and little liking for North Americans, while most United States citizens living there had only superficial contact with the people with whom they were doing business.

Having discussed this deplorable situation with everyone who would listen to him, Rockefeller attended the annual meeting of the Standard Oil Company of New Jersey, which brought together some three hundred company executives from all parts of the world. The sessions were devoted largely to bringing the executives up to date on company problems and developments in technical fields. Rockefeller didn't have anything to contribute along the line of new techniques but when he offered to make a speech no one was going to refuse him the opportunity.

He spoke on the social responsibility of corporations. The general idea that he expressed was that the corporation held property at home and abroad by the will of the people. Of course, he added, there were laws that said the corporation owned this or that but, if the people did not feel that the property was being used in their interest, they would in some way and at some time find ways to change the laws.

"In the last analysis," he continued, "the only justification for ownership is that it serves the broad interest of the people. We must recognize the social responsibilities of corporations and the corporation must use its ownership of assets to reflect the best interests of the people. If we don't, they will take away our ownership."

This was perhaps the most unpopular speech ever made to such a meeting of the Standard Oil Company of New Jersey, although none of the officers put it exactly that way to young Rockefeller. They merely felt, as did most business leaders of the day, that it was their job to run the company as efficiently and as profitably as possible. But there were a few executives like Eugene Holman, then chairman of the board of Creole, who were sympathetic toward the speaker. It wasn't difficult for Rockefeller to pick them out of the crowd, and he remembered them. He also gained greater confidence in his own viewpoint in 1938 when oil company properties were expropriated by Mexico, a country which felt that American business was not serving the interests of the people and which therefore changed the laws to take away American ownership.

These general ideas had been implanted in Rockefeller's mind after only a brief acquaintance with Latin America, and he did his best to make executives of the Creole and Standard Oil companies aware of the problem. Progress against the company old guard was slow, although they found it difficult to ignore the influence of a Rockefeller, even when it was a young and inexperienced and impatient Rockefeller. In this connection, it is noteworthy that, in the past, when Mr. Rockefeller, Jr., believed that a course was right or that a certain thing should be done, he was not hesitant to use his influence or the Rockefeller name if necessary to carry out his ideas. Mr. Rockefeller's second son, Nelson, was also willing to use his influence and he did, although in most instances his approach was as a friendly, enthusiastic and persuasive collaborater who was sure everybody would agree with him if only they knew all the facts. To make sure that he had the facts right he took a refresher course in Spanish and went back to South America in 1939.

II.

The ability to speak Spanish—poorly then, but fluently in time—enabled Rockefeller to confirm his original ideas. The Creole Company had followed the British concept of a self-contained compound. Camps were built inside barbed-wire fences and North American employees as well as foreign laborers lived behind a guarded gate. The company provided virtually everything from power plants to imported food. There was no attempt to become part of any locality. The company usually started operations well removed from any town. But within a short time a honky-tonk squatter town would spring up outside the gates—a town of saloons and places of amusement, of crime and disease and sickness. One such town in Venezuela grew to a population of twenty thousand but had no sewers, no schools and no water system. It was not likely that the company would gain a sympathetic view of the country or that the country would develop any friendliness for North Americans under such conditions.

In one city, Rockefeller went to luncheon at the home of the manager of a large United States company and was seated between the manager's wife and a high official of the country, neither of whom could speak the other's language. After acting as interpreter for them for a few minutes, he casually inquired how long the manager's wife had been in the country.

"Oh, I've been here twelve years," she replied. "And before that we were in Mexico for eight years."

"How is it that you don't speak the language after such a long time in Spanish-speaking countries?" he asked.

"Why should I?" she replied. "Who would I talk to in Spanish?"

She then began discussing the activities of the North American colony in the city and related the adventures of a minor United States diplomat who got drunk every Saturday night and on one occasion tried to break into the presidential palace.

The indifference of his compatriots toward the countries in which they worked and lived depressed Rockefeller. He observed that missionaries, educators and representatives of philanthropic foundations were almost the only United States citizens who tried to understand the culture or the aspirations of the people. He noticed, too, that many Europeans had a far better understanding and much closer relations with Latin America than did the United States businessmen. This was especially true of the Germans, who had married into important families in various South American countries, took an active part in local affairs and had great influence in political, social and government affairs in some countries.

Another thing that impressed Rockefeller was the feverish activity of the Communists in Latin America, particularly in labor circles, in universities and in the press. They attacked oil company activities as a capitalistic plot to exploit the workers and on occasion aimed their fire at Rockefeller and expressed the opinion he was in Latin America for nefarious purposes. Frequently, on the day after such attacks appeared in a Communist newspaper, a smiling, bare-headed young man would climb a flight of narrow stairs to the newspaper's editorial office, shake hands with the first person he met in the cluttered city room and say: "I'm Nelson Rockefeller and I'd like to meet your editor." This was definitely not the way a Communist editor expected his capitalistic target to react and Rockefeller usually was able to take advantage of his stunned surprise to explain the purpose of his visit to the city. He didn't expect this to have any effect on the editor's opinions but it gave him a chance to know the people who were attacking him and, in some instances, it opened the way to long-term acquaintance with newspapermen whom he liked even when he disagreed with them. Of these newspapermen, perhaps the most important was Rómulo Betancourt, a non-Communist, who was editor of *Ahora* and leader of the minority Democratic Action party in Venezuela.

Betancourt charged that Rockefeller was aiding the oil companies' efforts to be exempted from the wage and profit-sharing provisions of the new constitution, that poor tenants had been evicted from land acquired by the companies and that the Rockefeller heir was "exploiting our country with his specious, hypocritical" statements about trying to promote the well-being of humanity in the world.

> After looking over his vast oil properties . . . he will return to his office atop Rockefeller Center, to the warm shelter of his home, to resume his responsibilities as a philanthropist and Art Maecenas [Betancourt wrote]. Behind him will remain Venezuela producing 180 million barrels of oil for the Rockefellers. . . . Behind him will remain Venezuela with its half million children without schools, its workers without adequate diets . . . its 20,000 oil workers mostly

living in houses that the Department of Fomento (Development) states should better be called "over-grown match-boxes"; Venezuela with its three million pauper inhabitants, victims of frightful epidemics.

## III.

Betancourt's estimate of Rockefeller was not one that would stand the test of time. In Venezuela, the young oil scion had discovered a number of Creole executives who thought as he did. One of them was Arthur Proudfit, who was in favor of reorienting the company toward closer co-operation with the community. With Rockefeller's support, Proudfit's influence steadily increased and he eventually became president of the company. Another was the then manager, Henry E. Linam, who had been a poor boy in the oil fields of the Southwest and had gone to Venezuela as a driller.

Linam was a rough-and-ready character who carried a gun during the early days but who liked people, especially the Venezuelans. He quickly learned the language and made friends with the native laborers. Later, as he climbed to better jobs in the company, he lived in the native section of Caracas instead of in the so-called North American colony. His children went to Venezuelan schools. His friends included both high government officials and workers in greasy clothes from the oil fields, and any one of them might greet him on the streets with a hearty *abrazo* that amazed Rockefeller.

Many North Americans regarded Linam as a maverick but he was well known for his ability as an oil man and he was both fearless and kindly. Among other things, he ignored the tradition that only North Americans had the ability to handle drilling and rigging operations in the oil field and, after he became manager of the company, all the Creole drilling and field maintenance operations were handled by Venezuelan workers.

Linam, in later years, recalled that on his tours of Venezuela Rockefeller had a remarkable ability to meet people in all walks of life and to feel at ease with them as well as to make them feel at ease with him. Once Linam and Rockefeller were visiting a drilling operation in one of the oil fields and the latter wandered away to question members of a crew about their work. The driller watched for a few minutes and then strolled over to talk to Linam.

"I hear the field superintendent is being promoted," he said in Spanish.

"Yes," Linam replied.

The driller nodded toward Rockefeller. "I guess this man's going to be the new superintendent," he said. "Well, I think he's going to be a fine boss."

One government official in Venezuela told Linam that Rockefeller had endeared himself to the people because he conformed to the customs of the country and had learned to speak Spanish. Then, using an old Spanish saying, he added: "The important thing is that he does these things without any hint of being more popish than the Pope."

"This is a rare yet very important trait among the Latins," Linam commented. "They appreciate a foreigner who understands and who has the courtesy to conform to their customs. But they quickly detect insincerity when one tries to be more Latin than the Latins."

Gradually, men like Proudfit and Linam came to the top in Creole and gradually the relationship of the company to the community was changed. One of the first signs of the new order was the hiring of a dozen Berlitz teachers of Spanish in New York. They were sent to Venezuela to carry out an order that every company executive had to learn Spanish. Another step was to provide medical assistance for the squatter town inhabitants outside the barbed wire fence. The North American employees were encouraged to make friends in the communities in which they worked and to take part in civic activities. Venezuelans who could neither read nor write were soon trained to handle skilled mechanical operations and later their sons, with high school education in company-operated schools, worked in power plants and oil refineries and some of them received advanced training for jobs that in the United States are usually filled by graduates of Massachusetts Institute of Technology. With substantial funds from the company and the state governments, the shanty towns outside the compound slowly developed into cities, with water and sewerage, paved streets and schools. Whereas in the 1930's most of the natives suffered from malaria, hookworm and other tropical diseases and 90 per cent were undernourished, medical programs supported by the company so improved health conditions that workers gained from twenty-five to thirty pounds after a few months of proper diet and, within only fifteen years, the children in the oil camps averaged a little more than four inches taller than their parents.

There was, however, a still broader problem that interested Rockefeller. The Creole Company had grown rapidly in the 1930's and it would soon be a dominant economic factor in Venezuela. The company could maintain that position only if it contributed effectively to the general growth of the country's economy and helped raise the standard of living. In 1939, Creole hired a North American engineering firm to make a survey of the Venezuelan economy and to blueprint the bottlenecks that were stifling normal economic development. The survey showed that, while hundreds of millions of dollars had been pumped into the oil industry, little or nothing had been done about developing agriculture or other industries. Most food and supplies had to be imported. It was obvious that drastic measures were called for to bring the general economy up to the level of the oil industry if Venezuela was to gain an economic balance. But, at this point, the Creole Company was not in a position to be of special assistance. Its business was producing oil, not acting as a bank for economic development. The company, mindful of the expropriation of oil property in other Latin American countries, was willing to do its part, but it had its limits. This posed a problem that would attract Rockefeller's intense interest in the future.

IV.

The reorientation of the Creole Company did not, of course, take place suddenly. When Rockefeller returned to New York from his 1939 trip to South America he was convinced that there was an urgent need to improve both the business and diplomatic representation of the United States in Latin America. It is doubtful that he realized how formidable an undertaking that would be but not long afterward he had an opportunity to learn some of the frustrations that were to accompany efforts to put his ideas into practice. When the Mexican government expropriated the property of United States oil companies, the executives of the Standard Oil Company bitterly condemned the action as without legal justification, but there wasn't much they could do about it. A man seriously concerned about the Mexican government's action was Walter Douglas, a director of the Southern Pacific Railroad, who had worked in Mexico and was a friend of President Lázaro Cárdenas. Douglas told Rockefeller he believed a solution to the oil dispute might be found on a personal rather than a legalistic basis. He suggested that Rockefeller find out whether the oil companies could agree to a basis for settlement and that, if they could, he and Rockefeller go to Mexico to discuss the problem with Cárdenas.

Rockefeller took up the suggestion with the officers of the Standard Oil Company and, in the next few weeks, worked out terms for a possible settlement. The following month, he and Douglas, accompanied by their wives, went to see Cárdenas at his home in the little town of Juquilpan de Juárez, in the state of Michoacán. Cárdenas, a big, handsome man, was leader of the agrarian movement in Mexico and had put through reforms which broke up the big land holdings and helped to meet the Indians' craving for ownership of farms. He spent much time in the farming land, talking with local councils and listening to the ideas of the people. He and his wife had moved into a new home in Juquilpan de Juárez the day before the Rockefellers and Douglases arrived and they were not yet settled, but they greeted the party warmly. The ladies went into the garden, while the three men sat down to talk. Rockefeller decided not to take the initiative in regard to the oil problem. Instead, he told Cárdenas that, as president of the Museum of Modern Art, he was hopeful of putting on a show portraying the early cultural history of Mexico.

"But," he added, "it will cost $40,000 and the museum only has

$20,000 available. Do you think the Mexican government might put up $20,000,"

Cárdenas nodded. "Yes, we will do it," he said. "And I believe the Mexican railroad would provide free transportation to the frontier."

Rockefeller then said that the Mexican labor law provisions in regard to seniority were handicapping the work of certain United States foundations because young Mexican doctors trained in the United States were not permitted to fill top positions for which they were fitted. As a result, Mexico was not getting the full benefit of a program designed to improve health conditions in rural areas. The President knew nothing of the problem but he was deeply interested and promised that the necessary exceptions to the law would be made. The ladies returned from the garden, and still there had been no talk of oil.

While they were having tea, Cárdenas suggested that the visitors remain all night but even after dinner Rockefeller did not mention the oil problem. The next morning he arose early and went for a walk in the garden where he was joined about seven o'clock by the President, who brought up the oil expropriation issue. They talked for four hours, with a break for breakfast.

"I want to say I'm here as a private citizen, and have no official connection with the oil companies," Rockefeller said. "I believe the situation is unfortunate and that both sides have made mistakes."

Surprisingly, Cárdenas said: "You are the first United States contact I have ever had with the oil companies except for a lawyer [Donald R. Richberg] who was sent here to negotiate but who said frankly that he knew nothing about the oil industry, nothing about Mexico and did not have any authority to act." The President spoke with deep feeling but there was only a trace of bitterness in his voice. "Your businessmen don't associate with our government officials or with our business community. Nor do the British. I have a friend who plays golf. For seven years he had a locker at the golf club next to that of a leading British businessman. They never exchanged a word."

The conversation continued with frankness. It was, Rockefeller said later, one of the most instructive talks he ever had on the problem of relations among peoples. Cárdenas said that the actions of foreigners in Mexico, while creating great bitterness, were not the reason for expropriation of oil properties. "The real reason," he went on, "is not easy for you to understand. You have to remember that in the background is the seizure of Texas in 1836, the United States action in taking New Mexico and California in 1846, in sending your Army against Villa in 1916. Then you have to remember that our revolution ended the domination of the Spanish ruling class in Mexico and restored the self-confidence of our people. That was our liberation from domination in our own country."

There remained, however, the economic domination of the United States. The expropriation of oil properties, he continued, was a symbol of Mexican liberation from domination from without. Expropriation restored a sense of dignity and self-respect and independence, and that "is often more important to our people than is their own physical or economic well-being." The oil properties could not be returned to the former foreign owners, he emphasized, and no settlement could be made that would in any way jeopardize the self-respect regained.

"We must retain ownership even if the oil has to stay in the ground," he added. "Better that than for the people to lose their dignity."

Rockefeller had never heard talk like this before: a calm and dignified but intensely earnest exposition of the human element in international relations. Cárdenas expressed an emotional, almost a spiritual viewpoint but his youthful listener felt that it was just as important as the vast economic factors involved as far as the Mexicans were concerned. He could not take issue with the President's convictions, but he did discuss terms of a possible settlement and found Cárdenas interested. They agreed on various details but not on the one point—majority ownership—that was of vital importance to both sides. Each side offered to settle for 51 per cent ownership, but neither would accept 49 per cent.

Rockefeller later believed that both Cárdenas and the oil companies had taken the only positions possible in view of their basic convictions. The companies suffered heavy loss but the economic loss to the Mexican people in the following years was also great. On the other hand, both the companies and the country gained something. The Mexican expropriation was a kind of turning point for petroleum companies in the foreign field. They learned the importance of the proper observance of their social and political obligations abroad and the lesson would be taken to heart in the future by more and more United States industries in foreign countries. The economic loss, Rockefeller remarked later, was offset many times over by the improvement in relations between the United States and Mexico and, ultimately, in inter-American relations generally, basically because the United States government did not force the issue as might have been done in an earlier day.

The Mexican people gained in confidence and self-respect. And Nelson Rockefeller gained considerable—a far better understanding of the human element in world affairs as well as a lasting friendship with Lázaro Cárdenas.

v.

It was during these years in the latter 1930's, when Rockefeller was learning something of Latin America, that he was strongly influenced by the small group of friends—businessmen, economists, bankers—with whom he regularly discussed problems of United States activities abroad. The Group, as it became known, had an indefinite membership. There were perhaps four or five men who formed the nucleus, including economist Beardsley Ruml, architect Wallace K. Harrison, oil executive Jay Crane, and banker Joseph Rovensky and lawyer Tom Armstrong. But membership was constantly expanding and retracting, and the Group as a whole reflected a wide variety of ideas and philosophies. This made it more difficult for them to reach a collective opinion on problems but, at the same time, it provided a broad, realistic viewpoint as to what might be done to improve international relations and, especially, relations among the peoples of the Americas.

It was a basic belief of the Group that world peace and our own national security could be established only by striking at the roots of economic and social problems and by developing a positive, long-range program of international co-operation; a program that would help underdeveloped countries to help themselves in the interest of all. This called for mutual knowledge of each other's way of life, customs, traditions and aspirations; for an understanding among peoples and joint striving toward common goals. The Group tended to think in terms of action; but action was not easy. On one occasion, Rockefeller and Ruml went to Washington to discuss the situation south of the border with two of President Roosevelt's advisers, Ben Cohen and Tommy Corcoran. They said they felt that there was a great deal to be done to strengthen ties with Latin America in view of the approaching war crisis in Europe. Cohen and Corcoran were very much interested but nothing came of the meeting at that time.

The Group also tried to establish a committee of business and financial leaders who, they hoped, would take leadership in efforts to improve relationships of United States corporations operating in Latin America. The corporations weren't interested and the idea died out. Earlier Rockefeller, with Robert Bottome, Carl B. Spaeth, Edward H. Robbins, William F. Coles and Kelso Peck, had formed a company known as Compañía de Fomento Venezolano and opened offices in Caracas with the idea of attempting to finance local industrial development, and thus contribute to raising the general standard of living in Venezuela. But, by the time they got started, World War II was under way in Europe and action was almost impossible.

Only one project was undertaken and that as the result of a remark made to Rockefeller by President Eleázar López Contreras one day as they were riding through Caracas. The capital city had only one shoddy hotel at that time and this fact embarrassed the government.

"I've had proposals from a couple of United States groups to build a gambling resort hotel to attract tourists," the President remarked, "but I'd rather we had no hotel at all."

Rockefeller was sympathetic and said he would try to interest a

North American firm in building a hotel.

It didn't take much trying to discover that no hotel group in the United States wanted to build in Caracas. So the Compañía de Fomento Venezolano undertook to promote a new hotel, with the aid of the oil companies, which put up one-third of the required capital. Another third was put up by Venezuelan investors. Rockefeller, with the help of his family, put up the other third. Construction of the million-dollar Avila Hotel was started on the supposition that 73 per cent of its patrons would be tourists, but it was not finished until after the Japanese attack on Pearl Harbor plunged the United States into the war. The tourist trade was ended for the duration and the project appeared to be faced with failure, but Rockefeller felt he had a moral obligation to carry out his agreement to open the hotel.

In New York, Rockefeller's father had been studying the outlook for the hotel and decided that it was bad. He also decided that, because of the family association with the hotel, he had a moral obligation to the Venezuelan investors and, in view of the bleak prospects, he offered to buy back at par all of the stock sold to Venezuelans so they would not suffer a loss. Some of them sold to him, but others did not. The hotel opened on schedule and, from the first day, was a financial success, much to the surprise of Mr. Rockefeller, Jr. This apparently prompted some Venezuelan investors, who had taken advantage of Mr. Rockefeller's offer, to claim that it had all been a trick to get them out of a good thing.

"The experience," remarked the younger Rockefeller, "was a lesson in relations with local investors that would be useful to me in the years to come."

At the time, however, he was busy on other fronts. Even before war enveloped the United States, Rockefeller had plunged into the Washington bureaucratic jungle on a path that was to lead him to what has often been called the second most important political job in America.

# SIX

# Washington Duty

On the humid evening of June 14, 1940, Nelson Rockefeller walked unobtrusively into the White House carrying a brief case that contained, among other things, a three-page memorandum. He was conducted immediately to a room that had once been President Lincoln's study. Now it was the quarters of a long-time White House guest, Harry L. Hopkins, who was expecting him.

A gaunt man with brooding eyes and a melancholy smile, Hopkins had become President Roosevelt's close advisor and political fixer, a man with a great talent for getting things done despite his already shattered health. Since the beginning of World War II in Europe in 1939, Hopkins had been the President's eyes and ears and often the executor of his policies. He seemed to have a finger in everything—the administration's vast efforts to assist the Western Allied Powers to resist the aggression of Adolf Hitler's armed forces, the unofficial campaign against powerful isolationist sentiment in the United States, the push for stronger national defense and the movement to elect Mr. Roosevelt to an unprecedented third term, come next November.

128

Rockefeller had talked to several presidential advisors earlier about his own views and the views of the Group on Latin America. As soon as the European war started the British navy set up a blockade of Germany that cut off a third of Latin America's trade. Furthermore, the war isolated Latin America from its normal European source of supply for machinery and manufactured goods. About the only thing coming from Europe was Nazi and Communist propaganda, and that was disseminated on a huge scale. Unless economic help were given, Latin America would be a fertile ground for Axis propaganda and, in time, a possible point of penetration for Axis military invasion of the Western Hemisphere. With such dangers in mind, Hopkins, probably on the President's suggestion, had asked Rockefeller to draw up recommendations for a United States program of action. After consultation with the Group, the drafting was started by Beardsley Ruml but before he could complete it the German blitzkrieg against Holland, Belgium and France changed the face of war in Europe, put the British Isles in peril of invasion and greatly increased Nazi prestige in various South American countries. On the night Rockefeller visited Hopkins at the White House, the Battle of France was in its final stages and Hitler's military triumph was all but complete in Europe.

Hopkins received him gravely. His face was lined and he seemed tired as he sank back in his chair. Rockefeller pulled out the memorandum, entitled "Hemisphere Economic Policy," and Hopkins asked him to read it aloud. It began:

> Regardless of whether the outcome of the war is a German or Allied victory, the United States must protect its international position through the use of economic measures that are competitively effective against totalitarian techniques.
>
> If the United States is to maintain its security and its political and economic hemisphere position it must take economic measures at once to secure economic prosperity in Central and South America, and to establish this prosperity in the frame of hemisphere economic cooperation and dependence.
>
> The scope and magnitude of the measures taken must be such as

to be decisive with respect to the objectives desired. Half measures would be worse than wasted; they would subject the United States to ridicule and contempt.

As Rockefeller read, Hopkins showed an increasing interest. The memorandum outlined a broad program that included emergency measures to absorb surplus Latin American products; reduction and elimination of tariffs to stimulate a free flow of trade; measures to encourage investment in Latin America by private interests and by the government; a program to add to the government's 230 consular agents and otherwise improve services and boost personnel in Latin America; the appointment by the President of a small advisory committee of private citizens with direct access to the Chief Executive and of a small interdepartmental government committee to execute the program under direction of an executive assistant to the President. In addition, the memorandum said a vigorous program to improve cultural, scientific and educational relations in the Americas, with the co-operation of private agencies, was essential.

Hopkins had many questions to ask. The conversation became animated as Rockefeller's enthusiasm poured out and it was several hours before the meeting broke up, with Hopkins saying that he would talk to "the boss." When Rockefeller returned to New York, he didn't know whether anything would come of the meeting. France soon fell. Britain was desperately preparing for invasion by the Nazis. The full attention of Washington—of the world—was centered on Europe, and it seemed unlikely that Hopkins or anyone else would have time to think of the problem of Latin America.

President Roosevelt, however, indicated the extent of his concern by acting almost immediately. The memorandum from Rockefeller and Ruml was sent to the Secretaries of State, Commerce, Treasury and Agriculture, accompanied by a note from Mr. Roosevelt saying that it was "one of the many memoranda" he had received on the subject. He said that he considered our economic relations with Latin America a matter of great urgency and he asked each of the department heads to report to him not later than June 20 on "the action which this Government should take."

Mr. Roosevelt was not satisfied with the replies he received. He read the Rockefeller-Ruml memorandum to a meeting of cabinet members when Secretary of State Hull was away and the department was represented by Under Secretary Sumner Welles. As an authority on Latin America, Welles was upset by the idea that private citizens had prepared the memorandum and he was opposed to any new agency that would intrude into his particular area of operations. The President, however, on June 28 appointed James Forrestal as an administrative assistant with the task of dealing with inter-American affairs. On July 8, Forrestal called Rockefeller in New York, where he was celebrating his thirty-second birthday.

"Your memorandum has been considered by a cabinet committee," he said, "and the President has received recommendations on it. Can you come down here to talk about it?"

The following evening, an excited Rockefeller met Forrestal for dinner in the garden of the F Street Club. Forrestal asked a few pertinent questions and then let his guest talk. Rockefeller was bubbling with ideas and opinions about United States policy. He explored the possibilities of economic collapse turning the Latin American countries against the United States if we failed to assist them and he emphasized the Nazi propaganda line that the *Yanquis* were interested only in exploiting their southern neighbors. When it came to the problem of what the United States might do, Rockefeller was not very clear as to details. There were many areas in which he lacked both information and experience. But he had not the slightest hesitation in urging the administration to get busy at the job. If he impressed Forrestal as tending to be impulsive, the older man gave no indication of his reaction. As a matter of fact, he probably had already made up his mind that the Rockefeller-Ruml memorandum was a reasonable basis of approach to the problem and he doubtless knew that both Hopkins and Mrs. Anna Rosenberg, who was close to the President and who had worked on labor relations problems at Rockefeller Center, had commended it to Mr. Roosevelt.

"Nelson," Forrestal said at last, "the President is ready to take action. What would you think of coming to Washington to work with me on this program?"

To suggest that Rockefeller had not considered this possibility would require considerable imagination. Yet, he was young. He was a Republican. He was powerfully conditioned to the idea that the Rockefellers kept out of politics, and he was well aware that for years the Rockefeller name had been as much of a liability as the Rockefeller money had been an asset in political affairs. Later, he would say that he had never really thought of working for the government and that Forrestal's question surprised him. But, in the summer of 1940, Washington was an exciting goal for most young men who had ideas and ambitions. It seems most reasonable to assume that whatever surprise Rockefeller felt was mainly due to the fact that he would get the nod from a Democratic administration. In any event, he hesitated.

"I'll have to think about it," he told Forrestal. "This is a kind of crossroads. Can I let you know in a few days?"

Forrestal agreed and Rockefeller went back to New York to consult with his family. Then, traveling incognito under the name of "Mr. Franklin," he secretly took an airplane to Salt Lake City to talk to Wendell Willkie, the Republican nominee for the presidency, who was on a swing through the West. He wanted to consult with Willkie but he had no more than started to explain the situation when the big, hoarse-voiced Midwesterner interrupted him.

"If I were President in a time of international crisis," Willkie rumbled, "and if I asked someone to come to Washington to help me in foreign affairs and if that man turned me down—well, I don't need to tell you what I would think of him. Of course, you should go!"

About this time, the President decided to shift Forrestal to the Navy Department as Under Secretary and Rockefeller was asked to become head of the new Latin American program. He returned to Washington on July 25 to see Mr. Roosevelt.

"Are you sure you want me for this job," Rockefeller asked, "in view of my family's connections with oil companies in Latin America and the fact that I'm a Republican?"

Mr. Roosevelt dismissed the question with a wave of his cigarette holder, saying that that was his responsibility and adding: "I'm not worried."

"If I'm going to get a job done," Rockefeller continued, "I have to pick the people who will work with me on the basis of their ability and experience instead of on the basis of their political affiliations."

"You'll have an absolutely free hand," the President replied. "There'll be no political interference."

Rockefeller began to relax in the warmth of the Roosevelt smile. He asked what basic policies would be laid down for guidance of the program in addition to the Good Neighbor concept fostered by Secretary of State Cordell Hull and Under Secretary Sumner Welles.

"Forrestal is working on that," Mr. Roosevelt said. "You can get it all from him."

They talked for a short time. Rockefeller concluded that the President had a rare appreciation of the importance of the cultural aspect of foreign relations and an understanding of and interest in Latin America. He accepted the assurance that there would be no political interference and there never was. He walked out of the White House in a soberly confident mood, thinking that this was an opportunity and a responsibility. It is interesting to note that for the first—but not the last—time he had spotted a governmental problem that was being neglected, had come up with a plan for solving it and then had been given the job of executing the plan. It was a pattern that would become familiar in his later career.

II.

It may never be known just what Mr. Roosevelt and Hopkins really thought about the young man they were putting in charge of a new and highly experimental agency. The Washington bureaucratic establishment was such and the President's methods were such that his choice may have been influenced by many diverse and hidden factors. For instance, he was moving into a campaign for re-election. He was facing a great war crisis, with Republican isolationists a real worry. He was unhappy about certain attitudes of his Secretary of State, and he was in the habit of setting up new bureaus or agencies to get action on problems that were being muffed or neglected by established government officials. The President must have been very much aware of Rockefeller's youth and political inexperience.

But Rockefeller also was a realist. He had enthusiasm and energy and an uninhibited self-confidence, plus an overriding optimism that made him temperamentally akin to the President. They got along well together, and Mr. Roosevelt on one occasion was reported—doubtless inaccurately—to have remarked that if he could keep the young Republican under his wing for a few years he'd "make a man of him."

On the other hand, there wasn't much doubt about what the rest of Washington thought. The politicians decided Mr. Roosevelt was indulging another whim by bringing in a rich boy, and a Republican to boot, to do some unimportant job. The bureaucrats promptly agreed that there was no necessity for creating another agency that might infringe on their territory and that Rockefeller was a dilettante looking for publicity. The newspapermen were interested because it looked like another amusing story: a kid with a name who would soon sink hip deep into the capital's swamp of futility, but he might be worth writing about while he lasted. In addition, there was a generally held opinion that nobody would ever hear much about the new agency, which the President established by executive order on August 16 as the Office for Coordination of Commercial and Cultural Relations between the American Republics. Even in the alphabetical New Deal era, no agency ever had the misfortune to start out under such a cumbersome name and it soon became known as "the Rockefeller Office" and later as the office of the Coordinator of Inter-American Affairs or the CIAA.

The CIAA was created as a separate agency, not under a White House administrative assistant. The coordinator's job was to "maintain liaison between the Advisory Commission of the Council of National Defense, the several departments . . . of the Government . . . to insure proper coordination of . . . the activities of the Government with respect to Hemisphere defense, with particular reference to the commercial and cultural aspects of the problem." The coordinator was instructed to cooperate with the Department of State. He was advised that he would be responsible directly to the President, and that he would serve "without compensation."

If Rockefeller was an innocent lamb among the bureaucratic wolves of Washington, he probably did not realize it at the time. He came to the job with a clear conscience, an intense desire for action and an ability to get things organized. It was important that he had no axes to grind and no prestige to protect; and probably it was important that he was ignorant of the pitfalls ahead and that, for the most part, he was plunging into a field that was virtually unexplored.

Remembering Mr. Roosevelt's instructions, Rockefeller went to Forrestal and asked what basic policies had been worked out for guidance of the CIAA. Forrestal by this time was moving into the Navy Department and he merely grinned sardonically. "That," he said, "is your first assignment—to work out the basic policies." But he invited Rockefeller to live at his house in Washington until he could make other arrangements and he continued as a friend and advisor after becoming Under Secretary of the Navy. Association with Forrestal opened Rockefeller's eyes to the operations of government officials and, by being a careful listener, he picked up many helpful hints on what to do and what not to do.

At first, Rockefeller was amazed by the way the government was run. There were, for example, no clear lines of authority and no clear areas of assignment such as he had been accustomed to in the business world. One day he sat in a meeting of the Advisory Commission of the Council of National Defense at which President Roosevelt had announced he was going to appoint a chairman for the Office of Production Management. The President discussed the job for a long time, referring in flattering terms to most of the administration officials present. Finally, he turned to William S. Knudsen, the former General Motors executive now serving on the Advisory Commission, and said:

"Bill, I'm appointing you chairman."

Then, before anybody could say anything, he turned to Sidney Hillman, the labor leader on the Advisory Commission, and added:

"And I'm appointing Sidney Hillman as co-chairman."

"Now, Mr. President," Knudsen interjected, "just who is responsible for what and what is the meaning of co-chairman?"

Mr. Roosevelt launched into another monologue and, after a while, concluded: "In case there is any disagreement between you two, I am going to put you both in a room and lock you in there until you come to an agreement. Then we'll go forward from there."

Such a method of operation made Rockefeller realize that Washington was not much like the business world.

Eventually, Rockefeller set up his own household on Foxhall Road in Washington and, because of the shortage of living quarters, he invited a number of his associates to live temporarily with him. "The place soon developed into a kind of boarding house for Rockefeller staff members," Geoffrey T. Hellman reported in *The New Yorker*.

> Sometimes there were as many as fifteen house guests. Evenings were devoted to discussions of what progress was being made on the Latin-American front and to topics that ranged from weighty economic projects to how to handle such well-wishers . . . as the man who suggested that the problem of hemispheric solidarity could be solved by making all unmarried North Americans marry South Americans, thus providing for a really cousinly future.

This phase of Washington existence didn't end until the autumn of 1941 when Mrs. Rockefeller and the children moved into the Foxhall Road house and the boarders had to find other quarters. There were five children now: Rodman, who was nine; Ann, seven; Steven, five; and the twins, Michael and Mary, who were only three years old.

The children and Mrs. Rockefeller had, as was customary, spent the summer at Seal Harbor in Maine, to which Rockefeller commuted by plane for as many weekends as possible. The children were growing up as their father had at Pocantico Hills and at Seal Harbor, where they lived not in the rambling Rockefeller summer house on top of the hill but in a handsome, roomy home of glass and stone built in modern style among pine trees on a spit of rocky land beside the harbor. There were other differences, too. They did not build a log cabin in the woods as a place for games but they had an enticing spot of white sand around a swimming pool that was cut out of high rocks beside the beach. They learned to sail in the old *Jack Tar* which their grandfather had bought secondhand twenty-five years earlier, but there were other, modern boats available at their boathouse, including a seventy-two-foot British patrol craft that Rockefeller had personally redesigned as a pleasure boat that sleeps sixteen persons. Yet, life at Seal Harbor remained simple as compared to the more famous New England society resorts, and Mrs. Rockefeller impressed on her children the same principles of self-reliance and industry and tolerance that she and her husband had learned in their youth.

Rockefeller's working habits were unique in Washington, where few government officials with the possible exception of John Nance Garner were early risers and where the business day normally began sometime around ten o'clock. He started for his office about 8 A.M., lugging one or two heavily packed brief cases to his car and getting behind the wheel, his mind busy with a dozen problems other than that of driving an automobile. On the way to work he normally stopped three or four times to pick up members of his staff, partly because gasoline rationing made transportation difficult in Washington and partly because he wanted to start talking business. Running on schedule like a bus, he would take aboard his first administrative assistant, Janet Barnes, at one corner and, a few minutes later pick up Percy L. Douglas, an assistant coordinator, or Larry Levy, a young staff attorney. All the time, he would be talking at high speed about various office problems and driving at a speed too great for safety.

"He drove as if he were piloting a Paris taxicab," one of his regular passengers remarked later. "He seemed to be paying no attention to the traffic. He drove too fast. He drove too close to other cars. The rest of us were always cringing and mentally putting on the brakes. He didn't seem to give a damn. But he never had an accident. The only trouble I recall was that one day he ran out of gas and, when we got some from a filling station, he didn't have a cent in his pocket to pay for it."

At first, the CIAA offices in the Department of Commerce building were meager. Rockefeller had a large office on the third floor and the rest of his rapidly growing staff—it eventually numbered several thousand employees in the United States and abroad—was crowded into a few rooms on the fifth floor. Not a few of the staff that Rockefeller assembled were men he had worked with in the past, including Rovensky, Harrison, Spaeth, Robbins, Peck and John E. Lockwood, who became general counsel. Later an advertising man, Don Francisco, was named as head of the radio division; John Hay Whitney, later ambassador to London, as head of the motion picture division; Major General George C. Dunham, an outstanding expert on malaria control, as head of the Inter-American Institute; John S. Dickey, later president of Dartmouth College, as a special assistant; Karl A. Bickel, former president of the United Press Associations, as special advisor; Harry W. Frantz, a South American expert from the United Press, and Martha Dalrymple of the Associated Press, as press section assistants; and, later, Victor G. Borella of the Rockefeller Center staff as assistant co-ordinator. Rockefeller also hired a slight, prematurely gray former newspaper man named Francis A. Jamieson on the recommendation of his brother Winthrop.

Jamieson came from a politically-minded New Jersey family. He had won a Pulitzer Prize for his coverage of the Lindbergh kidnaping case for the Associated Press, worked as a campaign assistant to Governor Charles Edison of New Jersey, and was an employee of fund-raiser John Price Jones when he assisted Winthrop Rockefeller in directing the 1938 campaign of the Greater New York Fund. The coordinator gave him a trial as director of the CIAA press division and was so well satisfied with the results that they were together for the next twenty years.

Another important associate in the early CIAA days was a prominent Texas businessman, Will Clayton.

Rockefeller's penchant for "getting organized" whether merely for the purpose of going out to lunch or for a continental propaganda campaign made him one of the most formidable coordinators ever to crash the gates of official Washington. He coordinated everybody and everything in his own office to the nth degree and valiantly sought to bring into his orbit representatives of every other agency remotely connected with Latin American activities. He also was ever ready to reach out for any new ideas or projects that might be lying around unattended for the moment on the theory that practically anything could be coordinated into the CIAA, an attitude that appalled and frequently irritated the capital's established bureaucrats.

But underlying all this was Rockefeller's deep conviction as to the importance of Western Hemisphere unity and solidarity to the future security and freedom of the United States and the other American republics. He was fully aware of the degree of Nazi penetration in the Western Hemisphere. He understood the extent to which Communist propaganda had undermined United States prestige and exploited anti-United States sentiment throughout Central and South America. He felt the United States government needed to mobilize its forces to encourage more information and better understanding; to cushion the shock of the loss of Latin America's European markets; to strengthen the forces of democracy and raise the standard of living of the people of the Western Hemisphere through cooperation in the fields of health, education and food production; and to counteract and eliminate Nazi and Fascist economic and propaganda penetration.

A sidelight on Rockefeller's coordinating was the introduction of an elaborate army-type briefing room equipped with all the maps, charts, graphs, mechanical layouts and photographic projectors that the advertising world of Madison Avenue associated with "visual aids." A briefing room and visual aids were interesting innovations for two reasons: first, they were, originally at least, scorned by veteran government officials, who contended Rockefeller was wasting their time and the taxpayers' money and, second, they were to become a permanent part of Rockefeller's governmental operations. The CIAA briefing room was a chamber large enough to seat two dozen persons around a table and as many more around the walls when necessary. A young architect, Harmon Goldstone, was summoned by Rockefeller from New York to design the room and get it into operation. Charts and graphs were set up to show the objectives and the progress of all projects, movie projectors were installed, photograph display equipment was introduced and adequate lighting was designed. Eventually, the briefing room was staffed by five research directors, twenty-two designers of visual aids and various administrative helpers directed by Nadia Williams.

There were regular staff meetings in the briefing room for which elaborate preparations were made. Each project director, for example, had to make a weekly or monthly report. A director, George Dudley, set up the briefing room program, saw that preparations were made on schedule and often rehearsed the speakers in the use of visual aids prior to the staff meeting. By the time the coordinator and the staff and invited guests from other departments assembled, the brief- ing was skillfully fitted together so that it could be run off like a performance at the Radio City Music Hall. Rockefeller believed that the system not only kept the personnel of his and other agencies informed of what was going on but enabled them to avoid duplicat- ing or interfering with each other's work. The more he used the system, the more he was convinced that it was efficient and valuable and, in the coming years, he would struggle (often vainly) to in- troduce it into other government departments as a method of speeding up and improving operations.

Rockefeller also presided over a daily conference of top personnel at 10:30 A.M. This, too, was carefully organized to move at top speed according to a prepared agenda. The coordinator usually would start talking about the first item on the agenda and, by the time he finished, he would have outlined what he thought should be done. Or, if he was uncertain what should be done, he would throw the idea to the meeting for discussion and later investigation. During his first days in CIAA, Rockefeller was fairly well surrounded by persons who were familiar with his general ideas and this gave some ob- servers the erroneous impression that "yes men" fared well in the CIAA.

"In the beginning I think most of us figured that it was Nelson's show," one associate said later. "We wanted him to run it and we wanted to go along with him as far as possible. His ideas and plans were formulated in long bull sessions and conferences and he had a pretty good idea of what each of us thought by the time he made up his mind. Then he would tell us to do it and he would not worry much about what obstacles had to be overcome. Frequently, it took a lot of doing, and sometimes, of course, his ideas were complete busts."

The rest of Rockefeller's day was a crowded schedule of conferences, visits to various departments and agencies, trips to the Hill to talk with members of Congress, meetings of the Inter-Departmental Committee on Inter-American Affairs, frequently a visit to the White House and, almost every Thursday afternoon, an informal call at the office of Secretary of Commerce Jesse H. Jones to seek and receive advice not only on how to survive the tangle of Washington bureaucracy but on how to get things done. Rockefeller had met Jones at a poker party at which the former surprisingly won $20, and they got along well. The coordinator demonstrated a remarkable talent for making friends with diverse personalities in Washington. He could talk with and learn something from a Communist newspaper editor from South America just as easily as he could deal with a Latin investment banker who wanted nothing less than a 20 per cent return on his money. His close relationship with such a conservative Texas Democrat as Jones in no way interfered with his friendship with Jones's bitter enemy, Vice-President Henry A. Wallace, and both men were to come to his aid at times when he desperately needed their assistance.

Rockefeller normally left his office around six-thirty o'clock and, not infrequently, had dinner guests with whom he wanted to talk policy. These sessions sometimes continued until late at night, and sometimes broke up only when the host fell asleep in his chair. Later, he might dig into his brief cases or put them on a bedside table for investigation early the next morning.

Rockefeller had long been bothered by sinus trouble and the climate of the capital aggravated the affliction. At home, he worked under a sun lamp and he usually carried a pocketful of pills and nose drops. Almost his only outdoor exercise was tennis and the only time he could spare for it was early in the morning. He and Henry Wallace

—both left-handed—often met very early on the tennis courts and usually they wanted two other players for doubles. The younger men in the CIAA who had made the mistake of admitting they played tennis were frequently "invited" to show up at dawn ready for a lively tussle on the courts, with or without hang-overs. They appeared, usually chauffeured by sleep-dazed wives, struggled through a strenuous set with the indefatigable Rockefeller-Wallace combination, dragged themselves home for a shower and breakfast and then headed for a hard day at the office.

For Rockefeller, tennis before breakfast was simply a tune-up for work and, if rain kept him off the court, he substituted a brisk twenty minutes of setting-up exercises in his dressing room. He also usually had time to plow through some of the papers in his brief case and he seldom missed the opportunity—in Washington or anywhere else the family was together—of seeing his children for at least a few minutes before breakfast. Ordinarily, the children showed up in his dressing room and joined him in the morning calisthenics. Since they were young during the war and were likely to be in bed by the time he got home in the evenings, these pre-breakfast sessions were the best opportunity the youngsters had to talk about what they were doing or to make a plea for a bigger allowance or some special privilege.

The children were not held in as tight a rein as Rockefeller had experienced when he was a child but the general pattern was much the same. They had allowances ranging from a quarter to a dollar a week, they were encouraged to do specific jobs to earn extra money and they were required to keep accounts of income and expenditure as their father had done. Rockefeller was more likely to talk to the children about broad ideas and attitudes (or perhaps plans for a vacation trip on which they would learn something new) than about the little things of everyday life. (Their work in school, their parties, their swimming lessons and their little quarrels were problems that they took up with their mother.) Then, before breakfast, there were family prayers or perhaps Rockefeller read from the Bible.

Weekends were crowded because the Rockefellers had many guests

from Latin America and they usually held a kind of "open house"
on Sunday evenings for staff members and almost any other Washington officials—like Henry Wallace—who were interested in Latin
American affairs. Spanish or Mexican motion pictures were shown
on a home screen and recordings of Spanish songs were played,
largely for the benefit of the Rockefellers and others who were
learning to speak the language. Everybody was urged to join in singing. It was a lot of fun and, according to one regular participant, it
was also highly discordant in the musical department.

Rockefeller had a remarkable ability to concentrate completely on
what he was doing, so that when he played tennis the worries of his
office were wholly forgotten and when he was sailing a boat along
the Maine coast he left all other problems behind. As a result, brief
periods of "time off" enabled him to renew his energies and his
enthusiasm and he could return to work wholly refreshed.

Rockefeller's mother viewed his entry into official life in Washington with pride but also with some trepidation, which she tried to
conceal. When he first went to the capital, she wrote him a chatty
letter of encouragement and then, in a suddenly serious mood as if
she were reminding her son not to leave his clothes scattered about
his room, added: "From now on I imagine that you will have many
confidential papers. Probably it will be better if you do not leave
them about. I am sure I really don't need to tell you this." This
motherly advice to a man privy to secrets of the Council of National
Defense might have caused a tremor among agents of the Federal
Bureau of Investigation had they read the letter, but Mrs. Rockefeller probably knew her children better than anyone else. When
her son was too busy to write regularly, she sought other means of
getting news of him.

> I am most anxious to hear how you are [she wrote on September
> 18, 1940]. Couldn't you get Benjy or Miss Phillips to send me just a
> little note telling me the latest news about the condition of your
> cold?
> . . . There are so many good causes to which I feel that we should
> contribute that I am trying to economize. My latest thought is that
> I had probably better begin with myself and not use the long distance

telephone quite so much. I must say that it is a real sacrifice on my part because I love hearing your voices.

On September 24, Rockefeller's secretary wrote to his mother:

> . . . About Mr. Nelson—as you know, he is working terribly hard down here. He is in the office before nine every morning and often doesn't leave until after six-thirty in the evening. After that he entertains at dinner almost every evening. He is thinner after his two months down here. However, his sinus is much improved and his spirits are ever so much better these last two weeks. He spends his weekends in Pocantico where he is apparently able to rest and relax completely for he always comes back on Mondays very much refreshed. He is doing a splendid job down here and, as always, is putting every ounce of enthusiasm and energy into his work, which is now beginning to show the results of his efforts. We are all very proud of him and I am sure his family must be also.

Mr. Rockefeller, Jr., was concerned a year or so later when his son decided that he did not have time to take a scheduled vacation. He wrote: "I would be untrue to you and my duty as a father were I not to give you my views on a matter so important to your present health and your future usefulness." The letter urged him to organize his office so that he would have a second in command who could take charge. "While you have a magnificent constitution and an iron will," his father concluded, "neither can withstand indefinitely the strain you are putting upon them."

In February of 1941, there was a luncheon at a New York hotel where young Rockefeller and Ambassador John Winant were the speakers. A crowd gathered to welcome the guests of honor, photographers climbed on chairs to record the event for the newspapers and there was a general hubbub before the luncheon got underway. On the edge of the crowd were a dignified gentleman in a black Homburg hat and a dark blue suit and a smiling woman who tried to peer over the heads of the reporters. Once or twice the couple made a timid effort to find a way through the throng but with no success. They finally abandoned the idea and went to their seats in the huge luncheon room.

When the luncheon was over the couple waited for a few minutes but again there were confusion and pushing around the speakers' rostrum, and soon they made their way out of the hotel and went home.

> . . . We were hoping for a chance to speak to you . . . but we were unsuccessful [Mr. Rockefeller, Jr., wrote his son on February 11th]. We didn't try after lunch because you were surrounded by others. . . . You made us both exceedingly proud of you. . . . I would be proud to be able to write and speak anything like as well.

Rockefeller replied with thanks and added, rather wistfully, that he would pass on the compliment to "the true authors" of his speech, who were two members of his staff, Frank Jamieson and Carl Spaeth. "I only wish," he said, "I could write as good a speech myself, but little by little I'll get there."

### III.

The work of the Office of the Coordinator of Inter-American Affairs, from 1940 until May 20, 1946, encompassed a wide range of often complicated projects, from bolstering the war-shaken economy of Latin American countries to producing a Walt Disney cartoon movie about South America and sending Lincoln Kirstein's American Ballet Caravan on a twenty-eight-week tour of other American republics. The coordinator's office set up the first full-scale government information program operating in foreign countries. It pioneered in the use of the various media of radio, movies, news and specially printed publications. It undertook the first extensive government-sponsored cultural exchange programs. It initiated extensive projects in the field of economic cooperation and organized in 1942 the Institute of Inter-American Affairs to cooperate with the other American republics in carrying out programs in the fields of public health and sanitary engineering, education and increased food production. It was a small agency, judged by wartime standards in Washington, and spent only a modest $140,000,000 of taxpayers' money in its five years of operation. But its history, as has been recited in detail elsewhere,[1] was an over-all contribution to the unity of the Western Hemisphere that marked a significant turning point in American foreign relations.

There were, along the way, a good many flamboyant enterprises and several unhappy mistakes. One of Rockefeller's first acts, for example, was to set up a research office to keep him confidentially informed on what was going on, politically and economically, all over Latin America. He had been impressed by a small South American news letter service run by two young men, and upon investigation he discovered that they had correspondents scattered in strategic spots throughout the continent. On advice of the State Department, Rockefeller bought the news service for $10,000 and hired the two owners to run the CIAA research bureau. They did an efficient job and held responsible positions. Later, after Rockefeller had left the CIAA, officials discovered that the two men were extreme left-wingers and that their news service had been used by the Communist apparatus in South America.

In later years, there would be some disagreement among first-hand observers as to how Rockefeller approached the CIAA job. "The job, in my opinion, was basically a propaganda job," one member of the staff said, "and it called for bold action, but I thought Rockefeller and his advisors were almost as careful in their approach as the State Department. Except for a few close associates, he was surrounded by New York advertising men and bankers and most problems were approached from a business point of view at first. They reflected a viewpoint that was, I am unhappy to say, current in the government and in the country at that time—the idea that you mustn't do anything to disturb business. Whenever anybody had a new idea, Rockefeller's first reaction was to ask whether it would hurt business—not his own personal business, mind you, but the business community generally. Only Pearl Harbor changed all that."

Another man who worked for the CIAA in the early days had a disagreement with Rockefeller over policy and quit. "I felt that we

---

[1] See my *Those Rockefeller Brothers* (Harper); *History of the Office of the Coordinator of Inter-American Affairs* (United States Government Printing Office).

As Coordinator for Inter-American Affairs, Rockefeller was strongly impressed by the work of United States Army medical officers who trained Haitian doctors to run a clinic for treatment of yaws. Here he is welcomed to a Haitian clinic by Dr. Eddy Lemoine, director, in 1944.

Rockefeller (center) confers with Latin American technicians in Venezuela in regard to projects being started in 1949 by his International Basic Economy Corporation.

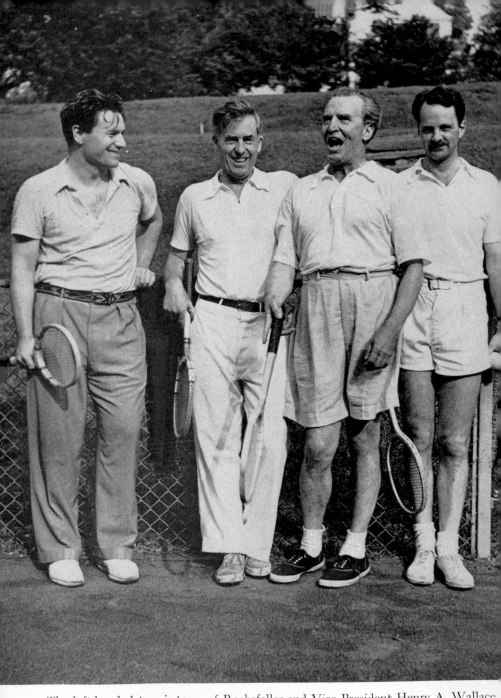

The left-handed tennis team of Rockefeller and Vice President Henry A. Wallace pauses during a match with Senator William Smathers and Percy Douglas, a member of the CIAA staff, in Washington during World War II.

Ranch owner Rockefeller photographed in 1947 while at work on one of his ranches in Venezuela.

An enthusiast about old automobiles, Rockefeller tries out an ancient machine during a journey in 1956 to Venezuela and Brazil.

A bureaucrat once remarked that "if you scratch a Rockefeller you'll find a chart." Here Under Secretary for Health, Education and Welfare Rockefeller uses visual aids to explain proposed legislation to a congressional committee.

As Under Secretary of the newly-created Department of Health, Education and Welfare, Rockefeller (right) dines with Secretary Hobby, President Eisenhower, Vice President Nixon and Mrs. Eisenhower.

Rockefeller was principal speaker at a meeting of the National Association for the Advancement of Colored People in 1959. Here he is greeted by NAACP officials Sam Pierce (center), first appointee Governor Rockefeller made to the bench, and Roy Wilkins (right), executive secretary of NAACP. (*Arthur Daley*)

Governor Rockefeller at a Labor Day parade with David Dubinsky (in ILGWU cap), Cardinal Spellman (at Rockefeller's right) and Mayor Robert Wagner of New York City (at Rockefeller's left). (*Arthur Daley*)

A view of Rockefeller's 5,000-acre ranch home in the mountains of Venezuela, where he often goes for vacations. (*Meyn, Caracas*)

Rockefeller's favorite sport is sailing. Here he is shown off the coast of Maine with two of his sons, Rodman and Steven, both expert sailors. (*Richard Meek*)

Always in a hurry and usually behind schedule, Rockefeller leaps from a helicopter that saved him a half hour by flying him from the State Fairgrounds to the Syracuse airport. (*Arthur Daley*)

Governor Rockefeller on the porch of the family boathouse at Seal Harbor, Maine. Inside the weathered boathouse is a small but beautifully designed art gallery containing some of his prized modern paintings, tapestries and wood sculpture. (*Alfred Eisenstaedt*)

Politician Rockefeller in action in a crowd during a New York City parade. (*Arthur Daley*)

were pulling our punches," he commented, "and trying to sell South America a soft program about the great beauty of the United States instead of hitting hard on the fact that we were building fifty thousand airplanes and were going to be able to take care of ourselves. When I quit, I was given the impression that I was 'deserting' and had let the team down."

On the other hand, there were plenty of persons on the CIAA staff who later remembered Rockefeller as exceptionally aggressive and open to bold ideas. "I never understood," one of them said, "how some people got the idea that he was either timid or naïve when he first went to Washington. He lacked political experience but he had had plenty of dealings with the smartest, most cynical and most sophisticated operators in New York and South America and he knew the field he was working in. His open friendliness may have sometimes made him look naïve but, as time showed, he knew how to protect himself in the clinches."

The early phase of Rockefeller's work in Washington was complicated in certain respects by the fact that he was venturing into a new field—and one that was highly vulnerable to newspaper and congressional charges that he was wasting the taxpayers' money. Newspapermen found it was easy to write humorous articles about a government agency that engaged in such "boondoggling" projects as sending exhibitions of modern art to Brazil or hiring Moe Berg, a former big league baseball catcher who spoke seven languages and had an LL.D. from Princeton University, to investigate the effect of sports competition on international relations. "The Brazilians," quipped one Washington reporter, "are said to have advised Washington that the next time we send a good-will mission to Rio de Janeiro they will immediately declare that a state of war exists with the United States."

Congressmen, too, were suspicious and critical of the unorthodox ideas of the rich young New Yorker who was buzzing all over Washington with plans for spending money to provide our neighbors to the south with a free picture magazine, with musical concerts, goodwill tours by motion picture stars and exhibitions of sculpture. The rumblings from the Hill caused Rockefeller little concern at first. He was reasonably confident that he knew what he was doing, and he frequently did, but obviously the CIAA was engaged in many experiments and just as obviously some of them were going to go wrong. The coordinator soon learned that there were a number of famous personalities in Washington jobs who quivered in their boots when they had to face a congressional committee, but he himself was inclined to take such matters lightly, until one day when he was asked to attend a Senate Appropriations Committee hearing on a supplemental appropriation of $100,000,000 for a dozen different defense agencies, including his own.

As usual, he had too many things on his schedule that day and he was late in arriving at the hearing. The heads of the other agencies, except for OPM administrator William S. Knudsen, were already present and the committee was in session. As Rockefeller entered and found a seat as unobtrusively as possible he heard the rasping voice of the chairman, Senator Kenneth D. McKellar, reading something that sounded vaguely familiar. Furthermore, McKellar was reading it in a slow, ponderous and sarcastic manner that would have aroused the fears even of a man who had never heard of the Tennesseean's skill at cutting bureaucrats into small pieces. It was, Rockefeller soon discovered, a highly legalistic section of the bill devoted to the granting of special powers to CIAA, including the right to distribute free newspapers, recordings, motion picture and other material as well as "other gratuitous assistance as he [the coordinator] deems advisable in the fields of the arts and sciences. . . ."

McKellar finished with almost a sneer. He laid down the paper and folded his hands on the table and looked balefully over his gold-rimmed glasses at the assembled bureaucrats, almost licking his lips in anticipation.

"Now," he rumbled, "if you want to build ten thousand motion picture concerns in the Republic of Mexico, you could do it under this bill. Couldn't you?"

Wayne Coy, representing the Bureau of the Budget, was in charge of defending the bill and Rockefeller presumed that he would do the talking. But instead Coy turned and pointed to the back row and said: "Mr. Nelson Rockefeller is here and he can explain this program."

"Go right ahead," McKellar said grimly.

Having arrived late and not having expected to testify, Rockefeller was not prepared to go right ahead. He did not, for instance, realize at the time that McKellar apparently had misunderstood the bill and was under the mistaken impression that the CIAA would get most or all of the $100,000,000. Actually, the agency was getting little or nothing in this particular bill.

"I would like to say first, gentlemen," he began, "that I think we have got to keep in mind, at least certainly from our point of view, it is one of the major objectives we have, that we are dealing with a total war. The military aspects of that war are like the part of an iceberg that floats above the water. . . ."

When he had, more or less, run out of steam without having explained anything, the chairman interrupted to point out that various agencies were spending money in Latin America.

> *Senator McKellar:* What I am afraid of is that we will have so many departments giving these people money that we will not know where to head off.
> *Mr. Rockefeller:* . . . our interest is the coordination and cooperation of the twenty-one American republics in the interest of national defense.
> *Senator McKellar:* That is a very general statement, Mr. Rockefeller. . . . Would you offer them money if they would give us good will?
> *Mr. Rockefeller:* I break it down in my own thinking, sir, to three objectives. . . .
> *Senator McKellar:* Well, in other words, you would lend them money; is that the idea?
> *Mr. Rockefeller:* No, sir; I spoke too quickly.
> *Senator McKeller:* Would you lend them money?
> *Mr. Rockefeller:* No, sir . . .
> *Senator McKellar:* This [the bill] says that you have the right to grant them money. Do you make grants to help out private institutions down there, and public institutions?
> *Mr. Rockefeller:* Let us take an example. . . .

McKellar, however, obviously wasn't interested in taking any examples. He wanted direct answers and he wasn't getting them. Coy broke into the exchange in an effort to take some of the heat off Rockefeller as well as to protect the bill. He managed to shift the questioning around to Dr. Vannevar Bush, who had considerable prestige with the senators, and he sent a messenger to bring Knudsen to the hearing as quickly as possible because Knudsen had a soothing way with congressmen who were worrying about the taxpayers' money. The hearing dragged on without doing much to repair the damage but at least complete disaster was avoided.

Rockefeller's reaction to this fiasco was typical. He blamed himself —there wasn't much else he could have done—for being unprepared but he was neither bitter nor intimidated. On the contrary, his respect for Congress and particularly for the committees of Congress was greatly increased by the discovery that they included men who worked hard, knew what they were talking about and had a kind of intuitive ability to ask questions that dug to the heart of a highly complex problem. "I learned plenty that day and later," he once remarked, "and I developed a great respect for committee members. They forced executive agencies to keep reviewing their work and we knew we had to justify whatever we did. They gave us a tremendous sense of responsibility to the people."

The experience also did much to convert Rockefeller into an expert witness at congressional hearings. He never again was caught short on such occasions; in fact, he was always loaded for bear, with facts, figures, charts, photographs and exhibits of an elaborate character such as were seldom used at that time by committee witnesses. His clash with McKellar merely convinced him that the best way to get along on the Hill was to know his subject, speak as frankly as possible and defend the ideas and actions in which he believed. McKellar was perhaps the most irascible and dangerous of congressional chairmen at the time, a man with long experience, a penchant for feuds and an ability to flay a foe with consummate skill. Rockefeller had differences with him later, but in the long run they became good friends. McKellar not only supported all the CIAA budgets but, on one occasion, restored $50,000 which the Bureau of the Budget had cut out for reasons of economy. He also came to Rockefeller's defense on an important occasion when Senator Hugh Butler, a Republican of Nebraska, sought to create a national scandal in regard to wartime expenditures in Latin America.

Rockefeller made a habit of keeping in touch with committee chairmen and other congressmen between hearings, inviting them to study what the CIAA was doing and to meet visitors from Latin America. When Butler decided to make a tour of Latin America in 1943, accompanied by a ghost writer, he asked Rockefeller for information regarding activities in the countries to be visited. The coordinator telephoned him promptly.

"I'd like to come to your office and bring some material," he said, "and we could talk about it."

He had luncheon with Butler, gave him an itemized list of CIAA projects in each country, prepared a seventy-five-page report for him and started him off for Cuba with a feeling that he had done a good public relations job. Butler covered twenty thousand miles and twenty countries at high speed, returned to Washington and wrote an article for *The Reader's Digest* in which he bitterly attacked ten government agencies and departments, including the CIAA, and said that he was astonished and appalled that the United States had spent $6,000,000,000 in three years on boondoggling projects in an unsuccessful attempt to "buy" good will in Latin America. He went on to recite in great detail how funds were being wasted and listed expenditures of $259,000,000 by the Rockefeller office. The charges, which Butler repeated in part in two Senate speeches, were headlined across the nation and were used as a springboard by various political writers for attacks on the cultural program of the CIAA.

Rockefeller protested promptly and vigorously to Butler and then got his staff to work on figures. When he next appeared before a congressional committee one of the questions asked him, probably by prearrangement, was in reference to Butler's charges. The coordinator let loose with a barrage of facts to show that the funds thus far available to CIAA for all purposes totaled only $128,444,946, that

NELSON ROCKEFELLER   A BIOGRAPHY

Butler's statements—"however sincerely offered"—were riddled with errors, that his conclusions were misleading and "may seriously jeopardize our international relations." He acknowledged that his agency had made mistakes but he denounced "criticism that misleads the American people."

"And believe me, gentlemen," he added, "I am not saying anything here that I have not said to the senator personally because I feel very strongly about it."

More important, however, was the fact that McKellar arose in the Senate and disclosed that he had vainly attempted to persuade Butler not to make the charges because they were misleading. He then defended the various agencies involved with detailed statistics and added:

> Mr. Rockefeller is a young man of unimpeachable integrity, honesty and excellent ability. . . . He has indomitable energy, is a fine personality and is one of the best witnesses of those who appear from time to time before the Senate Appropriations Committee. The President could not have found a better man for the particular and highly desirable work which Mr. Rockefeller has been doing in Latin America. Mr. Rockefeller has made a splendid success as Coordinator of Inter-American Affairs and much of the success of carrying out our Good Neighbor policy and good will policy in Latin America is due to him and his excellent work.

Coming from McKellar, this was a considerable accolade and indicated that Rockefeller had been successful in his efforts to make a good impression on Congress generally and to cooperate with its committees. It was not, however, a matter of mere charm, nor was it a one-way street. "There was a job to be done," Rockefeller said later, "and when I was doing something I believed in I didn't intend to be pushed around. Any time I couldn't do what I believed in I was ready to step out."

On more than one occasion, members of Congress discovered that the Rockefeller charm was tempered by self-confidence and a growing ability to take care of himself when the going got rough. When the Democratic administration's foreign loan policies were under discussion, Representative Harold Knutson, a Republican of Minnesota, tried to needle Rockefeller in regard to Latin American operations of the Chase National Bank.

"I suppose," he said ponderously, "that it is pretty embarrassing to you, Mr. Rockefeller, to have to be asked about the Chase Bank."

"It doesn't embarrass me in the least," the witness replied. "I do not represent the Chase Bank."

On another day some years later, Senator William Langer, a Republican of North Dakota, told Rockefeller at an executive session of a Senate committee that he had voted against his confirmation and "I've been thinking of suing you for years. Your great-grandfather sold my father $200 worth of fake medicine" when he was a "herbal doctor" out west.

"How long did your father live?" Rockefeller asked.

"Well, he was in his nineties when he died."

"That," the witness remarked, "wouldn't help your case very much in court."

At one hearing a reference to John D. Rockefeller, Sr., was made by Representative Charles L. Gifford, a Massachusetts Republican, who attacked Rockefeller as "just another New Deal bureaucrat" supporting the administration's reciprocal trade policy.

"You seem to have got religion," Gifford snapped sardonically. "You seem to believe—and yet your grandfather was known as a shrewd and ruthless trader."

Rockefeller stood up indignantly. "You may say what you please about me," he said, "but I resent what you say about my grandfather. He was a great man. I accept your first adjective in describing him but I reject the second."

The next morning, Rockefeller's father read an account of the hearing in his newspaper and promptly wrote his son a note.

"Your quick reply," he said proudly, "was, I think, perfect. . . . How I should like to have been present . . . and how proud both of your grandfathers would have been at the way you handled yourself."

# SEVEN

# Bureaucratic In-fighting

The office of the Under Secretary in the Department of State was a quiet, orderly chamber in 1940 under the direction of Sumner Welles, and the Under Secretary's secretary lifted a warning eyebrow one day at a young man who bustled in as if he were in a great hurry.

"I have an appointment with Mr. Welles," the young man began, taking a quick look at his wrist watch. "I was . . ."

"I'm very sorry," the secretary replied firmly and without any indication that she was sorry, "but the Under Secretary has an appointment and there's really no chance of seeing him."

"There must be some mistake because . . ."

"No. He has an appointment with the Coordinator for Inter-American Affairs, Mr. Rockefeller," the secretary insisted.

"But I am Mr. Rockefeller."

The eyebrows lifted again but without embarrassment.

"You don't say! I was looking for an older man."

When Rockefeller finally was admitted to his office, Welles stood up and bowed formally. Then he sat down without a word and waited. This was his habit as long as Rockefeller knew him. Except

154

for one occasion when Welles was talking animatedly in Spanish with a group of South Americans, he never saw the Under Secretary's façade of formality break. Welles would listen attentively to questions or suggestions and answer quickly and precisely. When the business was finished, he would stand and bow and that was it. In time, Rockefeller found him an easy man to work with, but at first Welles shared a general opinion among Washington bureaucrats that the new coordinator was a meddling outsider who had dashed into the capital with a staff of high-powered publicity experts and was skillfully wheedling funds out of Congress while the State Department was having a hard time getting sufficient money to carry on far more vital wartime programs.

The trouble between the CIAA and the State Department began early. President Roosevelt's original executive order had said only that the CIAA was "charged with the formulation and execution of a program in cooperation with the State Department." Rockefeller and his top aides, with youthful brashness, put the widest possible interpretation on this and decided that their agency not only was independent of the State Department but on a par with it. The department, probably on the theory that the new agency would soon burn itself out, did nothing much to discourage this idea for several months. By that time, the CIAA had survived an initial period of bureaucratic futility and despondency and was getting its program moving.

One of its projects was an advertising campaign in Latin American newspapers. The United States had no information program abroad whereas the Germans were getting wide attention in the South American press, usually by paying for articles that appeared in the newspapers. The CIAA didn't want to "buy" news space, so it tried to keep on the ethical side of the fence by buying advertising space to tell the story of the United States and, if possible, create sympathy for and understanding of this country. This was done by preparing a series of advertisements showing a Latin American couple traveling in the United States, explaining what they saw, how they were treated and how important good relations were in the Western

Hemisphere. It is important to note that Rockefeller made sure that this project was seen by an Assistant Secretary at the Department of State and that he approved it, putting his "O.K." on each advertisement.

Unfortunately, the advertising program could not be launched until a time when the war made travel abroad very difficult, and it seemed far-fetched to run advertisements of a Latin American couple on a pleasure tour of North America. The contracts had been made, however, and Rockefeller finally decided to go ahead. The reaction was all bad. One United States embassy sent in a report that the advertisements were absurd and, furthermore, were running in one of the biggest pro-Nazi newspapers in South America; in other words, the United States was subsidizing an enemy publication. The newspapers at home made a big thing of this and some criticized the Rockefeller operations. Welles, probably having been waiting confidently for just such an amateurish blunder, moved into action by way of the White House. "It was," Rockefeller remarked long afterward, "his chance to get rid of the CIAA and he almost did."

On April 22, 1941, Rockefeller received a letter from Mr. Roosevelt. It was a formal "My-dear-Nelson" kind of letter but it laid down the law and concluded:

> . . . I am aware of your own personal intentions to cooperate for the purpose of furthering the highest interests of the country. . . . And I also know of your intentions to consult with and to obtain the approval of the Department [of State] concerning activities to be undertaken by your Office . . . but I have observed impairment of our total effort, particularly in regard to activities which, while directed from within this country, are carried out in the other American republics.
>
> I therefore desire that you take appropriate steps to institute arrangements for assuring that in all instances projects initiated by your Office shall be discussed fully with and approved by the Department of State, and a full meeting of minds obtained before action is undertaken or commitments made. . . . I know that you will fully share my judgment that the steps requested are essential to the success of the Administration in attaining its objective in inter-

American affairs, in behalf of which I am sure I can count on your
contribution.

Very sincerely yours,

Franklin D. Roosevelt

The order, which clearly confirmed the department's authority as
to determination of basic policy as well as to authorization of each
specific project, rocked Rockefeller back on his heels harder than
almost any previous event in his life. He sat at his desk, reading the
President's words again and becoming more and more discouraged.
It was obvious that the President had not been told that the State
Department had okayed not only the project but each of the advertisements. It was also obvious that the department official who okayed
them had not spoken up, and probably not even Welles knew that
approval had been secured. Rockefeller decided that he was not
going to say anything about that because there was no question
that the whole campaign had been a blunder. He was, however,
deeply troubled by the tone of the President's letter because it was
not a sympathetic or friendly correction but a stiff reprimand. If he
had lost the confidence of Mr. Roosevelt, his usefulness obviously was
ended almost before it had begun.

As he studied the letter, he was struck by something familiar in
the style. He decided that it was the style of Welles's office and
that Welles had dictated the letter for Mr. Roosevelt, and he felt
better. But he had to be sure. He picked up the telephone and called
his friend, General Edwin M. Watson, the White House appointments secretary.

"Pa," he said, using Watson's nickname, "I need to see the boss."

"Yes, Nelson," Watson replied, "you sure do! Come on over."

When Rockefeller arrived at the White House, Mr. Roosevelt
was sitting behind his big, cluttered desk with a smile on his face.
Perhaps he was amused; perhaps he was pleased that Rockefeller had
come up fighting after being dumped on the floor in round one. But,
for all of his friendliness, he wasn't taking any nonsense from his
young Coordinator of Inter-American Affairs.

"Look, Nelson," he began before Rockefeller could say much, "I

know that you're in a difficult situation in regard to State and I
knew it was going to be tough when I set up your office. But understand this—it is up to you to get along with them because if it ever
comes to a showdown between your office and State I will have
no choice but to back the department and Mr. Welles." He paused
and took a deep drag on his cigarette. Then, almost as if he were
asking a favor, he added flatteringly: "You have got to handle your
problems in a way that doesn't give them an opening to take the
kind of shot they've already taken at you—or to create a showdown
in which I'll have to make a decision."

Whatever intentions Rockefeller may have had when he entered
the White House had been dissipated in the glow of the President's
confidential manner. He felt that he still had the President's sympathy and he knew where he stood.

"That's fair enough," he said. "I'll see it doesn't happen again."

Thereafter neither Welles nor Rockefeller seemed to hold any
antagonism toward each other, possibly owing to a friendly gesture
by the latter on the following day. He went to Welles's office and
was admitted to the presence of the Under Secretary.

"It's clear that you're the boss," he told Welles. "Now tell me
what I should do to coordinate our work."

This attitude of cooperation seemed to impress Welles. Although
the relationship between the two men continued to be strictly formal,
the CIAA and the department worked together smoothly thereafter.
Welles did not have any great interest in the economic and social
work of the CIAA, and Laurence Duggan, head of the Division of
the American Republics, took over most of the details of cooperation
for the department and strongly championed Rockefeller's objectives.

From that time on every CIAA project was written in memorandum form, stating the objective, the manner in which it was to be
carried out, the number of people involved and the estimated cost.
This memorandum was sent to the State Department over Rockefeller's signature. After State had reviewed or modified it, it was
countersigned by Welles or Duggan. Then copies were sent to
ambassadors in the countries affected with instructions that this was

an approved U. S. program, and that its execution should have their wholehearted support.

## II.

Rockefeller wasn't caught short again, but he did have a few more first-rate rows with representatives of the State Department, largely because the old-line ambassadors were strongly conditioned against such untraditional activities as were normally pursued by the CIAA.

One of the traditionalists was George Messersmith in Mexico City, an able and highly respected diplomat but a stubborn man who didn't want anybody, and especially a Rockefeller who was still wet behind the ears, horning in on his territory. The CIAA had done rather well with its projects in Mexico, particularly in connection with efforts to stimulate the Mexican motion picture industry so that it could replace the strongly pro-Nazi Spanish and Argentine films in Latin America. John Hay Whitney, head of the CIAA Motion Pictures Division, had arranged for Hollywood cooperation in building laboratories, studio space and other facilities in Mexico, and seven RKO studios were constructed later as the industry developed with the assistance of CIAA financing. None of this was approved by Messersmith, who felt that the information program started in Mexico by the CIAA should be under his control. Eventually, the controversy between the embassy and the CIAA men in Mexico City became so acute that Rockefeller flew there to see what could be done about it. The ambassador was not friendly, and after their initial talk, the coordinator felt that his field men in Mexico were being throttled but that there wasn't much he could do about it. Messersmith was too tough.

That evening, however, Rockefeller went to a party attended by members of the embassy staff, one of whom drank too much and, in a reckless moment, boasted to the visitor from Washington that Messersmith was planning to take over the functions of the CIAA in Mexico. His detailed description of the plans convinced Rockefeller that he knew what he was talking about. The next day, the coordinator again called on the ambassador, but this time it was the visitor who was tough.

"I don't believe we're getting anywhere," he said, "but we've reached a point where we're going to fish or cut bait. Either we are going to run our own program in Mexico without interference from the embassy, or we are going to pull out. I have no intention of supplying the money for these projects and taking the responsibility for them and then letting somebody else run the show. But if we have to pull out of Mexico, you can be sure that we will explain why we did it."

He then recited the details of Messersmith's plans to gain control of the program. The ambassador knew when he had been bested at bureaucratic in-fighting. He agreed to a system of CIAA operation in Mexico that left the agency free to manage its approved projects and to make its own mistakes, for which Rockefeller took full responsibility.

Rockefeller's efforts in Mexico later proved to be of importance because of the need for increased wartime traffic over the Mexican railroads. Except for the Southern Pacific properties, all of the railroads had been taken over by the Mexican government and were managed by the labor syndicates. The management was not efficient, and in January of 1942 the CIAA received an emergency appeal from its representatives in Mexico City to do something about getting defense materials moved to the United States. Tonnage was greatly increased due to the war, trains were running twenty-four hours behind schedule and there was an average of one wreck an hour. In cooperation with the State Department, the CIAA arranged for Walter Douglas to make a survey and decided that the only solution was an outright grant under U. S. direction to make improvements and to furnish technical assistance.

Eventually, about sixty-five United States technicians were moved into key spots where they could cooperate with Mexican railroad personnel, the system was reorganized, repaired and put back into action—much to the delight of the Mexican railroad workers, who had been menaced by a high accident rate, poor health conditions and inefficient management. Among other things, the reorganization turned up millions of dollars' worth of equipment which had been purchased, dumped in railroad yards and forgotten. Bridges were rebuilt or strengthened, terminals were enlarged, hundreds of thousands of defective cross ties were replaced, and better roadbeds were laid. In all, about $7,500,000 was made available by the United States for the purpose of putting the roads, which employed some fifty-five thousand workers, on a sound basis.

There was an interesting sequel to the Mexican railroad project in 1943 when President Roosevelt became the first Chief Executive to visit Mexican soil, meeting with President Avila Camacho at Monterrey in April. Among other things, they named a joint development commission for economic cooperation to facilitate wartime integration and to lay plans for the postwar development of Mexico's economy. Rockefeller was a member of the commission, which planned a variety of projects for new public works, for expansion of industrial plants and building of new industries. In view of the emphasis on industrial expansion, Rockefeller was distressed that there was no labor representation on the commission despite the fact that two big unions, CTAL and CROM, had gained great power.

At the second meeting of the commission in Mexico City, he talked to the leaders of the two unions and asked permission to visit their headquarters and meet members of their governing boards. He found the headquarters in an old, ramshackle building and climbed three flights of stairs to a big room where a dozen men sat on wooden chairs around a table.

"I'm Nelson Rockefeller," he said in Spanish to the man nearest the door and shook his hand. The man was silent and obviously suspicious. So were the others, but Rockefeller shook every hand before he sat down.

He explained the work authorized by the two Presidents. The Mexican labor leaders sat in silence. Rockefeller mentioned his affection and admiration for the Mexican people. Silence.

"The reason I came here," he went on, taking a deep breath, "is that I don't know whether the people want this kind of industrial program. This is your country, not mine. If the people are not interested in industrialization I want to know it now." The group stirred and there was a murmur of comment. "It is important," Rockefeller continued, "that you face the fact that this has been predominantly an agricultural country but that the proposed economic development program means more industrialization, more machinery to take the place of unskilled labor. For a time, some jobs will be lost but in the long run the whole country will benefit.

"The decision really is up to you. If you want to remain an agrarian economy, say so frankly and we will drop out. If you want to be an industrial nation, then we're ready to help."

All of the indifference of the group was gone. Animated discussion broke out, arguments developed. Rockefeller sat back in a rickety wooden chair and listened, fascinated by the opposing ideas, by the clash of theories. No immediate decision was possible but eventually the majority agreed that the best interests of labor in the long run would be served by the economic development program. More important, their indifference to the commission had changed to intense interest. But how could union leaders support a plan that meant loss of jobs even temporarily?

"We can't get out and actively support the program," they said, "but we assure you we will not oppose it."

On that basis, the commission went ahead. A short-term program of twenty projects calling for investment of around $24,000,000 was carried out and a postwar program of fifty-nine projects costing some $383,000,000 was set up. At the end of the war, Mexico had accumulated a large dollar reserve and had ordered materials in advance for twenty-two carefully planned projects, so that the country was able to get a running start on a postwar program that gave the national economy a big lift. Except for certain utilities, all of the projects were developed by private companies.

Of the many difficulties encountered by the CIAA as it struggled to carry out its program in Latin America, one other ambassadorial crisis is worthy of mention because it demonstrates Rockefeller's flexibility in changing his tactics to meet a particular situation. One United States ambassador resented the coordinator's activities so intensely that he delayed a year in forwarding a government invitation for Rockefeller to make a formal visit to Rio de Janeiro. Eventually, the invitation reached Washington through other channels and Rockefeller accepted. When he arrived at the capital he discovered that the ambassador had told the foreign ministry that it was not necessary for anyone to meet the visitor at the airport and that there was no reason for any speeches to be made at an official luncheon.

Rockefeller had worked hard on a speech emphasizing that mobilization in the United States was making it difficult to deliver goods to Latin America, that everybody was going to have to get along with less but that, by close cooperation, everybody would be able to keep going. When he arose to speak, however, the ambassador created what could only be called a diversion. He asked for cigarettes in a loud voice and began talking across the table to a government official, ignoring the guest of honor. Instead of trying to talk above such interference, Rockefeller delayed his prepared speech and made a five-minute talk in praise of the ambassador. He congratulated the government on having such an able representative from Washington and said, without much regard for the truth, that the ambassador was extremely close to President Roosevelt. The ambassador told Rockefeller later that it was the finest speech he had ever heard and thereafter he took a great interest in the CIAA program in the country.

III.

Once when Rockefeller was having a particularly difficult time protecting his agency from encroachment and possible destruction by other bureaucrats he stopped in to chat with Jesse Jones about his troubles. Jones listened sympathetically until the younger man said that he was thinking about going to the President for a solution.

"Don't ever take your problems to the President unless you have an answer that he can approve or reject," the Texan said. "He doesn't like people who leave problems on his desk. But if you take your problem in and say, 'Mr. President, here's my answer to this problem'—then you're all right."

Rockefeller took Jones's advice in his relations with Mr. Roosevelt and, as he gained experience, he discovered another rule to follow at the White House. As he put it later: "You couldn't ask the President to intervene and settle a jurisdictional dispute between two agencies or departments, because he didn't like the idea and he didn't have time. But you might settle it through an intermediary if you had friends around the White House." Fortunately, Rockefeller had such friends.

"Rockefeller survived the early days in Washington," a close associate remarked later, "because he had an intuitive understanding of the power structure at the top. He never lost the capacity to put himself in the position of the head man and thus to know what action to take in a critical situation. He baffled many lawyers and bureaucrats because he was not a 'word man' and did not think in abstract terms. He couldn't read a legal document and immediately grasp its meaning. But he was constantly amazing the experts by his knowledge of detailed facts and figures when dealing with complicated problems or specialized subjects. He was sure-footed when the going was rough. Not a few rival bureaucrats thought they had him trapped and hog-tied at various times, only to discover that he was off and running with the ball." Rockefeller preferred making friends to making enemies and Elmer Davis, director of the Office of War Information, once remarked that he was "one of the few persons in Washington who won't knife you when your back is turned."

One of the important challenges to the CIAA was posed by the appointment of the First World War hero, Colonel—later Major General—William J. Donovan, as Coordinator of Information in July of 1941. The colonel also operated in the cloak-and-dagger field, but his clash with the CIAA arose from the fact that he wanted to take over all government information work. Rockefeller regarded his own regional program as vital to operation of his agency and could see nothing but the end of his office if Donovan gained control. Worried, he followed his customary practice of going to the other fellow to try to work out an agreement for cooperating.

"There is one thing you can say for the CIAA operations," Rockefeller remarked years later, "we didn't have any pride of position. Nobody had to come to us because we were always ready to go to them."

Going to Donovan, however, wasn't very fruitful. The colonel was not impressed by Rockefeller's suggestions and made his attitude clear during two talks. The third time they talked, however, there were new developments of the kind Rockefeller had feared. A presidential order outlining the powers of the COI had already been prepared.

"You know, Jimmy was talking to his father," the colonel said in reference to James Roosevelt, who worked in Donovan's office, "and the President told him he believed the whole information setup ought to be taken over by one office. So, I think there will be a transfer of the Latin American information program from your office to ours. Jimmy will tell you all about it."

This was a hard blow to Rockefeller and he tried to cover up his anger.

"I'm not interested in talking to Jimmy," he said, but Donovan summoned him anyway, and Roosevelt confirmed he had talked to his father about the new setup when they were on the President's boat on the Potomac the previous day. The COI was to have full authority.

"Did you remind the President of the executive order which he signed creating the CIAA and giving it authority over its own information program?" Rockefeller asked.

"No, I didn't mention that."

Rockefeller turned to Donovan. "Bill, I don't think it is fair to the President to present this thing to him from only one side, simply getting him to agree to a principle without discussing the problems and the agencies involved. I think we ought to go together to see him and work it out."

"No," Donovan replied. "The President has made a decision and that's that."

"All right. I want to make it clear that I don't feel it is in the interest of the President. But if you want to take unilateral action, I want you to know that I will follow the same procedure."

As soon as Rockefeller left Donovan's office, he made a few telephone calls that confirmed that the COI was being given such broad authority that it might well absorb the CIAA information program. Then he called a council of war in his office and asked Anna Rosenberg to attend. Mrs. Rosenberg, an advisor to CIAA, knew the information program was vital to the success of the CIAA and a few hours later she departed for the White House with the draft of a statement. It was issued the next morning over the signature of the President and it made clear that the creation of the Office of Coordinator of Information was not intended "to supersede or to duplicate or to involve any direction of or any interference with" the activities of certain established government agencies, including the CIAA.

Later, the two agencies worked out a method of cooperation that was only partly satisfactory and which led to clashes over control of broadcasting channels for Latin America and was responsible for numerous newspaper articles about the President's efforts to "coordinate the coordinators." This was not finally settled until October of 1941, when Mr. Roosevelt wrote Donovan that:

> I continue to believe that the requirements of our program in the [Western] Hemisphere are quite different from those of our programs to Europe and the Far East. In order that information, news and inspirational matter going to the other American republics . . . may be carefully adapted to the demands of the Hemisphere, it should be handled exclusively by the Coordinator of Inter-American Affairs in cooperation with the Department of State.

Donovan, who later became director of the Office of Strategic Services, was considerably ruffled and was distinctly cool toward Rockefeller for a couple of years. But one day Rockefeller walked into his office and stuck out his hand.

"Seems to me it's about time to bury the hatchet," he said. "We're on the same side in this war."

"I guess you're right," Donovan said, shaking hands. The two men remained on good terms until Donovan's death.

## IV.

There was another and still more formidable threat to the CIAA in 1942 when the Bureau of the Budget attempted to get all information agencies under one tent. On the surface, at least, this seemed a wise move and newspaper comment generally was favorable to a consolidation. The Office of Facts and Figures had been set up late in 1941 under Archibald MacLeish to keep the nation informed on national defense matters. After some controversy, the CIAA worked out a formula for cooperation with MacLeish's agency. The following March, however, there were reliable reports that the Budget Bureau had prepared an order for the President centralizing all information activities. Rockefeller called on a friend at the bureau and asked if the report was true.

"Yes," was the reply. "There is an order going to the President for signature. It puts all of the information programs into one office. Some of the stuff Donovan is handling and some of your program will be under a new agency called the Office of War Information, which will take the place of the Office of Facts and Figures."

Back at his own office, Rockefeller called in several aides, including Enrique DeLozada, a Bolivian who was a member of the staff and later became Bolivian ambassador to the United States. The coordinator for once was depressed.

"It's serious, I guess," he said. "I saw the order that's been drafted and Harold Smith [Director of the Bureau of the Budget] is taking it to the President this afternoon. If it goes through, we might as well close up."

Gloom settled over the room, but only for a few minutes. Then Frank Jamieson wondered out loud who had appointments with Mr. Roosevelt prior to Smith's visit to the White House. He made a quick check and discovered that Henry Wallace was having luncheon with the President. The gloom lifted a little. Wallace was very much interested in Latin America and had done a great deal to improve relations south of the border. He also was a frequent visitor at the Rockefeller home and had strongly supported the work of the CIAA.

"I think he might put in a word for us with the President if he knew the facts," Jamieson suggested. A few minutes later, DeLozada rushed to Wallace's office and rode in a taxicab with him to the White House, explaining the situation and the threat to CIAA. Wallace understood and was sympathetic.

Rockefeller called Karl A. Bickel, chairman of the CIAA news section, and asked him to talk to a dozen key officials, including Secretary of Navy Frank Knox. Then the coordinator himself went to see Under Secretary Welles after drafting in longhand a note to White House Secretary General Watson:

> March 7, 1942
>
> General Watson—I would like to see the President in advance of his consideration of a proposed executive order on War Information which would remove my Office from one of its two primary fields of operation in the Western Hemisphere. While I recognize that there is a need for propaganda directives by a central agency, the removal of this Office from operations can only be construed by me as indicating that the President has changed his concept of this work and that my job is ended.

Welles and Rockefeller later went to the White House. The Under Secretary talked to Mr. Roosevelt and the coordinator was shunted off the main track to make his plea to presidential advisor Sam Rosenman and Budget Director Smith.

"The decision has been made," Rosenman and Smith said, "and it looks like it is final."

Rockefeller was little short of furious. Hot words were exchanged.

"I understand the idea that functionally it would be good to get all these information services under one roof," he said. "But what you don't understand is that the situation in regard to Latin America is different. The CIAA has to dramatize the idea that here is a United States organization dedicated and devoted to the grave regional problems of the Western Hemisphere. It cannot do that unless it has control of its own information program."

"Nobody is criticizing the CIAA," Rosenman replied, "but this is just a part of the evolution of these wartime agencies."

"The CIAA," Rockefeller retorted, "has become the symbol of the President's special interest in Latin America. If you break it up—and don't think this won't ruin it—it will be a serious, self-inflicted propaganda defeat for our country. And if this decision sticks—I'll get out."

Welles's talk with Mr. Roosevelt made it clear that he and Secretary of State Hull opposed infringement on the CIAA's information program. "I . . . believe," he wrote later, "that the Office of the Co-ordinator of Inter-American Affairs should remain as a separate and autonomous agency of the Government. . . ." Welles had discovered that he could work effectively with Rockefeller's office and he apparently did not desire to change a satisfactory arrangement.

The President delayed action and later took the problem up with various cabinet members. Both Knox and Wallace came to the defense of the CIAA's position. As a result, the order prepared for Mr. Roosevelt was not signed. Eventually, it was redrafted and, when issued on June 13, 1942, it included a paragraph stating that "the authority, functions, and duties of the Director [of the newly created Office of War Information] shall not extend to the Western Hemisphere exclusive of the United States and Canada."

Later, the President remarked rather ruefully to Rockefeller: "Well, you must be doing a good job if you can get such diverse fellows as Welles and Wallace on your side."

It was the last real threat to the CIAA. "That was the closest we came to being abolished," Rockefeller commented later, "and it made me realize that personal friendships and balances of power are important, too. I suppose we were lucky in the whole thing. All of us in the office were young. We didn't have any prestige to preserve so we didn't worry about protocol, and I guess we made up in energy what we lacked in political experience. But the most important thing, I'm sure, was that we really believed in what we were doing."

EIGHT

# The Battle for Latin America

During the war, Rockefeller had several talks with President Roosevelt that were outside the realm of official business. On August 13, 1942, the President and the coordinator had luncheon at the White House.

"I'd like to ask your advice on a personal matter," Rockefeller told him. "I'm ready to go in the army now or at any time unless you, as Commander in Chief, want me to keep on with my present work."

Mr. Roosevelt brushed off this statement. "I'll let you know when I want you in the army," he said sharply, "and that would be only if there were some special job for which you're especially qualified."

The President's brusqueness vanished. "You stay put," he went on. "I don't know of anyone who could take over the work you're doing. Don't forget that many vitally important jobs are being done by men in civilian clothes—including that of the Commander in Chief."

He then began reminiscing about the First World War and when he was Assistant Secretary of the Navy. He said that he had worried —just as Rockefeller now worried—about whether he should join

170

the armed forces, and he had gone to President Wilson to ask his advice, just as Rockefeller had come to the White House on this day. Mr. Wilson told him to stay put.

Another conversation with Mr. Roosevelt was on May 19, 1943. Rockefeller's record of the conversation showed that they discussed the possible use of Brazilian troops in the European war and whether the North African port of Dakar might one day be set up as a permanent military base designed to protect the security of Latin America from transatlantic invasion.

They also discussed the projected Pan American Highway as a means of developing inter-American tourist trade in the future. The President was very much interested and believed that hotels and camps should be built along the highway—making sure, he added, that nothing would detract from the native atmosphere or the beauty of national monuments. He suggested that Chambers of Commerce ought to be interested and that probably the United States Congress should appropriate funds for building such hotels on the grounds that in the long run the increased tourist trade would mean increased sales for United States products.

The talk shifted to the Soviet Union and the President expressed the opinion that as long as Premier Joseph Stalin was in power he would soft-pedal the international Communist movement, although he would not publicly disown it. After Stalin, he speculated, others might adopt a far more aggressive international program. He was not pessimistic about postwar relations with Russia. Referring to Maxim Litvinov's analogy, he said that Communism had gone 20 per cent of the way toward capitalism since 1917 and that it would eventually go 40 per cent of the way. Meanwhile, the United States had gone 20 per cent of the way toward Socialism and would probably go another 20 per cent under his administration. That, he concluded, would create a 40-60 relationship between the two opposing ideologies and bring them close enough together so that there could be a working arrangement between the two nations.

"My feeling," Rockefeller replied, "is that the liberal leadership of this hemisphere should be provided by the United States and that it is not to the interest of any American country to have the people look to or be led by a nation outside the hemisphere."

The President said he agreed. Mr. Roosevelt added that he felt Americans had always kowtowed too much to the British because we had an inferiority complex. After the war, he added, the United States would have to do a better job of selling and of delivering more for the money to compete in international trade.

## II.

Of the many projects undertaken by CIAA, a few are worthy of special mention because they illustrate different facets of Rockefeller's character or because they influenced his thinking in later years. Prior to Pearl Harbor, Harry Hopkins asked the CIAA to do a survey of Nazi penetration into political, business and financial circles in South America.

"Keep in mind," Hopkins told Rockefeller, "that we made a mistake in handling this kind of thing in the First World War. At that time, many Germans were local agents of United States firms in Latin America. As soon as we got into the war, we blacklisted all enemy business firms. This immediately disrupted our channels of trade in Latin America and worked serious economic hardships on many friendly countries. Perhaps this time we can plan for United States companies gradually to weed out their German agents."

Rockefeller and Assistant Secretary of State Adolf A. Berle, Jr., organized a mission to make a survey. It included Percy L. Douglas, on leave from the International Division of the Otis Elevator Company and a member of the CIAA staff; John Lockwood, also on the CIAA staff; Percy Foxworth, chief of the Latin American division of the Federal Bureau of Investigation; and George Butler of the Department of State. They visited eighteen countries in three months and reported back that many United States firms were represented in Latin America by Nazis or pro-Nazis and that they often used their advertising budgets to support anti-American newspapers and their profits to finance anti-American propaganda. They also were part of a widespread German espionage network in many instances.

Douglas and Rockefeller made confidential calls on perhaps a score of top industrialists and explained the results of the survey.

"We're asking you voluntarily to change your foreign agents where the evidence is definite," Rockefeller said. "Sometimes this will mean breaking contracts and a loss of money, to say nothing of vast inconvenience. We don't offer you a penny of reparation. It's strictly a matter of patriotism."

All of the top officials agreed to cooperate, but the head of one of the largest United States industries operating in South America turned the matter over to his Chief of Export Division, who had already been publicly criticized for close contacts with Nazi government officials and who had nineteen strongly pro-Nazi agents in South America. When CIAA representatives talked to this export chief he listened politely, thanked them for their information and said there wasn't anything to be done.

"We are a strictly nonpolitical business," the chief added, "and we're not interested in taking sides."

Rockefeller was astonished and his astonishment turned to anger when further negotiations failed to change the chief's mind. A short time afterward he invited the chief to Washington and arranged a meeting in which Welles and Berle as well as CIAA personnel participated. Welles explained the dangers of the situation with impressive forcefulness. He laid it on the line that a matter of national security was involved and that the whole program would be greatly handicapped if not wrecked by the failure of one of the nation's big industries to cooperate.

"No," the chief replied. "We're not interested in getting involved in politics." He said it arrogantly, Rockefeller thought, and the meeting ended. Rockefeller, however, had no intention of giving up. As the others departed, he called the chief aside and forgot the restraints of diplomatic procedure.

"Look," he began, "we are trying to work this out on a cooperative basis in the national interest. I think you are doing a great disservice to private enterprise generally." He paused but got no response. Then the Rockefeller hardness came through. "Well," he went on, "there is one alternative. That is to make a public statement and say that of all American businessmen involved you are the only one who hasn't cooperated." He added, pointedly: "I just can't conceive how an intelligent businessman can take a position like this— especially in view of the number of stockholders in your company."

The man remained outwardly impassive. A few days later, however, Rockefeller received a message from the company's headquarters. It was short and to the point: "The Company has decided to move its nineteen agents."

In about six months, more than a thousand undesirable agency accounts in Latin America were dropped or replaced by United States firms. Rockefeller wrote to seventeen hundred firms which had business contacts in Latin America, asking them to cooperate. By the day of Pearl Harbor, 85 per cent of the business which had been passing through the hands of pro-Nazis had been shifted elsewhere—often at considerable cost to United States businesses. But when war came there was little disruption due to blacklisting.

The war caused a shortage of newsprint everywhere and CIAA went to bat for Latin American newspapers in order to keep many of them from closing, and perhaps also to encourage them to print many thousands of news stories and cartoons and mat photographs which the agency distributed each month to about twelve hundred daily and weekly papers south of the border. A still more serious problem, however, arose when United States firms quit advertising in Latin America because the war prevented them from shipping products there. This threatened many newspapers and radio stations with bankruptcy because as much as 40 per cent of their income was from North American advertising. Rockefeller discussed the problem with a number of the biggest advertisers and suggested that they resume advertising in Latin America—high war taxes made it inexpensive— as a gesture of good will. They agreed, but said the United States Treasury had ruled such advertising would not be a legitimate tax exemption if they were selling nothing. Rockefeller then got Secretary of the Treasury Henry Morgenthau to write him a letter saying that, if the issue arose, he would rule in favor of exempting the advertising expenditures. Copies of the letter were sent to sixteen hundred United States exporters. Soon thereafter most of them restored their original advertising in Latin America of approximately $11,000,000 a year, and by the end of the war this total had climbed to $20,000,000.

"These are comparatively small things," Rockefeller said, "but they represent what can be done only if we have somebody interested and have the mechanism for getting action. Something that seems small to us may be of life-or-death importance to others, and doing something about it means the difference between good relations or bad, between unity or disunity."

### III.

The CIAA information program in Latin America devoted a great deal of attention to democracy and freedom and what they meant to the Americas. But talk, of course, was not enough. It was essential to demonstrate the United States attitude by deeds in order to combat Nazi charges that the United States would desert its southern neighbors as soon as the war emergency ended. One way in which the United States moved to meet this problem was by developing a cooperative inter-American health, nutrition and education program. There was an important political idea behind the program: better health and better education would tend, in the long run, to strengthen democracy in lands that were frequently plagued by dictatorship and would thus mean progress toward the unity and security of the Western Hemisphere.

The manner in which this idea was born and the way in which it later developed into a world-wide effort to strengthen democracy in the struggle against totalitarianism—particularly Communism—constitutes one of the most important and exciting chapters in Rockefeller's career. The story continues over many years but its beginning in the Office of the Coordinator for Inter-American Affairs can be stated rather simply. The United States in 1941 announced that it was providing $150,000,000 in lend-lease funds for Latin America. This promptly aroused fears in some quarters that the money would be used to strengthen various dictators who were then in power in a number of Central and South American countries. Rockefeller and the CIAA were bending their efforts toward furthering democratic principles in Latin America. They believed that it was of vital importance to the United States to have the support of the people in a war emergency and to convince the people that they would be better off under democratic government. They came to the conclusion that, to offset the danger of strengthening dictatorships, the United States should spend an equal amount—$150,000,000—to further democratic aims by attacking the problems of illiteracy, disease, and other causes of backwardness in Latin America. This, they argued, would further our interests in the event of a war emergency because it would strengthen democracy, provide technical assistance to increase agricultural and other production and reduce the health hazards that would be encountered by any of our armed forces that might be sent to Latin America to protect the Western Hemisphere. The overall importance of the proposals, however, was that the strengthening of democratic government was essential to our future security—a theory that had never actually been accepted or implemented by the United States government in the past.

Rockefeller believed that such a program might be financed by the Reconstruction Finance Corporation because it was partly designed to increase production of strategic war materials, so he took up the idea with Jesse Jones. The RFC chief expressed the belief that there was merit in the plan, but when it came to putting up perhaps $50,-000,000 without a good prospect of getting it back someday he promptly shied away. Rockefeller suggested various ways in which he might justifiably provide the funds but without success. Finally, Jones decided there was only one way to get rid of him.

"I can't do it," he said, "but if you're convinced it ought to be done I'll tell you how."

"I'm convinced," Rockefeller replied.

"Well, the President has the money in his emergency fund and he has the authority to have it allocated for this purpose. But to make it work you would have to get Congress to give you the power to set up corporations as they've done for the RFC. If you need me, I'll help you on the Hill."

A few weeks later, Rockefeller got together a book of charts, statistics and data on the program and went over to the White House to see Harry Hopkins. He got there before breakfast and Hopkins, in a dressing gown, was sitting up in bed in his room, which adjoined the President's bedroom. The coordinator handed him the book and began talking with his usual enthusiasm. When he had finished, Hopkins asked a few questions. Then he got out of bed, stuck his feet into a pair of bedroom slippers and, picking up the book, went padding out of the room to see Mr. Roosevelt. He was back in a short time, perhaps ten minutes.

"Okay," he said, "the President will make an initial allocation of $25,000,000."

Slightly dazed, Rokefeller gathered up his materials and went about the business of getting Congressional approval. Senator McKellar was disturbed about the proposal when first approached but, as he had promised, Jones came to Rockefeller's aid and the necessary authority was granted. Meanwhile, Rockefeller had gone to Sumner Welles and explained that he had the $25,000,000 and needed advice. Welles pointed out that the desired objective could best be achieved by a cooperative effort of the American republics rather than by unilateral action on the part of the United States. A conference of the American republics was to be held in Rio de Janeiro in January of 1942 and Welles suggested that it should be asked to adopt a resolution for joint action to achieve the goals Rockefeller had in mind. After discussion with other Latin American representatives, such a resolution was proposed at Rio de Janeiro and adopted. It invited the various republics to act jointly or bilaterally to further democratic principles by economic, technical and other assistance.

In response to this resolution, the United States established the Institute of Inter-American Affairs, which became an instrument of great significance in hemispheric relations. It was given formal approval by the President on March 24, 1942, and later made numerous agreements with Latin American governments for technical and other assistance as a means of moving toward the goal of stronger democratic government. Eventually, half a dozen corporations were set up to handle various phases of the program with funds contributed by the United States. In each instance, the projects were started with the United States putting up most of the money but decreasing its contribution each year until the work could be financed entirely by the local government. By 1945, projects had been arranged in eighteen countries, in which the United States spent some $40,000,000 while the other countries put up $24,000,000 in cash and as much again in materials and equipment. Actually, this was the forerunner of what later would be known as the Point Four program of foreign assistance.

An example of how the program worked was provided in Brazil. German U-boat warfare was highly successful in the South Atlantic in 1942 and the sinking of many Allied ships—plus a severe drought—created a critical food shortage in Northern Brazil, which had no other means of transport from its southern states. At the same time, the United States had completed arrangements with Brazil to build a series of air, naval and military bases along the northern coast to guard against Axis invasion and to protect an aerial supply line to North Africa. When Rockefeller arrived in Brazil in the early autumn of 1942 the experts of the Institute of Inter-American Affairs had made a survey of the rubber-producing Amazon Valley and the northern coast. They recommended a huge public health service program throughout the three-thousand-mile-long Amazon basin and a drive to improve farm production in seven states of northern Brazil. The local farmers had only the most primitive tools—a machete to cut weeds and a sharp stick to make a hole in the ground for planting seed. Their farm stock was poor and they couldn't produce enough food to supply the people in normal times, to say nothing of United States armed forces along the coast.

The institute's field men had done excellent preliminary work that enabled them, within a week after Rockefeller's arrival, to conclude arrangements with the Brazilian government for a joint program to which the institute contributed $5,000,000. Field teams went to work the next day. Within a short time, bulldozers and other heavy equipment lent by U.S. Air Force engineers at bases on the coast were clearing large tracts for planting. Demonstration farms were established and modern water systems were installed at three key centers so the workers would no longer have to drink contaminated water from the Amazon. Many thousands of baby chicks and pigs were flown into the area. It was planned to give them to native farmers but the gift offer aroused suspicion and it was decided to exchange the healthy stock for the scrawny native chickens and pigs in order to assure the farmers that everything was on the level. This worked well, and there was soon a demand for more stock than could be supplied. But perhaps the most vivid illustration of what the program achieved was provided by a very simple move—the distribution of seventy-five thousand ordinary hoes. This, the experts estimated, *quadrupled* the manpower productivity of the farmers who, for the first time, used a hoe instead of a sharp stick to plant seed.

In two years, production of food stuffs in the seven states was changed from a deficit to a surplus that not only met local needs but supplied the armed forces, permitted expansion of the wartime rubber-producing program and permanently boosted the living standards of the people in a strategic area that was regarded as vulnerable to Axis invasion. The institute continued its program in various Latin American countries until 1948, working on more than two thousand projects, training some ten thousand persons for all kinds of jobs from midwife to sanitary engineer and completing some fifty-four cooperative agreements. It was merged later with the Inter-American Education Foundation, Inc., which became an integral part of the mechanism of inter-American relations.

## IV.

The CIAA inaugurated a number of projects which, toward the end of the war, were gradually shifted to other agencies and departments, sometimes on Rockefeller's suggestion and sometimes over his vigorous protests. "He is a man," one government official remarked, "who doesn't let go of anything easily." Once he had seen a project or a division shifted elsewhere, however, Rockefeller usually was ready to cooperate to see that it functioned smoothly. For example, the commercial and financial divisions of CIAA were coveted by the Board of Economic Warfare. The BEW was the inspiration largely of Henry Wallace and Milo Perkins and it was designed to speed up procurement operations and build up stockpiles of strategic materials by buying on a preclusive basis and at set prices the entire output of certain commodities.

When BEW was first established there was conflict with CIAA but an arrangement was worked out at one period for the two agencies to have a kind of joint control over what had been the CIAA's commercial and financial division. Under this system, the division was jointly directed by two men. One was selected by Perkins. The other was a CIAA staff member, a close friend for some years of Rockefeller and earlier a "boarder" at the Rockefeller home in Washington. Some coolness had developed between Rockefeller and his friend prior to the BEW arrangement and, not long afterward, the coordinator was informed that the joint directors of the commercial and financial division were working on a plan for turning the division into a separate agency without responsibility either to the CIAA or the BEW. This was later described by the CIAA staff member as "a healthy disagreement concerning alternative courses of action on which reasonable persons could understandably differ." The coordinator, however, did not regard the idea of a separate agency as either healthy or reasonable. He promptly consulted with Perkins and both of the men involved were separated from their jobs. There came a time later when Rockefeller, then in the State Department, prevented his former friend from getting a department job for which other officials thought he was well qualified. Normally, Rockefeller was inclined to fight hard for what he thought were his rights but, once a decision had been reached, to forgive and forget. But if he some way—justly or unjustly—became convinced that an intimate member of his "team" had acted disloyally, he was unlikely either to forgive or forget.

"Rockefeller did many wonderful things for many persons and nobody ever knew about it," an official who served with him said much later. "But he was then young and intense and I thought he sometimes showed a vindictive streak that cost him the services of some able men at the time. There was one Latin American ambassador whose methods he did not like and with whom he had differences when he was coordinator. When Rockefeller moved later to the State Department he had that ambassador shifted to a distant post where he held a lesser rank."

In the spring of 1944, Rockefeller arranged for a meeting in New York of the Inter-American Development Commission, an agency of all twenty-one American republics formed in 1940 to work out ways of replacing markets lost due to the war. As chairman, he presided over the New York meeting and was presented with the gold medal of the Pan-American Society in recognition of his efforts toward inter-American unity and cooperation.

As usual, his working schedule was so crowded that he hardly saw his parents while he was in New York and their longest glimpse of him was from the floor of the banquet hall when he received the medal. But the next day, his father wrote him:

> I was very proud of you last night—proud of the recognition given you by the Pan American Society in awarding of its gold medal; proud of the appreciative words spoken about you; proud of the wholly charming, modest manner in which you accepted the gold medal on behalf of the other members of the conference and the large group of your associates rather than as an exclusive tribute to yourself . . . and above all, proud of the many expressions of affection and devotion to you that were made to me by individual members of the conference. . . .
>
> When you started on this work and many people said to me, "Yes, but it is impossible," you will recall that my answer always was, "It may be impossible but it is necessary." Because you believed it was necessary and vital, you have made it possible and,

by grinding, unremitting, indefatigable hard work, have brilliantly
turned the impossible into the possible.

I never was surer of the importance of friendly relations among
the various countries of the Western Hemisphere than I am today.
You have proved to the world that such relations are possible. . . .
And so, with a full heart of pride, joy and gratitude, I say: "Well
done, my son, you have wrought a good work . . . you have
brought added credit to the family name."

Affectionately,<br>
Father

In the autumn of 1944 Rockefeller made a trip to the Caribbean
Islands that he will never forget. The little Negro Republic of Haiti
was plagued by many grave problems including the fact that 80 per
cent of its population suffered from yaws, a contagious skin disease
having many analogies with syphilis that literally sapped the vitality
of the nation. The Inter-American Institute was cooperating with
the Haitian government in a campaign to combat the disease, and
Rockefeller was invited to visit a clinic in a distant corner of the
country. He flew from Port au Prince to a small airfield and then
drove along the coast, through coconut and palm forests and past
glistening white beaches. After a few miles, his automobile began
passing lines of pedestrians, all going in the same direction. They
were a pitiful procession. Some seemed barely able to drag themselves
along. Some hobbled on crutches or held to the arms of companions.
Some rode donkeys led by children. The procession became heavier
as the visitors approached the hutlike clinic building in the hills,
where at least a couple of thousand persons had gathered for a special
occasion.

The little clinic originally had been founded and run by a U.S.
Army medical corps colonel and two assistant medical officers who
lived virtually in exile in one of the poorest sections of the country
and who had treated with great gentleness and understanding the
unfortunate victims from whom others turned away in horror. Natives
had been trained, however, to do the work and on this day the army
officers were turning the clinic over to three young Haitian doctors.

There was a brief ceremony. Then one of the elders among the patients arose and made a moving speech in which he recounted what the clinic had done for the people. In a trembling voice, he thanked the army doctors and the people of the United States for the service they had rendered his community. A great cheer went up from the crowd of patients. As the old man sat down, Rockefeller saw that he was crying softly. He saw, too, that the city-bred government officials whom he had accompanied from Port au Prince were impressed.

"It was one of the most moving scenes I ever witnessed," said Rockefeller, who ignored the danger of infection in order to shake hands with many of the patients. "This was a different kind of foreign relations than had ever been practiced by our old-school diplomats. It had a sense of reality and it gave meaning to the word democracy."

# NINE

# A Struggle for Unity

While Rockefeller was still on his Caribbean tour, he received a telephone call from Washington the second week in November. It was from Edward R. Stettinius, Jr.

"Nelson," said Stettinius, who had been Under Secretary of State, "Secretary Hull has resigned and the President has asked me to take over. Can you come back to Washington at once?"

Rockefeller said yes and caught a plane. When he reached Stettinius' office, the new Secretary was in the midst of reorganizing the Department.

"Nelson, the President wants you to go in as assistant secretary in charge of Latin American affairs," Stettinius said.

At the moment, Rockefeller did not notice that Stettinius had said it was Mr. Roosevelt who chose him but later General Watson told him that "it was the boss who wanted you, not the new Secretary." At the time of the meeting in Stettinius' office, Rockefeller was very much interested in going into the State Department but he hesitated. To understand his hesitation, it is necessary to look back at State Department policy, particularly in regard to Argentina.

II.

Argentina had been a difficult problem since the European war started. The Rockefeller office had sought to counteract powerful Nazi and Fascist influences in that country by helping Argentina to dispose of large wheat and meat surpluses, but at the 1942 Rio de Janeiro conference of American republics, the Buenos Aires government refused to agree to a resolution calling for mandatory severance of relations with the Axis powers. Under Secretary Welles felt there was danger of splitting the conference wide open and he worked out a compromise that merely "recommended" rupture of relations with Germany, Italy and Japan. Hull bitterly opposed this plan as "more appeasement" but the President finally approved it, on the ground that hemisphere unity was essential to our security. Hull and Welles were on opposite sides of the fence thereafter and Welles finally was forced to resign in 1943.

Then, in June, 1943, the army overthrew the Buenos Aires government and established a junta of colonels to run the country temporarily. This regime went through various transformations but gradually it emerged as a pro-German dictatorship in which the behind-the-scenes power was wielded by Colonel Juan Perón. Argentina continued as a base for propaganda and espionage activities of the European Axis powers. Early in 1944, Rockefeller had a long, friendly talk with Hull regarding Argentina and expressed fear that enemy activities there would destroy the progress that had been made toward uniting the Western Hemisphere behind the Allied war effort. Hull was tremendously occupied with many problems and he asked the coordinator to take it up with Under Secretary Stettinius. Rockefeller submitted a memorandum in January, 1944, emphasizing that Nazi propaganda in South America was broadcasting charges that the United States would desert the other American republics when World War II ended. He said our current program had created an atmosphere of cooperation that was essential to our security and welfare but that it depended on a dynamic United States policy and that we were in danger of losing Latin American support because of a lack of leadership in support of clear and precise objectives that would assure permanent inter-American cooperation.

Stettinius expressed a sympathetic attitude toward the proposals and referred them to subordinates who had no power to act. In other words, nothing was done. When, in June of 1944, the United States asked all American republics to withdraw recognition from Argentina, four Latin American governments refused to do so for fear of retaliation and the unity of the Western Hemisphere was shattered. Perón's prestige increased and his tricky methods of operation infuriated Secretary Hull, who declined to accept proposals by various Latin American diplomats, including Ezequiel Padilla, the Mexican foreign minister, for some kind of joint action to deal with the situation.

Meanwhile, on May 29, Hull had announced that the United States, Great Britain, China and Russia were considering plans for a world organization. But the State Department had not consulted in advance with other American republics and this led them to wonder whether we were abandoning the inter-American system in favor of a world organization run by the big powers, which they feared would leave the small nations without adequate protection and representation.

On August 19, Rockefeller went again to talk to Hull. "I believe that there are only two courses open to us," he told the Secretary. "We must apply economic sanctions, jointly with other Allied nations, against Argentina and give full support to any other American republics against which the Argentina government might take reprisals; or we must call a conference of foreign ministers of all the American republics, put the Argentine situation up to them and be guided by their joint decision."

Hull didn't want a conference and he said the boycott problem had been considered by the cabinet, which had decided that a boycott of Argentina could be undertaken only if the United States was willing to ration meat more tightly in order to supply Great Britain. It was decided that that was impossible.

"But our position is inconsistent," Rockefeller argued. "Personally, I believe the people of this country would be willing to make the sacrifice of eating less meat in order to combat Nazi penetration of the Hemisphere. And I believe it would help rather than harm the administration in the coming election."

"The decision has been made," Hull replied.

The talk with Hull left Rockefeller depressed. He finally came to the conclusion that he could do nothing but reassert to Hull in writing his own feelings. Several associates warned him that it would do no good, that Hull was so bitter about the situation that such action probably would lead to Rockefeller's ouster from the government. Finally, Rockefeller went to talk to the President and was surprised to learn that he was well aware of what had been happening. He expressed no objection to Rockefeller's plan to reiterate his ideas to the Secretary of State, which Rockefeller did in a memorandum on September 5, 1944, setting forth detailed recommendations for a firm policy of inter-American action.

The Secretary never replied to or commented on the memorandum, but he was not henceforth friendly to Rockefeller. His health was failing and, after again vainly trying to persuade the British to agree to a boycott of Argentina, Hull resigned in November, 1944, and Stettinius telephoned Rockefeller to come home and be Assistant Secretary.

Rockefeller proposed that, in reorganizing the department, Stettinius give one person full authority and responsibility to integrate all activities in regard to Latin America. The new Secretary did not agree. He said that Will Clayton would take charge of economic activities, while Rockefeller would be concerned with political affairs. Rockefeller respected Clayton and knew he could work with him. He delayed his decision until he had talked with Harry Hopkins, who told him that the President was ready to back a strong policy that would re-establish Hemisphere unity. Rockefeller then turned the CIAA over to Wallace Harrison and moved over to the State Department.

"I really had no alternative," he said later. "I had been criticizing for months. Now I couldn't refuse to accept the responsibility."

On December 20, the Senate considered the President's nomination of Joseph C. Grew to be Under Secretary of State and of five others, including Rockefeller, to be Assistant Secretaries. A number of senators spoke against one or all of the nominees, some of whom were criticized as being too far to the left and some of whom were described as right-wing representatives. Senator Robert La Follette, usually regarded as a liberal, charged that confirmation of the six would "tend to destroy the hope of the American people for a just and democratic peace." Although Rockefeller was not picked out for any special attack, nine senators voted against him and sixty-two voted for his confirmation. Now he had both the responsibility and the opportunity.

III.

It could not be said that Rockefeller ever made himself popular in the Department of State except with a distinct minority. He had long disagreed with the traditional methods of diplomacy. He chafed under legalistic restraints and objected to what he believed were overcautious, halfway measures toward achieving a goal. He believed a people-to-people program to encourage mutual knowledge and understanding among nations should be an important factor in the conduct of foreign relations and he seldom ceased to pester both career and political diplomats to do things differently, to try something new. His methods and his attitude were often criticized by department officials.

Yet, the record will show that Rockefeller's needling and his persistence even in a rather secondary official role were of significance in later years in the struggle of the Western democracies against Russian Communism. Had he not made himself unpopular in 1945 it is quite possible the United States and its allies would have been in a far less favorable position vis-à-vis Soviet Russia a decade later. This should not necessarily be taken to mean that the youthful Assistant Secretary of State had vision superior to that of more experienced diplomatic officials. He was dedicated to the idea of unity and cooperation in the Western Hemisphere, and his comprehension of what that meant to the security of the United States was the basis of his actions. That it eventually would mean far more to the security of the Western world was, perhaps, a result that neither he nor others could foresee so clearly in 1945, any more than they could foresee an alliance that would be called the North Atlantic Treaty Organization. But the fact remains that NATO might never have been possible if it had not been for the "meddling" of Rockefeller in 1945.

The knowledge that Stettinius had selected Rockefeller only because of the President's suggestion was seldom a handicap to the new Assistant Secretary but it made Rockefeller wary in the first days. He discovered, however, that his superior had very little time to interest himself in Latin American affairs and was more than willing to have Rockefeller present when he discussed such problems with Mr. Roosevelt. Rockefeller felt that his job was to take a firm stand toward Argentina. His first proposal was that the Allied powers should refuse to purchase Argentina's output of 400,000 tons of fats and oils— mostly for Great Britain—unless the Buenos Aires government cooperated in the war effort against the Axis. Except for Clayton, everybody opposed this idea in view of the world shortage of fats, and the British would have nothing to do with it.

Even before his confirmation by the Senate, Rockefeller had revived a proposal by Foreign Minister Padilla of Mexico for holding at Mexico City an inter-American conference of foreign ministers to deal with political and economic problems—a suggestion on which Hull had not acted. He discussed the proposal at a department staff meeting and he also consulted with an old friend, Rafael Oreamuno, former minister from Costa Rica, who pointed out that for several years there had been very little personal contact between the State Department and Latin American diplomats. He gave Rockefeller the names of three ambassadors and suggested he invite them to luncheon at his home.

"I'll come, too," he added, "and I think the general conversation will lead us to the main problems."

When the five men gathered for the luncheon on December 21, 1944, Rockefeller asked them frankly for their ideas. The group was uncertain as to whether an inter-American conference at Mexico City would be successful in restoring unity.

"The Argentine question would have to come up," one of them pointed out. "There's no chance that the various nations would be united on that subject. The United States and some other republics might join in denouncing dictatorship in Argentina, but you may be sure that the small countries who are neighbors of Argentina would not do so. They are afraid because they have the example of Bolivia. When the Bolivian government refused to cooperate with Argentina there was an uprising [probably with the help of Buenos Aires] and the United States did nothing to aid the established government. It was overthrown and others fear the same fate if they openly oppose Argentina."

The conversation then turned to the possibility of providing for joint action by all of the American republics to protect the political and economic security of all.

"That is the key to a solution of the dilemma," one ambassador said. "If only the United States would agree that the conference would consider an inter-American basis for solving problems of peace and security as well as economic problems, we might be in a position to take a common stand on the Argentine situation."

"I believe," Rockefeller said, "that the United States may be prepared to proceed along those lines."

The ambassadors looked at him with disbelief as if this were merely the naïve viewpoint of a new and inexperienced State Department official. But Rockefeller, probably remembering his talk with Hopkins and knowing the President's firm attitude, convinced his guests that he was serious. Once they felt he knew what he was talking about, they shed their despondency and the meeting took on an atmosphere of confidence and enthusiasm. They worked for four hours on an agenda and other details of a projected conference of American republics which were cooperating in the war effort. Later Rockefeller gradually extended his conversations to the other American republics' representatives and gave each the feeling of having been consulted and of having contributed to the plans. Step by step, the Mexico City conference program was pieced together and no piece was included unless it reflected the general thinking of the American community, except for Argentina, which was not consulted.

"About all I contributed," Rockefeller remarked, "was a willingness to listen and to understand their problems and their viewpoints."

Rockefeller encountered opposition at State Department staff meetings in connection with his hope of developing a united moral force among the American republics on the understanding that the United States would be prepared to give economic, political and military support in event the smaller nations were threatened, presumably by Argentina, with aggression. The department's main attention was centered on the Dumbarton Oaks conferences, at which the groundwork was being laid for formation of the world organization that eventually would be called the United Nations. Our experts at these sessions included Leo Pasvolsky, special assistant to the Secretary of State for International Organization, and Alger Hiss, executive secretary of the Dumbarton Oaks program. They and most other department experts regarded plans for the world organization as so vital to the future and as involving so many delicate issues that they opposed—for good reasons—the introduction of any new factors that might make the work more difficult. They were not in favor of the Mexico City conference because they feared it would arouse the suspicions of European leaders and might prejudice preparations for the world organization. In the minds of some experts, regional blocs were contrary to the whole idea of a United Nations.

In January, 1945, Rockefeller and Stettinius twice called at the White House. The President was preparing to go to Yalta for his historic meeting with Prime Minister Churchill and Premier Stalin, and Stettinius had much to discuss with him in that regard. Then the Secretary sat back and worked on his notes while Rockefeller took up the question of the Mexico City conference. To summarize the two conferences, Rockefeller said that the Latin American countries were worried about Big Power domination of the United Nations but that they were willing to support the principles of the Dumbarton Oaks program in a formal resolution at Mexico City, provided the United States would support further development and strengthening of a regional inter-American system.

Rockefeller felt that the President was pleased by the attitude of the other American republics, and that he did not share the viewpoint of the International Division of the State Department that a mutual defense pact might damage prospects for a world organization. Mr. Roosevelt said he did not see why there should be any conflict between regional agreements and the world organization, according to Rockefeller's notes on the conversation. He added that the Mexico City conference could lay the foundation for harmonious integration of regional agreements in the framework of the United Nations and that this integration could be confirmed at San Francisco.

"But the major powers," he told Rockefeller, "may misunderstand what is planned at Mexico City and you should call on their ambassadors there and inform them fully and assure them that the conference will not detract from the plans for the world organization as worked out at Dumbarton Oaks."

In regard to Argentina, Rockefeller told the President that the United States should express its determination not to establish relations with Buenos Aires "until its government demonstrated by unqualified acts its intention to observe its inter-American obligations and abandon threats to hemispheric peace." The President approved this policy and initialed the proposed agenda for the inter-American conference at Mexico City.

Rockefeller had still another idea which he presented in a memorandum. It proposed to test Perón's good faith by urging him to turn over the Argentine government to his Supreme Court temporarily while honest elections were held to select a new government. If that were done, the new government would be recognized by the other American republics and Argentina would be invited to attend the Mexico City conference. The President approved and initialed the memorandum. He expressed deep concern that, after the war, the peoples not only of the Western Hemisphere but of the world should have an opportunity to realize the objectives of the Atlantic Charter and that there should be progress toward economic cooperation and mutual security.

Rockefeller visited the White House on one other occasion before Mr. Roosevelt and Stettinius left for Yalta. Former President Eduardo Santos of Colombia, a liberal statesman with integrity and courage, arrived in Washington that January. He was an old friend of Mr. Roosevelt but the President was so busy preparing for his journey that his aides discouraged the idea of an appointment for the Colombian statesman. Rockefeller finally called General Watson and appealed for ten minutes for Santos. Watson arranged it, but specified that Rockefeller should be present.

Mr. Roosevelt appeared to be very tired when they entered his office on January 9, but he listened attentively to Santos' frank observations. There was a very real fear, the Colombian said, of aggression in Latin America, particularly in Chile, Uruguay, Colombia, and in Central America. All of these nations, he went on, were faced with the problem of illiteracy and hunger yet all were spending far too much—perhaps a third of their federal income—for military purposes. As a result, military dictatorships were being encouraged and democracy was thwarted.

"The best hope for the future," he said, "lies in the idea of President Wilson for a mutual guarantee of borders. Do you think that you or Secretary Stettinius might mention such an idea at the Mexican conference?"

"I understand this problem," the President replied, "but it would be more appropriate if Colombia introduced a resolution. In that case, the United States would support the resolution. But it is difficult to define aggression. In my own opinion, aggression would be when an armed man crosses the frontier from one country to another."

"I agree," Santos said. "I believe Colombia might introduce the resolution but we probably would want to have Venezuela join with us."

The President nodded. "This is a wonderful example of the spirit of cooperation in the Western Hemisphere," he added. "I think I will

discuss the principle with Stalin and Churchill in Yalta." He turned
to Rockefeller. "Will you follow up on this talk for us?" Then, as
his visitors departed, he raised his hand in salute and said: "God
bless you!"

The Assistant Secretary was only too willing to follow up but he
continued to encounter opposition from the department's International Division, which argued that regional agreements of this nature
might easily wreck the conference at San Francisco. Rockefeller stood
his ground and, when hard pressed, said: "My instructions come from
the President. If you want to change this policy, you will have to
take it up with him."

## IV.

On February 16, 1945, Rockefeller chartered an airplane and invited the Latin American ambassadors to fly with him to Mexico for
what was called the Inter-American Conference on Problems of War
and Peace. The chartered plane was the kind of grandiose gesture
frowned on by old-school diplomats, but by this time Rockefeller's
diplomacy was being conducted largely on a basis of close personal
acquaintance with the ambassadors and none of them were worried
that he couldn't afford the junket. They ran into storms en route,
had to land a couple of times to wait for the weather to clear and
were much more like a group of close companions—most of them
were comparatively young—than a delegation of striped-pants diplomats by the time they reached the Mexican capital on February 18th.

This feeling of close harmony was increased rather than dissipated
during the conference. For one thing, Rockefeller quickly discovered
that his hotel suite was wired for sound with an interesting assort-
ment of microphones concealed in odd spots. This, it turned out,
was not necessarily a sinister attempt to learn state secrets because
the suite had been wired ever since the hotel was built, but of course
the system might have been used by someone if it had gone unde-
tected. Rockefeller also was informed that certain tables in certain
popular restaurants had concealed microphones and that visiting

diplomats might be conducted to these tables. All of this information he passed on to his Latin American colleagues and this served to strengthen their confidence in his sincerity and honesty.

The conference itself was conducted more harmoniously than might have been expected. Secretary Stettinius, just back from Yalta, flew down to Mexico City to lend his prestige to the Washington delegation, although he had been so occupied by other vital matters that it was impossible for him to catch up with Latin American developments and much of the conduct of the sessions as well as of press conferences was left in Rockefeller's hands. This was not always a comfortable position for either Rockefeller or Stettinius, who was an able salesman of the President's ideas but was not a policy maker and occasionally lacked a detailed knowledge of what he was selling. As a result, he sometimes had to turn to his Assistant Secretary to clarify obscure points at press conferences or elsewhere; this inevitably led to a certain strain on relations between the two men.

Early in the conference, the delegates conferred secretly on the question of inviting Argentina and authorized Foreign Minister Manuel C. Gallagher y Canaval of Peru, to transmit to the Buenos Aires regime the terms on which it could be represented at Mexico City—turn over the government to the Supreme Court pending honest elections and declare war on the Axis powers.[1] There was sentiment among the Latin American countries for inviting Argentina to the conference. President Avila Camacho of Mexico deplored the absence of Argentina in a public speech and there were street demonstrations by Mexican students favoring the Buenos Aires regime. The United States, however, felt strongly about the pro-Axis activities of the Argentine government and, with the support of other American republics, insisted that it should change its policies and agree to the terms transmitted by Gallagher in order to be ac-

[1] Rockefeller had little doubt at the time that Perón would refuse such a proposal. Earlier, he had, with the approval of President Roosevelt, sent a secret and completely unofficial emissary to Buenos Aires to sound out the military dictatorship, in which Perón was the power behind the scenes. Perón's reply was to point out that the president of the Supreme Court was then old and ill and that he could not "turn the government over to a corpse." He said, however, that he would call free and honest elections.

cepted in the community of American nations. The Argentine government, then headed by President Edelmiro Farrell, did not reply immediately.

Meanwhile, the sessions in Mexico City developed few major problems. The conference adopted resolutions to continue inter-American wartime cooperation and voted to support the coming conference at San Francisco to form a world organization. The United States backed a resolution to strengthen the system of inter-American cooperation.

The main work, however, centered around what became known as the Act of Chapultepec, which provided for a guarantee of the boundaries of the American republics. The drafting of this act was in the hands of Senator Warren Austin, for the United States, at the beginning of the sessions. Basically, it set up the thesis that an attack on one American republic was an attack on all and would be jointly resisted. Rockefeller felt that the preliminary work was going so well that there should be some newspaper publicity of an off-the-record nature. He explained the situation to James Reston of the *New York Times* and said that the theory of a joint guarantee of boundaries was "in the bag" because Senator Tom Connally would approve it when he arrived in the next few hours.

Connally arrived, but he was so tired that when Rockefeller asked him to read the prepared text he angrily snorted that he wasn't going to read anything that day. "Don't try to rush me, young man," he warned. Well aware of the rivalry between Connally and Austin, Rockefeller could see the Texas senator blowing sky-high if he read in the newspapers that the act had been agreed on before he even arrived in Mexico City. He called Reston and asked him to kill the story.

"Sorry," Reston replied, "it's already in print in New York."

Rockefeller spent a bad night and felt even worse the next day when he discovered Reston's story on page one of the *New York Times*. The senator, however, finally approved the draft.

Pasvolsky was still opposed to the Act of Chapultepec and he was so vigorous in his argument that the United States delegation was threatened with a split at one briefing session, despite the fact that policy had been agreed on in advance. When the session broke up without firm action, Rockefeller was indignant and he bitterly said so to Pasvolsky in the presence of Stettinius.

"If you're going to work against the agreed position of our delegation and the agreed position of the State Department," he said angrily, "you better go on back to Washington. I'm responsible to the Secretary for the conduct of the United States delegation here."

Pasvolsky did not reply but neither did he protest later when Stettinius and the members of Congress on the delegation overruled objections and put the united delegation on record as favoring a mutual defense agreement to be implemented later by treaty. Later the Act of Chapultepec was adopted by the conference. Rockefeller signed it for the United States.

The results of the Mexico City conference exceeded Rockefeller's hopes in that it set up a framework for future development of economic and social and defense cooperation. It also set the scene for action in regard to Argentina.

It was not until late in the second week of the conference that Gallagher hurriedly called a meeting to say that Argentina had turned down the ambassadors' proposal. This impressed the delegates as demonstrating that Argentina had no intention of cooperating in the war effort against the Axis. The success of the conference had raised morale among the delegations of the other republics and they enthusiastically agreed to draft a resolution that would express sympathy for the people of Argentina but would also express concern over the attitude of the government. Adolf A. Berle, Jr., U.S. Ambassador to Brazil, began drafting the resolution in Rockefeller's hotel suite but soon half a dozen ministers were joining in, working on various sections. Colombian Ambassador Alberto Lleras Camargo, an old newspaperman, took off his coat and began punching at a typewriter to weave the different sections together as they were completed. Papers littered the floor. Diplomats loosened their neckties as they wrote and rewrote a sentence or a phrase. By the time the work was completed, the scene was more like a newspaper office at press time than a meeting of dignified diplomats considering problems of international significance.

While the draft was being retyped, Berle invited Rockefeller to go outside for a breath of fresh air. They walked along a broad avenue and finally sat down on a concrete bench in a small park. There, beyond earshot of any curious delegates, Berle said that he believed Rockefeller should be extremely careful about considering any overtures that Argentina might make to the United States.

"I know that there is a kind of undercover group who will be trying to get the Perón government accepted without any real change," he said. "I don't believe you should negotiate with them; certainly not now. Be cool toward them. Let them wait. The war is almost over and we don't need their help. They are still pro-Nazi and public opinion in the United States is not going to accept them. This conference has been a great success. You're now sitting on top of the world, so don't do anything to change that situation. Your desire for a united front in the hemisphere is sound and it is right to try to achieve it. But I think it would be a political error to rush into any negotiations with Perón and, anyway, I don't believe you can change Perón. He is completely cynical."

Rockefeller was silent for a few moments. "Thanks," he finally said. "I'll think about it. But I believe unity of the Americas means a lot."

Stettinius was tied up at a dinner that night and Rockefeller took the draft resolution to the home of Foreign Minister Padilla, chairman of the conference, about midnight. Padilla approved the draft, which was in effect an invitation to the Argentine government to reorient its policies, to cooperate in the war against the Axis, to sign and live up to the Act of Chapultepec, to provide democratic procedures and freedom for its people and to become a partner with the other American republics.

After a few changes the next morning, the resolution was presented and adopted. The conference ended the next day and shortly thereafter Stettinius and Rockefeller climbed aboard an airplane and flew to Havana to talk to a big, tough and aggressive diplomat, Spruille Braden, about the possibility of going to Buenos Aires as ambassador if Perón accepted and complied with the conference resolution.

# TEN

# San Francisco—World Politics

On March 16, 1945, Rockefeller strode briskly into the White House with a feeling that he had good news for the President as a result of the success of the Mexico City conference, but his buoyant mood began to evaporate as soon as he entered the big, oval office where Mr. Roosevelt sat behind his desk. The President had changed markedly since January. Momentarily, Rockefeller saw in him no spark of animation. It was as if an inner fire had gone out; as if he had been drained of all emotion. Then he aroused himself and the old glow of enthusiasm was there again.

The Assistant Secretary briefly reviewed what had been done at Mexico City and said that he assumed Perón, who then held the post of vice president, was a "strong man" in Argentina and would be chosen President in a free election, because he had cleverly exploited the resentment of the people, particularly the workers, against the old oligarchy of landowners and their political allies. He said he had met since his return with key ambassadors from Latin America and they had coordinated their position by drafting a memorandum to the effect that, if Argentina declared war on Germany and Japan and expressed conformity with the Act of Chapultepec and signed it, then the Perón government would be recognized and the United States would recommend that Argentina be invited to sign the joint declaration of the United Nations.

"The important thing," he added, "is to get the Argentine government to reorient its policies, and join in cooperation with the other republics and, if that is done in good faith, it will be natural to want her in the world organization. The memorandum was approved yesterday at a State Department staff meeting."

The President indicated that he was pleased with results of the Mexico City conference and he was interested, even a little amused, by the way the Argentine situation had been handled. He said he shared the belief that it was necessary to spell out the terms under which the Buenos Aires government would be admitted. He approved and initialed the memorandum. Showing some of his old enthusiasm, he talked briefly about the future of the Western Hemisphere and remarked that what he had seen at Yalta convinced him more than ever that responsibility for future leadership would rest with the new world.

Then, as Rockefeller departed, he sank back in his chair as if exhausted. Rockefeller and his wife dined the next evening at the White House and, in a crowd, the President seemed almost his old self. But they were not to meet again.

On March 27, Argentina's government accepted the terms laid down by the other republics, declared war on Germany and Japan, signed the Mexico City resolution and agreed to abide by it. On April 9, all of the American republics as well as Great Britain and France resumed full diplomatic relations with Argentina. Braden became the United States ambassador at Buenos Aires. Eighteen pro-Nazi newspapers in Argentina were closed and Axis assets in that country seized.

Rockefeller was a bit puffed up over these developments. He felt that Argentina's apparent reversal of policy was a real victory and demonstrated the moral force that could be exerted if the other republics stood united. This, however, was by no means the unanimous opinion of State Department officials, some of whom regarded the developments as a defeat for the United States. Hull, for example, had been extremely bitter toward the Perón dictatorship, and he strongly felt that the policy pursued by Rockefeller was too lenient toward an unscrupulous government. Furthermore, Perón had not yet demonstrated any real change of heart.

When Rockefeller, on April 9, brought up at a State Department staff committee meeting the question of recommending that Argentina be invited to sign the joint declaration of the United Nations—the last step that had been agreed to at Mexico City—Assistant Secretary James C. Dunn objected.

"But this is a commitment," Rockefeller said.

"Yes," was the reply, "but there is no time schedule for carrying it out."

Dean Acheson, Archibald MacLeish and others also strongly opposed a recommendation that the pro-Nazi Perón dictatorship be invited to sign the world organization documents, and most United States newspaper comment was along the same lines. Stettinius was well aware of Hull's views and hesitated to go against them. Rockefeller did not believe the issue was confined to such narrow limits. He could well agree with the argument that it was repugnant to recognize a pro-Nazi government, but he strongly believed that the united action taken by the United States and the other American republics in regard to Argentina was in the best interests of the Western Hemisphere. Hemisphere security was of vital importance, he felt, and he was—mistakenly—confident that the united stand of the American republics would force Perón to live up to his pledges.

"We made commitments with the full knowledge of the President, the Secretary of State and the staff committee," he pointed out. "The San Francisco conference is only a couple of weeks away and, from a practical viewpoint, we are courting political trouble by delaying. If we don't act, I do not believe we can persuade the other American republics to refrain from proposing Argentina for membership in the world organization at San Francisco."

But his arguments were not successful. Public opinion and political expediency dictated delay. This was not a viewpoint that Rockefeller could appreciate at the time. He was perfectly willing to "take the rap" of public disapproval, if necessary, rather than fail to fulfill his promises—a stubborn and politically dangerous attitude that did not appeal to more experienced department officers. And the President was resting in Georgia and not available to intervene, although he had approved Rockefeller's procedure.

Rockefeller did not change his mind about the desirability of carrying out the commitment to invite Argentina but the situation was unchanged when President Roosevelt died at Warm Springs, Georgia, on April 12, and Harry S. Truman became chief executive. Rockefeller had not seen Mr. Roosevelt since he dined at the White House, but he had had a letter from him on March 31:

> Dear Nelson,
> The termination of your services as Coordinator of Inter-American Affairs prompts me to send you this note. You have made a magnificent contribution to the unity of this hemisphere and its ability to emerge with renewed strength from a grave period in its history. The people of this country and, indeed, of the other American republics are well aware of the significant progress attained under your leadership.
> Accordingly, I extend my high appreciation for your work as Coordinator. I am particularly glad that you are continuing to serve the cause of the Good Neighbor policy in the capacity of Assistant Secretary of State in charge of relations with the American republics. I wish you every success in that enlarged role.
> Sincerely yours,
> Franklin D. Roosevelt

The President may have been a little slow in getting around to writing the note because of the press of world affairs, but Rockefeller was happy that he had it.

## II.

After President Truman had instructed Stettinius to carry on without change any policies that had been agreed upon by Mr. Roosevelt, a request was received from the Argentine government that the United States support her bid for an invitation to San Francisco. Stettinius was very busy at the time and nothing was done prior to the conference except that Rockefeller sent the President a memorandum reviewing the problem and recommending that we carry out our commitment.

Rockefeller was very eager—overeager, in fact—to achieve complete unity of the Americas. On April 18, he sent a special mission, headed by Avra M. Warren, director of the Office of American Republic Affairs in the State Department, to Buenos Aires to see how the Argentine government was carrying out its promise to cooperate in the war against the Axis. At that time, most neutral observers failed to see any change, but Warren made a two-day survey and took a favorable stand toward Argentina, saying that "it is gratifying to encounter an official and public desire" to live up to the Act of Chapultepec. Perhaps this was what Rockefeller wanted to hear and perhaps Warren knew it was what he wanted to hear.

Meantime, Stettinius had broken some bad news to Rockefeller. "In view of the unhappy feelings between you and members of the International Division," the Secretary said, "I believe it would be best if you did not go to San Francisco. You had full freedom in Mexico City and now they want the same freedom at San Francisco."

"I can't blame them," Rockefeller replied, remembering how bitterly Hiss and Pasvolsky had opposed him in the past.

Very soon after this, however, the Russians began to cast around among the delegations to see how many votes they could control or influence at San Francisco. The idea of trying to line up voting blocs may not have been exactly in the spirit of the Dumbarton Oaks conferences but there wasn't anything Stettinius could do about it except look around to see how many votes might support the United States in a crisis. The result was that the votes of the Latin American countries suddenly became exceedingly important. Remembering what had happened at Mexico City, Stettinius suggested that perhaps Rockefeller should go to San Francisco after all. Hiss and Pasvolsky very strongly objected, criticizing Rockefeller's attitude and methods of diplomacy, but the secretary overruled them and told Rockefeller to get ready to go for a few days to "talk to the Latin Americans and get the ball rolling." He departed on April 21, again with a chartered planeload of Latin American delegates with whom he had been working closely.

Like everyone else at the time, the Latin Americans were greatly concerned that Mr. Roosevelt's death had left the world, particularly the Western world, without strong leadership. They desired, according to their talks with Rockefeller, to take part and accept responsibility in the United Nations, but they were worried about domination by the Big Powers and the failure of Washington to complete the Argentine agreement. Most important in their minds, was whether the inter-American system as represented by the Act of Chapultepec could be smoothly integrated into the world organization. It was typical of Rockefeller that he made their problems his own and that this frequently brought him into conflict with other State Department officials who were gravely concerned with broader international issues and with the success of the conference as a whole.

Almost from the beginning, there were discord and conflict between the delegates of the Soviet Union and the Western powers over everything from electing a chairman to the recognition of the so-called Lublin (Communist) government of Poland, which the Russians had promised at Yalta to replace with a representative regime. This made the role of Stettinius and his top aides increasingly difficult. They were not prepared for the harassing and obstructionist tactics of the Russians and, in some instances, they feared that the conference would break up and the dream of a United Nations would evaporate. Rockefeller's role, of course, was a limited one, but because of the increasing importance of the Latin American votes he usually sat in on meetings of the United States delegation—of which he was not even a member—and on the meetings of the foreign ministers of the Big Powers. This, he felt, was an ironic climax to the efforts of Hiss and Pasvolsky to keep him away from San Francisco.

Without attempting to consider here the main problems of the San Francisco conference, there were several early developments that tended to strengthen the unity of the Latin American delegations. For example, during maneuvering and debate on selection of a conference chairman, Foreign Minister Padilla of Mexico made an eloquent and courteous speech in favor of Stettinius. Padilla was greatly respected by the Latin Americans and they were shocked and chilled when Soviet Foreign Minister Vyacheslav M. Molotov arose and delivered a tirade of abuse and ridicule not only against the Mexican but against Latin American traditions in general, charging that Padilla was a stooge for the United States. Probably nothing could have served to alienate the Latin American republics more than such tactics. They knew then what the Russians thought of them and they didn't forget it.

They also were impressed at the April 27 meeting of the steering committee by the overbearing way in which Molotov treated Jan Masaryk, the son of the liberator of Czechoslovakia, who was greatly admired in South America. Molotov practically ordered Masaryk to propose that the Polish Lublin government be invited to the conference. The Czech rose, ashen faced and humiliated, and with eyes on the floor spoke of the heroism of the Polish people. He did not offer a motion that the Lublin government be invited but Molotov jumped up and said: "I second the motion." The United States delegation seemed momentarily confused by these tactics, but Victor Andrade of Bolivia pointed out that no motion had been made. Molotov leaped to his feet again and pointed at Masaryk.

"Jan Masaryk seconds my motion," he said. Stettinius and Eden denounced the proposal as contrary to the Yalta agreements.

None of this performance was lost on the Latin American delegates, who received an impressive lesson in how the Communists treated small states under their control.

At the same meeting, Molotov proposed the admission of White Russia and the Ukraine to the world organization, as had been agreed on at Yalta, and his motion was adopted. It had been proposed earlier in private by the United States that the question of actually seating the two Russian states at the conference and the similar question of inviting Argentina be delayed for three weeks to see whether Perón lived up to his promises to reform his regime. But now Molotov ignored this suggestion and proposed that the Russian states be invited to sit in immediately. Stettinius hesitated, but Foreign Minister Lleras Camargo of Colombia quickly moved that the question be referred to the executive committee for study and this was done.

Molotov's action, however, had created a crisis because the Russians indicated they would use the question of inviting Argentina into the United Nations as a lever to force the admission of the Lublin Communist government in Poland. The Latin American delegates felt strongly that the United States was committed to support of Argentina on the grounds that the Buenos Aires government had met the terms laid down at Mexico City. Stettinius said that the obligation would be met but he did not want to get the Argentine issue mixed up with the Russian demands on White Russia, the Ukraine and the Lublin regime. The aggressive demands of the Russians and the apparent fear of the United States and Great Britain that Molotov might break up the conference on some pretext such as the Polish question caused considerable despondency and uneasiness among the Latin American delegations.

In an effort to overcome this muddle, which was delaying the work of the conference, three Latin American members of the Executive Council met with Stettinius, Eden and Molotov in Stettinius' penthouse headquarters atop the Fairmont Hotel on April 28. Padilla, as spokesman for the Latin Americans, expressed the hope that Molotov would agree to invite Argentina and to postpone seating of White Russia and the Ukraine.

"I will support the invitation to Argentina," Molotov countered, "if you will support the seating of the Lublin government."

"That is impossible," Padilla replied, pointing out that the Yalta agreement provided for selection of a representative Polish government prior to admission to the world organization. Molotov remarked brusquely that there was no point in further discussion, and the meeting broke up on the understanding that the executive committee would try to reach some kind of decision.

Rockefeller followed all of these developments with a good deal of impatience. He felt that a principal trouble was lack of leadership against the Russian maneuvers and lack of preparation on the part of the Western powers which, he felt, were too fearful that they would be accused of "ganging up" on the Russians. Having reached this conclusion, he had to try to do something about it despite the fact that he was already in disfavor with most of the State Department experts and that a wiser diplomat would doubtless have decided it was a good time to let the authorized officials carry the ball. He sought out Stettinius and argued that the traditional diplomatic approach had failed and that the time had come to apply some practical political tactics.

"You've got to get this thing organized," he said. "You've got to outline your problems and see how we can get organized to do something about them."

The harassed Secretary of State was unimpressed, but Rockefeller didn't give up easily. He carried the same argument to Pasvolsky and other department officials. They were even less impressed. Having been thoroughly rebuffed, the Assistant Secretary might well have retired to his tent, which would doubtless have pleased most of his colleagues. But instead he continued to meet daily with the Latin American delegates and they decided to do a little "organizing" of their own in a quiet way.

Ambassador Guillermo Belt of Cuba was a member of the conference steering committee and always sat next to Stettinius. Rockefeller normally sat directly behind Belt. The Latin Americans agreed that when the Russians became obstreperous at the next session, Rockefeller would advise with Stettinius on the next step and would inform Belt and the Cuban would then make a speech advocating that line of action. The other Latin American delegates would know that Belt was voicing Stettinius' ideas and they would vote for his proposition. In addition, Galo Plaza Lasso, who was later President of Ecuador, was designated to act as a kind of parliamentary whip. He brought an aide to the sessions and, if necessary, Rockefeller would inform the aide of the desired plan of action and he would drift around the room in order to inform the other Latin American representatives. If a speech was needed, for example, he would pass the word along to those who were to speak and give them the theme to be followed.

On one occasion, Molotov planned to propose admission of certain international labor representatives to the conference. The United States was opposed to such action but the State Department delegates decided to do nothing until the issue arose. The Latin Americans talked it over, however, and Galo Plaza Lasso remarked that "I can get my foreign minister to handle this." Later, when Molotov made the proposal, Rockefeller called Stettinius' attention to the fact that the Ecuadorean foreign minister was on his feet and "wants to be recognized."

The Ecuadorean was young, dark-skinned and obviously of Indian blood. He stood near Molotov and talked directly to the Soviet foreign minister. "This is an interesting idea," he said. "The workers did much to win the war." Then, after further praise of labor, he said that it had occurred to him that the soldiers also had done a great deal to win the war and perhaps soldier representatives should be invited to the conference. "And then," he added, "one of the great contributions to the war was made by mothers who gave their sons. Perhaps they have done the most and they should be represented. Labor, yes! Soldiers, yes! Mothers, yes! . . . But it occurs to me that, if these groups are represented here, we must ask ourselves whom *we* represent? In the last analysis, we were sent here to represent all of these groups and therefore, Mr. Chairman, I shall have to oppose the motion."

Molotov jumped to his feet. "I withdraw the motion," he said quickly, and sat down.

III.

The united front of the Latin Americans, which Rockefeller had predicted to the State Department, aroused no cheers from the United States delegation. Despite the obstructive tactics of the

Russians from the beginning, there was a great, unquenchable public yearning for a world organization that would work harmoniously in the interests of all for the preservation of peace. The idea of forming blocs of delegates was foreign to this general approach and the pressure tactics of the combined Latin American delegations were widely criticized. The Russians, who charged that the other American republics were puppets of the United States, were not the only critics. Some American newspaper editorials were highly unfavorable, complaining that the administration was yielding unwisely to pressure by its neighbors. And members of the United States delegation asserted that the Latin American block was giving the impression that the Americas were trying to "gang up" on the world, thus causing disharmony at the conference and handicapping the United States in its relations with the other Big Powers. Rockefeller was sharply criticized by State Department officers for his methods. "Sometimes nobody seemed to know what he was doing," an official said later. "He acted as if he were a separate delegation." At least one of Rockefeller's associates warned him he was likely to be fired from the State Department unless he changed his tactics.

Rockefeller argued that the turmoil had been caused by the Russian delegates, who were obstructive and who had used every trick in an effort to get their own way, and that an organized united front was the only way the smaller powers had of protecting themselves. For example, there had been little or no public protest against the Soviet Union's failure to observe the Yalta agreements or Molotov's refusal to cooperate by postponing the Argentine-White Russia-Ukraine problem or his offer to vote for Argentina if the Latin Americans would vote for the illegal Lublin government. Rockefeller urged Stettinius to publicize these facts but the Secretary declined.

The Argentine issue came to a head at the end of April. "I believed," Rockefeller said later, "that if we agreed to seat the two Russian states we also had to support the Latin American demand for an invitation to Argentina. Otherwise, the Western Hemisphere would be split wide open again and we might well lose the support of Latin American countries in later voting on vital sections of the charter. Furthermore, if Argentina were not admitted at this time, when the Big Powers did not have the right of veto, the Russians could later exercise the veto to keep her out and to prevent indefinitely the re-establishment of complete unity of the Americas. I certainly believed that in the assembly of the world organization —as differentiated from the veto-controlled council—we would need to have the confidence and support of small nations. I felt that the Russians were doing everything possible at San Francisco to prevent American unity." He also believed that the crisis could have been avoided if the United States had promptly carried out its commitment regarding Argentina.

There was a rather bitter debate at a U.S. delegation meeting on April 29 at which three alternatives were discussed. The United States might:

First, oppose seating of all three of the disputed states and thereby risk wrecking the conference if the Russians walked out, as some experts believed they might.

Second, vote against Argentina and for the two Russian states. This might well have been the most popular course with the United States press and public because Argentina was a pro-Nazi dictatorship. But it also would mean giving in to the Russians for the sake of expediency and it would mean betraying a moral commitment made at Mexico City.

Three, vote for all three states.

Senator Arthur Vandenberg at this time was leading a movement within the delegation for standing firmly against what he regarded as unreasonable Russian demands. A few days earlier he had cast a lone dissenting vote against seating the two Russian states at any time, and he spoke out strongly against the second alternative. In the end, the delegation chose the third alternative of voting for all three, and President Truman approved the decision.

The next day, April 30, there were consecutive meetings of the conference executive committee, the steering committee and of the conference itself in plenary session. At each meeting, Molotov proposed the seating of the two Russian states and his motion was adopted unanimously. Then at each meeting an invitation to Argentina was proposed and Molotov argued against it. Next, a representative of the Latin American countries presented the facts regarding the Mexico City conference and asked that the agreement made there to invite Argentina be honored. Then Stettinius announced that the United States would honor the commitments made at Mexico City. Then a vote was taken and in each instance the invitation to Argentina was approved over the opposition of the Russian bloc, the plenary session vote being thirty-two to four with a number of small nations abstaining.

The outcome was far from popular but at least the danger of a Russian walkout had been avoided and the conference was able to complete its formal organization and get to work on the bigger and more difficult problems before it. The next day Rockefeller flew to Washington to keep a previously arranged date with a congressional committee. He discovered that in the capital he was being severely criticized for his actions at San Francisco and some of his foes were saying he was pro-Fascist and anti-Russian.

This criticism may have been best illustrated by an editorial that appeared later in the Washington *Post* in connection with an article from Buenos Aires by Arnaldo Cortesi, correspondent of the *New York Times*. Cortesi's article recited in detail the dictatorial methods and acts of the Perón regime in suppressing democracy in Argentina. In praising the article, the Washington *Post* said:

> But for such men as [Cortesi], American opinion would have to accept the dubious word of the officials who run the Latin-American division of our State Department, Nelson Rockefeller and Avra Warren. Mr. Warren . . . was the man [who] went to Buenos Aires just before the San Francisco conference and gave out a soothing report on Argentine progress. . . . The regime which is described by Mr. Cortesi as having done things "recently that exceed anything that this correspondent can remember in his seventeen years experience in Fascist Italy"—this regime was railroaded into the company of "peace-loving states" in San Francisco by Secretary Stettinius and Assistant Secretary Rockefeller. The

next day Mr. Rockefeller justified the admission by extolling the "progress" report from Buenos Aires. We take it he referred to the oral report of Mr. Warren. All that the news recorded was [on the next day] the re-establishment of censorship, and from then on a steady stream to the concentration camp of the best friends this country ever had in Argentina.

Mr. Cortesi provides a shocking epilogue to the Stettinius-Rockefeller-Warren shenanigans. We don't know whether the heroes of the San Francisco exploit think themselves smart or merely cynical. All we know is that the bloc they have built up is built upon sand, and that, far from earning from our Latin American friends any encomium for putting together this jerry-built contraption, we are arousing their criticism and causing a great deal of disgust south of the Rio Grande.

There were, then and later, other similar editorials in other newspapers. Oddly enough, Rockefeller did not particularly blame these newspapers for their attacks because he felt the traditional State Department policy of secrecy prevented reporters from getting all of the facts behind the action on Argentina. He called at the White House and gave President Truman a report on developments at San Francisco, saying that both the Latin American delegates and Secretary Stettinius were receiving a great deal of unjustified criticism. The President was noncommittal, having already decided to replace Stettinius with James F. Byrnes following the conclusion of the San Francisco conference.

Some weeks later, on July 13, the New York Times correspondent in Washington, Arthur Krock, would agree with Rockefeller's remarks to Mr. Truman. Writing on the possibility that Congress might make a formal investigation of relations with Argentina and of the United States delegation's support of the invitation to Argentina, Krock said that

> the facts . . . will in this correspondent's opinion greatly disappoint the critics of Secretary Stettinius and Assistant Secretary Rockefeller for their part in the history. These critics based some of their demands for the replacement of Mr. Stettinius on his handling of the later phases of the Argentine problem and Secretary Byrnes has

been publicly advised to dispense with Mr. Rockefeller's excellent
services on the same ground. But observations here and at San
Francisco lead this correspondent to believe that if and when the
whole hidden chapter is revealed, both officials will be shown to
have dealt ably with the later phases of a most difficult problem,
which they inherited and did not create, and the inner records of
San Francisco, if they are opened, will assign whatever fundamental
blame there may be in the circumstances to other persons and
conditions.

Krock then referred obliquely to the fact that Molotov had sought
to serve his own ends by bringing up the issue of admitting the pro-
Communist Lublin government to the conference. "There may be
villains in this piece," the correspondent concluded, "but Mr. Stettinius and Mr. Rockefeller are not among them."

# ELEVEN

# New Regional Framework

Rockefeller returned to San Francisco on Saturday, May 5, and promptly ran into more trouble. Up to this point, his role in the dispute over Argentina had been a kind of minor-league affair in relation to the over-all problems of the conference. But now the question of regional agreements or alliances within the world organization began to assume paramount importance.

What had happened was that the Big Powers had agreed among themselves on twenty-seven amendments to the proposed charter of the United Nations, including one for "regional arrangements." In effect, this amendment would have permitted the formation of military alliances among Russia and other European nations against "enemy states" (Germany) or among Russia and China against Japan to prevent renewal of aggressive policies, without such alliances being subject to veto in the Security Council. But it did not exempt other regional treaties from the veto. In other words there would be nothing to prevent the Russian member of the Security Council from vetoing any Western Hemisphere alliance such as the mutual

215

defense treaty provided for under the Act of Chapultepec.
Senator Vandenberg wrote in his diary that under this amendment

> Europe would have freedom of action for her defensive arrange-
> ments (pending the time when the Peace League shall prove its
> dependability as a substitute policeman) but the Western Hemi-
> sphere would not have similar freedom of action under its Pan-
> American agreements which have a background of a century
> behind them and which were specifically implemented again by our
> 21 Republics a few weeks ago at Chapultepec. Therefore, in the
> event of trouble in the Americas, we could not act ourselves; we
> would have to depend exclusively on the Security Council; and any
> one permanent member of the Council could veto the latter action
> (putting us at the mercy of Britain, Russia or China). Thus little
> is left of the Monroe Doctrine.

Rockefeller had previously discussed the implications of the
amendment with Stettinius and made clear his opposition and he
was shocked that it had been tentatively approved during his absence
in Washington. He immediately telephoned one of the Secretary's
aides and asked for an appointment.

"The Secretary is exhausted," the aide replied. "He is not going
to see anyone over the weekend. Why don't you talk to Dunn or
Pasvolsky?"

Rockefeller decided after this conversation that his best hope of
getting a hearing was to talk to Vandenberg and Connally. After
some delay, he reached Vandenberg and invited him to dinner that
evening in his suite at the St. Francis Hotel. Just what Vandenberg
had intended to do about the proposed amendment is not clear from
his diary, except that he wrote that "it bothered me all day." Then
he added that "by a significant coincidence, Nelson Rockefeller
asked me to join him at dinner where he disclosed these same fears
and said the South American republics are up in arms."

In any event, at dinner Rockefeller told the senator that the
Latin American delegates had always feared the amendment and
were convinced some provision should be made to continue the
mutual defense concept of the Act of Chapultepec. Once he had

started talking, Rockefeller laid all of his worries before Vandenberg. He was not sure, for example, that the British or French were wholeheartedly in favor of the Act of Chapultepec, because it would serve to strengthen inter-American cooperation. He also talked about his past troubles with some members of the International Division of the State Department. These foes of regional agreements, such as the Act of Chapultepec, had strongly pressed the argument that peace could best be maintained by a universal organization rather than regional organizations, he emphasized. In theory, their position was sound, but was it purely a coincidence that it happened to please the Russians, whose regional pacts against Germany would not be invalidated? In any event, it was politically unwise because it would weaken security of the Americas, whereas recognition of the Act of Chapultepec would in the long run tend to strengthen the world organization.

Vandenberg was fully aware that respected members of the delegation had sincere and logical objections to regional pacts, but he could also see Rockefeller's point and he could envision the possibility of trouble with the United Nations charter in the United States Senate if it tended to nullify the Monroe Doctrine.

> The grave problem [he wrote later in his diary] is to find a formula which will reasonably protect legitimate regional arrangements without destroying the over-all responsibility of united action through the Peace League and without inviting the formation of a lot of dangerous new "regional spheres of influence."

As the evening wore on, Vandenberg decided that the only solution to this dilemma was to add a sentence to the proposed amendment that would exempt the regional agreements reached at Chapultepec (as well as the treaties against Germany and Japan) from the veto power of the Security Council. There was no time to be lost and he immediately began drafting a letter to Stettinius setting forth this idea. Rockefeller got on the telephone and asked the Cuban ambassador, Guillermo Belt, and the Colombian foreign minister,

Lleras Camargo, to join them. Both approved the letter, which said that Vandenberg was disturbed that the United States might be charged with deserting our obligations under both the Act of Chapultepec and the Monroe Doctrine. He added, pointedly, that this might threaten Senate confirmation of the United Nations charter. Then he proposed that the regional agreements made at Mexico City should have the same exemption as proposed for European defense alliances, without in any way prejudicing the legitimate interests of other United Nations governments.

It was midnight by the time the letter was typed. It was delivered to Stettinius at nine-thirty the next morning by Vandenberg.

## II.

The Vandenberg letter touched off an explosion in Stettinius' penthouse headquarters that could be heard all over San Francisco. The Secretary's weekend of rest and seclusion ended with an indignant outburst in which most of the United States delegation shared. Rockefeller's role in the framing of the letter soon became known. Almost everyone joined in the criticism, including John Foster Dulles, the principal Republican advisor on foreign policy, who wouldn't speak to Rockefeller for some time but finally got around to denouncing him for doing "a most dangerous and damaging thing."

"That letter," Dulles exclaimed, "might wreck the conference!"

"Well," Rockefeller said without much conviction, "I didn't write it. Van wrote it."

"It makes no difference," Dulles replied. "It was extremely unwise."

At the regular meeting of the United States delegation on Monday, there was obvious bitterness. The fact that the Assistant Secretary of State in charge of Latin American Affairs previously had been opposing the amendment was one thing. Rockefeller could be brushed off. But the fact that a powerful member of the United States Senate had been brought into the controversy was quite another thing and could not be brushed off, especially since Senator Connally promptly lined up with Vandenberg's position.

Vandenberg later described the meeting as follows:

> . . . Stassen felt my proposal would gut the international power by emphasizing regional authority. This view was generally held by the State Department, particularly by Pasvolsky who was bitter about it. . . . Dulles argued that there is nothing in Dumbarton Oaks which prohibits "self-defense" and that under the Chapultepec agreement "self-defense" in the Western Hemisphere is a partnership affair and that the Monroe Doctrine is still part of it. I served notice on the Delegation, as a matter of good faith, that if this question is not specifically cleared up in the Charter, I shall expect to see a reservation on the subject in the Senate and that I shall support it. . . . At the end of an acrimonious session . . . the subject was temporarily referred to a special committee of technicians.

The argument took up the delegation's time for the next week or so. Stettinius met with a number of Latin American delegates with no result except to convince the Secretary that they were completely sincere in their demand for exemption of inter-American defense agreements from veto by the Security Council. After a week in which little progress was made, Rockefeller decided to ask Harold Stassen to dinner because he felt Stassen had a knack for dealing with legalistic problems. Stassen, however, was in a cautious mood and his secretary was careless about handling the telephone. When she relayed the telephone invitation, Stassen's reply could be clearly heard in Rockefeller's office: "I can't say now. I've got to talk to the Secretary. Rockefeller got Van into an awful lot of trouble and I'm not sure I ought to go down there."

Later, Stassen accepted the invitation, but his host was irritated by that time and decided not to mention the regional problem. After dinner, Stassen asked: "Aren't we going to talk about Chapultepec?"

"I'd be happy to if you want to talk about it," Rockefeller replied.

He then discussed his own attitude toward regional alliances. Stassen became interested and finally came up with the idea that the inherent right of self-defense, coupled with the concept adopted by the American republics that an attack on one was an attack on all, provided a common meeting ground.

"I think that's the answer," Rockefeller said enthusiastically.

They worked the rest of the evening over the formula and the next morning Stassen presented the idea in a memorandum, which Rockefeller still has in his files. It was well received. Vandenberg, who, incidentally, did not mention Stassen's role in his diary, went to work on a substitute amendment and came up with the following:

> VI E. Self Defense
>
> 1—Nothing in this Charter shall be construed as abrogating the inherent right of self defense against a violator of this Charter.
>
> 2—In the application of this provision the principles of the Act of Chapultepec and of the Monroe Doctrine are specifically recognized.

The Latin American delegations were pleased, but the British and others objected to the specific mention of the Act of Chapultepec in the draft amendment. This led to one further crisis. Some leading Latin American delegates balked at the omission because they feared the United States might not go through with the inter-American defense treaty authorized (but not yet drafted) by the Act of Chapultepec. The importance of alleviating these fears was made clear when on three earlier occasions motions by Connally on various subjects before conference committees were defeated because the Latin Americans voted against him. Connally complained they lacked loyalty and gratitude.

"Well, Senator," Rockefeller replied, "you've got to make up your mind. You abused them first because they ganged up on our side and now you blame them when you get voted under. I can't tell them how to vote. But I believe they recognize that this charter has to go through and that they will stand by us whenever we convince them that it is to our mutual interest."

In an effort to achieve agreement, Stettinius invited the Latin American delegates to a meeting in his penthouse. He began by saying he had talked to the President, who gave assurances that the United

States stood ready to meet at Rio de Janeiro in August, 1945, to negotiate the inter-American treaty. He added that the Big Powers understood that the treaty would come under Article 51 within the framework of the United Nations Charter.

Connally then made a rather impassioned speech in which he told the Latin Americans that the United States had done much for them in the past and expressed regret that they did not seem to trust us to go through with the treaty. He made it clear that he believed they had "forced" the United States to agree formally to a specific date for the Rio de Janeiro conference and that this indicated a regrettable lack of faith.

This meeting and the statements made by Stettinius and Connally were important because later an announcement by Under Secretary of State Dean Acheson did postpone the Rio de Janeiro conference, although not owing to any fault of those present at the meeting. But on the morning of May 15, the Latin American delegates were satisfied with the assurances given and agreed to support the new amendment. After some further technical changes, it was unanimously adopted on June 9 and became a part of the United Nations Charter.

The significance of the regional alliance agreement was not fully realized at the time by all of the delegates. The Latin Americans insisted on it because they feared that in a crisis a veto by one of the Big Powers might prevent the world organization from taking action to protect them. Rockefeller shared their attitude toward the veto power and believed regional agreements could strengthen rather than weaken the United Nations. He was also highly suspicious of Russian intentions. Vandenberg and Connally were concerned that the Monroe Doctrine would be nullified without the regional amendment and that the charter would face defeat or reservations in the Senate.

In later years, however, the significance of Article 51 would be far greater than most of them had anticipated. It would provide the legal basis for the formation of the North Atlantic Treaty Organization and other regional alliances throughout the world in the long and desperate struggle of free nations to withstand the expansion of

Communism. Without Article 51, the unity of the Western world and the existence of the United Nations might well have been impossible in the 1950's.

### III.

Rockefeller was up to his neck in so much controversy at San Francisco that it seems unlikely he would have had any time for social activities, but he managed to make the rounds of cocktail parties and dinners, to visit Trader Vic's in Oakland, attend functions of the Bohemian Club, and to do his share of entertaining at the Burlingame Country Club and the St. Francis Yacht Club, to which he imported a group of  Hollywood entertainers, including Carmen Miranda.

> Nelson starts his working day with breakfast at 8 a.m. [a member of his staff wrote in mid-June]. Usually staff members are present and this gives all of us a chance to clear up pending matters and exchange reactions. There are night committee meetings regularly, so some of us are sleepy at breakfast, which is usually interrupted by phone calls from Washington. Nelson leaves to attend the morning staff meeting of the U.S. delegation at Stettinius' apartment. . . . Later individual or group conferences are held with various foreign ministers or ambassadors of Latin America. In the afternoon there are committee meetings or he may attend sessions of the Big Five in an advisory capacity. In the evening his social calendar is always crowded. A man of less rugged strength could scarcely stand the pace, but I think Nelson catches some rest before dinner.
>
> I think that Nelson's regular meetings with representatives of the American republics have had a very vital influence on the progress of the conference. . . . This role, of course, takes a nice tact, as the cooperation and support of other countries must be obtained without any coercion whatever, and in a manner to avoid any public impression that the U.S. is seeking to establish a Latin American bloc.
>
> Of course, there is a lot of embarrassment and difficulty along

with the good breaks. The U.S. policy toward Argentina . . . has been very sharply criticized by some of the prominent newspapers. . . . The policy grew out of very justifiable military and foreign policy interests of the U.S. and other American republics but Argentina's internal situation is vulnerable to criticism because of the lack of effective democratic leadership. . . . But I believe that the invitation to Argentina to attend here was well advised. The confirmation of her absence would have been a permanent blow to any program of solidarity among the American republics and Argentina would have started a bloc movement in the southern part of South America . . . but the current situation with its many negative reactions has been painful to those of us who share Nelson's responsibility.

No small part of the "negative reaction" originated within the United States delegation. One morning, a State Department official stopped Rockefeller as he headed for a meeting and said: "You're in a hell of a lot of trouble. The Secretary has a message from South America indicating that you've been giving the Latin American delegates information that violates security."

Rockefeller had a sinking feeling but he tried to smile. "I'll talk to him," he replied, aware that various members of the delegation would be happy to see him sent back to Washington.

Stettinius was indignant when he received the Assistant Secretary, and said that he was disturbed about security.

"I don't know what message you're talking about," Rockefeller said. "What have you read?"

"Well," the Secretary replied, "I haven't read it myself but I know about what it says."

"We can save a lot of time by reading it," Rockefeller said. They sent for the message to which Stettinius referred and it turned out to be a report to his home office by an ambassador who had quoted Rockefeller in regard to the attitude of the Russian delegation. How the message was passed on to Stettinius was not clear but it said nothing that was not generally known.

"There's nothing of significance in this message," Rockefeller protested. "I think somebody's giving you a song-and-dance."

Stettinius agreed but then he burst out with an opinion that was shared by others in the International Division of the State Department. "You talk too much with these people anyway," he exclaimed. "Damnit, you've got to be careful!"

Rockefeller agreed to be careful, particularly in view of the fact that another storm was building up in connection with the opposition of small nations to the veto privilege proposed for the permanent members of the Security Council. Dr. H. V. Evatt of Australia, Lleras Camargo of Colombia, and Guillermo Belt of Cuba were leaders in the fight against the veto by which any one of the Big Powers could prevent the world organization from taking action to prevent war or to force a settlement of a dispute between two nations by peaceful means.

Rockefeller shared the attitude of the smaller nations in principle and particularly opposed a Russian-backed plan to extend the veto to prevent even a discussion of disputes. He decided to put his views on record in a memorandum to Stettinius on May 22.

> It seems to me that the present veto power . . . can have the effect of completely isolating the United States from taking an effective part and exercising moral influence through the World Organization for peace and security in Europe and the Far East. . . . For example, a dispute might develop in the Near East where many of the permanent members [of the Security Council] have interests. Such a dispute might have world-wide implications, yet any one of the permanent members could prevent the World Organization from endeavoring to settle this dispute by peaceful means. I fear . . . there may be disillusionment and a feeling that the veto was carried beyond the original intent of President Roosevelt at Yalta. His preoccupation was primarily in protecting the right of the United States to control the use abroad of American armed forces. . . . It seems to me that . . . a modification might be . . . that the veto does not apply to pacific settlements . . . or an amendment specifying that action toward pacific settlement may be taken by a majority vote of the Security Council. . . . If, after we have exhausted every possibility along these lines we cannot bring about a change, then and only then will we be in a logical position

to appeal to the small nations for support of this Yalta agreement on the ground that it is essential to establishment of the World Organization.

After Rockefeller had made his views clear, both Connally and Vandenberg advised him that they could not get Senate approval of the charter without the veto provision and asked him to determine whether, for that reason, the Latin American delegations would go along. He relayed this information to the various delegates, saying that he did not desire to influence any who had taken a public position against the veto or who were firmly opposed on principle. The Latin Americans knew that Rockefeller had argued against the veto. But they wanted the world organization to come into being and some of them said that, if necessary, they would shift their position. In time, Rockefeller had enough votes lined up.

This did not satisfy all of the members of the United States delegation, who felt that they had been through a rough time with the Latin Americans and that the results had put them in disfavor with the American public. They insisted that there should be a unanimous Latin American vote as a kind of vindication. The delegates had been under great pressure for weeks, their nerves were frayed and there was much bitter discussion. Rockefeller, however, refused to agree.

"I'm not going to ask them to make it unanimous," he said. "We will have enough votes to put it through. But maintaining our good relations with Latin America is more important than getting some kind of moral vindication which would be dishonest anyway. If you want somebody to tell them to vote unanimously you can appoint anybody you want except me. I'll drop out of the conference."

For a while, Rockefeller thought that they might take him up, but in the end they didn't. On June 7, the Russians yielded in the argument over extending the veto power to prevent even discussion of disputes brought before the Security Council and the way was cleared for final acceptance, which came on June 13. Enough, but not all, of the Latin American nations voted for the veto formula.

The United Nations organization conference ended the last

week in June on a note of great rejoicing. Vandenberg and Connally returned to a great reception in the Senate, which broke its routine for fifteen minutes to permit members to congratulate them and shake their hands while packed galleries cheered. Hardly a shred of this enthusiasm extended to Stettinius or Rockefeller. Most comment on their roles was critical. Almost the only good word that Rockefeller heard before he left San Francisco was from the energetic Herbert Evatt of Australia, who came around to apologize for an earlier remark he had made concerning Rockefeller's lobbying with the Latin Americans.

"I said that your tactics were evidence of domination, imperialism and dictatorship by the United States," Evatt recalled. "But I've come to understand the Latins and your relations with them. It is new to me, but I want to tell you that these people really respect the relationship because it is a relationship of dignity. I was wrong about what I said earlier."

Not every newspaper criticized the Assistant Secretary of State. The New York *Journal-American* said on June 19 that there was a better relationship among the American republics and that "the United States has made many contributions to this vital understanding, for which major credit is due the CIAA under the capable direction of Mr. Nelson A. Rockefeller. The policies of the United States have been consistently sound, insofar as they have reflected the beneficial leadership of Mr. Rockefeller." Columnist David Lawrence on May 22 wrote that "the most significant achievement, of course, is our close relations with the Latin American countries, and in that field the skill and magnetic personality of Nelson Rockefeller has been an invaluable factor in keeping high the prestige of the United States at the San Francisco conference."

There also was a column by a reporter for a Negro newspaper, the Pittsburgh *Courier*, which related an incident at San Francisco:

A nice guy to know is Nelson Rockefeller . . . actually, the man is charming without intending to be so; charming and smart. . . . Yours truly asked him, "Mr. Rockefeller, is it true that Argentina will admit only pure whites to citizenship?" He turned, put his arm over our shoulder (really), while about fifty white newsmen and women looked on, and said that he didn't know, but if it were true he was against that sort of thing. Never would think he was close to money. Necktie looked like it was out of a five-and-ten. This Rockefeller has more than dough.

There would be other consolations for Rockefeller later. Vandenberg praised him and added that "I've never realized before how important the work of his [Rockefeller's] Department is in keeping our good neighbors united with us. . . . I do not see how anyone could be more efficient." Then, a few years later, when the Russians were using the veto time after time in the United Nations to obstruct interference with Communist expansion, there was a gradual shift of opinion in the Western world as to the wisdom of permitting one of the Big Powers to block the desires of the majority. Steps were taken in 1950 to diminish the effect of the veto by increasing the power of the General Assembly to act in an emergency. Rockefeller was pleased that he had not acted on Stettinius' suggestion that he withdraw his memorandum on the subject from the files of the Department of State.

Perhaps his greatest satisfaction, however, came one evening when he sat down at an official banquet and found himself next to John Foster Dulles. As they shook hands, Dulles recalled his bitter complaint at San Francisco that Rockefeller's activities threatened to wreck the conference.

"I owe you an apology," he added. "If you fellows hadn't done it, we might never have had NATO."

## IV.

When Rockefeller got back to Washington the Department of State was in the midst of a thorough shake-up. James F. Byrnes replaced Stettinius. President Truman had continued Mr. Roosevelt's policies and personnel in the department until the United Nations was organized, but now he wanted his own men. Some of the men he wanted were the most severe critics of Rockefeller, and one refused to serve unless the Assistant Secretary was dropped.

Byrnes was tremendously busy with many problems, including the Potsdam conference of Mr. Truman, Prime Minister Churchill and Premier Stalin. No staff meetings were held and very few staff members saw the new Secretary. Rockefeller had asked for an appointment before Byrnes left for Potsdam but didn't get one, so he went about his business as best he could. Braden had taken up his post as ambassador at Buenos Aires during the San Francisco conference and had immediately adopted a tough attitude toward Perón. The Argentine election campaign was approaching and the ambassador made it clear in many ways that he was looking forward to Perón's defeat. Rockefeller did not approve of all the ambassador's political activities because he felt the Argentine people would resent outside interference, but Braden's actions were generally applauded in the United States.

> Ambassador Braden expressed what has been in the minds of most Americans when he told a luncheon gathering in Buenos Aires of the Argentine Rural Society that "there are few peoples on earth so well prepared to exercise healthy democracy" as are the people of the Argentine [said the New York Times in praising the ambassador]. A positive step [for the United States] is to give the democratic elements in Argentina all possible moral encouragement to continue their fight for free elections and a government of their own choosing.

Actually, it did not work out that way. Perón welcomed the opportunity to campaign against the United States ambassador, and he also began to backslide on his promises to reorient his government and live up to democratic principles. While Byrnes was at the Potsdam conference late in July, Rockefeller felt that the Argentine situation again was threatening to disrupt Hemisphere unity, partly because Washington was not providing leadership, and he suggested that a statement or a speech should be made taking a firm position against Perón's divisive and pro-Axis tactics. Others in the department felt that the problem was too important to handle in the absence of the Secretary and the President, and, anyway, Rockefeller was still deep in the departmental dog house.

By the time Byrnes got back from Potsdam, the situation was worse. Perón had completely failed to observe the pledges he had made prior to being invited to the United Nations. The time had come to speak out strongly. Rockefeller had accepted an invitation to address the Pan American Society of Massachusetts and Northern New England at Boston on August 24, and for that occasion he prepared a speech that, in effect, was a reversal of the State Department's approach to the Argentine problem.

The speech expressed admiration for Braden's work in Buenos Aires. It said that the American republics had shown their willingness to work with Argentina and that they had expected Perón would reciprocate in good faith. Then it outlined what Argentina had done and had not done in carrying out her promises.

> This record shows that while steps have been taken toward carrying out the commitments, there are many important failures which have serious implications. Too often the action has appeared to be reluctant. Too often steps have been begun or promised and not carried through to completion. The fact remains that many vital commitments in which Argentina joined with her American neighbors still remain unfulfilled by her government. That the people are not in agreement with such a policy has been manifest in many ways . . . by their own words they have shown they share the same ideals held by the peoples of the other American republics. . . . They have expressed their abhorrence of tyranny and of dictatorships. . . . Their voice and their action are giving the people of the Americas the assurance that they will see to it that their nation will live up to its commitments.

Rockefeller had been trying for weeks to get an appointment with Byrnes to discuss the proposed speech. The Secretary apparently had no prejudice against Rockefeller and, in fact, later paid public tribute to "the splendid service" he rendered during the war. But he was overwhelmed at the time with tremendous world problems and he doubtless was not unaware of the criticism that had been directed at

Rockefeller in connection with the Argentine problem. In any event, the Assistant Secretary could not get an appointment until he sent Byrnes a copy of the speech he had written and a note saying it was important that they discuss it. Byrnes received him on August 23, but he was harassed and almost brusque.

"What is it you want?" the Secretary asked.

"I want to talk about Argentina," Rockefeller replied and started to explain his proposal for a change of policy.

"Frankly," the Secretary said, "there's no use talking. The President is going to accept your resignation."

"Well, Mr. Secretary," Rockefeller said, "I have given you a speech on Argentina which I am going to make tomorrow night."

"Oh, no; because you'll no longer be Assistant Secretary."

"All right, that will free me to make the kind of speech I would like to make as a private citizen and to tell the true story."

Byrnes was not happy about this prospect. "All right," he said, "the President won't accept your resignation until after your speech."

Rockefeller made his speech and the next morning his resignation, because of his desire to return to private affairs, was announced by the White House. He went to see Mr. Truman before leaving Washington. "I want to assure you, Mr. President," he said, "that I did not want to leave the State Department and that I do not want you to feel that I was unwilling to carry on under your administration. I just want to keep the record straight."

Rockefeller's departure from the department attracted some editorial comment.

> The record of Inter-American affairs of the last five years is all the proof that is needed of [Rockefeller's] success [the *New York Times* said editorially]. Since the San Francisco conference, Mr. Rockefeller has been under unceasing and ill-informed criticism because of his part in forcing through an invitation of participation for Argentina. His address at Boston last Friday night should provide the answer as to his own personal attitude toward the Argentine government. Until then he had accepted without answer the entire criticism for the San Francisco action. . . . He is

respected and, what is more important, well liked everywhere in South America. It is hoped he will carry on unofficially as ambassador of good will. . . . This country could not have a better one.

The *New York Times* also praised Braden, who was recalled from Buenos Aires to succeed Rockefeller as Assistant Secretary.

With Braden's appointment the State Department shifted its policy toward Argentina more or less along the lines set forth by Rockefeller in his Boston speech, but the new approach never did seem to get up a full head of steam. The tougher Washington attitude did nothing to weaken Perón at home and the whole concept of joint inter-American action was neglected. In February, 1946, Perón was elected President of Argentina. Furthermore, the August conference at Rio de Janciro was postponed by the Department of State despite the pledges that had been made to Latin American delegates at San Francisco and despite the protests of Connally and Vandenberg. This action further weakened the confidence of Latin America in the United States and the damage was not repaired until 1947, when the conference finally was held and the treaty implementing the Act of Chapultepec was signed.

> Somehow or other they don't pin medals on men who achieve for their country some of its most substantial successes [wrote columnist David Lawrence in September, 1947]. Everybody, for example, is happy in Washington nowadays over the new Inter-American treaty . . . yet this magnificent result could not have been attained if good relations had not been restored with Argentina. . . . Without Argentina there really would never have been a treaty or even a meeting at Rio de Janeiro. . . . Had it not been for the indefatigable work of Nelson Rockefeller when he was Assistant Secretary of State, and George Messersmith, when he became American Ambassador to Argentina, today's applause for the Rio treaty would never have been heard because there would have been no such agreement. . . . President Roosevelt was farsighted early in 1945 when he accepted and initialed a memorandum from Mr. Rockefeller recommending that the Argentine

government be invited to the meeting at Chapultepec and be given a chance to join the United Nations. . . . It was at San Francisco that Mr. Rockefeller carried out the wishes of Mr. Roosevelt in making the fight for admission of Argentina to the United Nations. . . . Mr. Rockefeller was bitterly criticized by the left wing press which didn't know he was operating under instructions covered in a memorandum approved by Mr. Roosevelt a few weeks before he died.

Although discouraged by his ouster from the State Department, Rockefeller was convinced that Latin Americans wanted close cooperation with Washington. He was convinced that they respected our way of life in an industrial age and that they wanted to be associated with that way of life, not just to seek material progress but to move forward in the democratic tradition.

"I believed," he said later, "that we could translate this relationship into a great postwar force that would help hold together the free world and give it a new sense of purpose and direction. We had the great power of a common effort toward common objectives, and the Latin Americans had come to feel secure in that association."

Rockefeller felt a kind of personal responsibility toward Latin America because he had made many speeches in which he emphasized the determination of the United States to carry on its cooperation after the war. One day a Brazilian journalist, Alfonso Schmidt, came to see him at his office at 30 Rockefeller Plaza in New York, and talked about what had happened to Brazil during the war. The Brazilians, he said, had had a tremendous rise of confidence and hope as a result of their close association with the United States. They felt they had arrived on the world scene. They looked to the future with enthusiasm. Then, the war ended and they found that the interest of the United States also was ending. Their confidence was shaken. They were uncertain about the future. As Schmidt talked, Rockefeller noticed that tears were sliding down his cheeks. He was talking about what he regarded as a disaster for his country.

"I knew that what he was saying was true," Rockefeller said later.

"It is hard for us to understand the Latin attitude but it was true."

In the following months, Rockefeller devoted a great deal of thought to the problem and discussed with his associates whether private efforts could make a small start toward aiding the economic development of Latin America. He kept thinking that there might be a cooperative program aimed toward raising standards of living and developing a greater faith and confidence in the future.

Gradually, he evolved a plan.

TWELVE

# The Private Citizen's
# Great Experiment

"You can have big thoughts and big ideas," Nelson Rockefeller once remarked, speaking of his own effort to make his mark in the world, "but when it comes to doing you usually feel that you are dealing only with little things. Well, little things can take you a little way forward if you're headed in the right direction."

Such an expression could be highly misleading to anyone unacquainted with the range of Rockefeller's ideas. What he regarded as a big idea, for example, might easily encompass the known areas of the world and veer off into outer space. A modest idea might involve only one continent or a large country and little things might be no more than revolutionizing the economy of the Fiji Islands or mechanizing the agricultural production of Brazil. "Nelson," an associate commented, "likes big, broad ideas and large-scale action. He knows how to get thing done in a big way—and when he makes a

234

mistake, it's likely to be a whopper, too."

When Rockefeller got back to New York after World War II he became chairman of the board of Rockefeller Center but it was obvious that such a job would not keep him busy. His four brothers had returned from war service, all of them rather grimly determined to show that the third generation of Rockefellers could maintain or exceed the family record for achievement. They were not, however, at all sure just how they were going to do it.

Family conferences are an old Rockefeller custom which, incidentally, is still followed by the fourth generation—the great-grandchildren of John D. Rockefeller, Sr. There had always been a conscious drawing together at regular intervals; on Sundays, for instance, it was more or less expected that all who were within striking distance would share the noonday meal at the home of Mr. Rockefeller, Sr., in the early days and later at the table of Mr. Rockefeller, Jr., a custom that was continued until after the five brothers were grown and married. After the war each of the brothers had his own special interests, but their affairs were so intertwined and their broad objectives so similar that they normally got together at least once every few weeks to synchronize their plans. The relationship among the brothers—John, Nelson, Laurance, Winthrop and David—and their sister, Abby Rockefeller Mauze, was a close one because they were bound by family interests, but they were distinctly different as individuals. All of the brothers were hard-working and ambitious and, in many ways, they were rivals. Each was determined to make a career of his own and none had any intention of being outdone by his brothers.

The late 1940's were a difficult period for all of them and for their father because they faced important readjustments. Before the war they were young men just getting started and David had barely finished his education. In 1946, they were men who had had experience in the vast, breath-taking effort that marked America's participation in the war. They had commanded men in action and directed large-scale wartime enterprises and conducted confidential missions. They were all adults now and they were eager to get back to their careers, to accept responsibility and to do big things.

Nelson was perhaps the most eager and the most aggressive at the moment because his particular wartime job had given him confidence in aiming at major objectives, and he brought a new sense of urgency into the family conferences. Mr. Rockefeller, Jr., however, was accustomed to moving with caution and he was not always in harmony with the ideas of his sons. When they and their sister proposed that they take over and run Rockefeller Center, for example, he was a bit surprised and disapproving. He definitely encouraged his sons to be enterprising and to accept responsibility but sometimes he wondered whether they were inclined to move too rapidly. It was Nelson who, once he was convinced of the wisdom of the move, took the lead in a campaign to convince Mr. Rockefeller and carried it on so vigorously that he sometimes verged on insubordination. In the end, his enthusiasm, his arguments and—definitely—his persistence prevailed and Rockefeller Center was taken over by the children, who eventually became its owners.

"Although Nelson and his father are not at all alike," one observer once remarked, "Nelson is a good persuader and he could always deal strongly with Mr. Rockefeller. He was always exploring, always wanting to do things and always challenging his father, perhaps more than any of the others. This may have distressed Mr. Rockefeller at times but it also fascinated him because he wanted his sons to have courage and initiative and, in the end, they always settled things in a cooperative spirit."

The regular meetings of the Rockefeller brothers enabled them to carry on their joint enterprises—they undertook a program for expansion of Rockefeller Center, for instance, in the next decade—and to plan new endeavors. But these meetings also were important in giving them an opportunity to iron out their frequent differences of opinion and to try to avoid stepping on each other's toes. Their ideas of what to do and how to do it were as disparate as the décor of their headquarters on the fifty-sixth floor of No. 30 Rockefeller Plaza, which is marked by a neat bronze plaque reading:

ROCKEFELLER
OFFICE
OF THE
MESSRS

Inside the big glass doors, the visitor who turns right enters a suite of traditionally furnished offices. There are gleaming paneled walls, fireplaces with bright brass pokers and tongs, comfortable leather chairs and not a few rare English and Colonial antiques. These are the offices of Mr. Rockefeller, Jr., and his eldest son, John 3rd. In the opposite wing are the briskly modern offices of Nelson and Laurance Rockefeller, with brightly colored walls, severely functional furniture and a generous scattering of modern paintings. In an adjacent corridor there are also offices for use when needed by Winthrop and David—in fact, so many Rockefellers are gathered here that the family name is seldom uttered by members of the staff, who avoid confusion only by addressing the brothers as "Mr. John" or "Mr. Laurance."

When "Mr. Nelson" was again established in his own small corner office, decorated with rare examples of primitive art and a couple of modern paintings, he joined with his brothers and sister in planning how to make the best use of their energy as well as their money. One step in this direction—led by Laurance—was formally accomplished in 1946 by the formation of Rockefeller Brothers, Inc., which was greeted by the gamin New York *Daily News* with a cheery headline: "The Rock Mob Incorporates!" Rockefeller Brothers, Inc., was originally a limited partnership company but it was later reorganized as a service agency and, in practice, was a kind of holding company for the ideas of the five brothers and their sister, Abby. The Company provided an outlet for the Rockefellers' venture or risk capital investments, designed to encourage technological progress by providing funds, managerial ability and engineering skill for new, pioneering industries. Such investments normally were for a period of five to ten years and when the new enterprise was on its feet (or had definitely failed) the Rockefellers would withdraw their original capital and profits (or take a loss) for reinvestment in another similar venture.

II.

Rockefeller's principal interest after the war was centered on Latin America, and his salesmanship succeeded in directing the attention of his brothers and sister to that area in a limited fashion. He was convinced that, despite past friction, the Latin Americans had been impressed and excited by the wartime glimpses they had had of technological progress in the United States. They admired the big tractors, the road-building machines, the bulldozers and the men who operated them. They wanted to share in the progress that had produced such machines in a democratic state, and the prestige of the United States was high at the end of the war. Furthermore, various Latin American countries had accumulated surpluses of funds because they had been unable to make normal purchases during the war. The failure of the United States government to take advantage of these circumstances after the war prompted Rockefeller to consider what might be done by private capital to bolster the Latin American economies and thus strengthen inter American political and cultural ties.

"The third generation of Rockefellers," a friend commented, "is still exporting the missionary idea, just as their grandfather did through his large contributions to foreign missions of the church."

But, if the missionary idea was still dominant, the techniques had changed drastically.

"In the last century," Nelson Rockefeller summed up, "capital went where it could make the greatest profit. In this century, it must go where it can render the greatest service.

"The really exciting and constructive new development in regard to Latin America at the end of the war was that progressive local businessmen were no longer thinking in the old European terms of cartels or of restrictive production. They were saying that if action could be taken to raise living standards there would be no more surpluses in Latin America but shortages. There was everywere a surging forward of the people seeking opportunity and a better future."

In this connection, it is noteworthy that there was more to Rockefeller's ideas than just the goal of raising living standards, more than mere "do goodism." As a capitalist, he was vitally concerned with the world-wide struggle of totalitarianism as represented by fascist dictatorships or by the Soviet Union as opposed to the forces of capitalistic democracy represented by the Western powers. Rockefeller had discovered Communism in its hard-headed and implacable form during the war and at the San Francisco conference, but it was probably a minor incident as far back as 1939 that was most important in molding his attitude in the ideological conflict.

Columbia University Teachers College wanted to abandon the Lincoln School, which Rockefeller had attended as a boy and which he had enjoyed. With his usual confidence, Rockefeller decided to step in and find a way to keep the school going in one form or another. This proved to be far more difficult and far more complicated than he had expected, because New York Communists, for reasons of their own, became active in a prolonged controversy over whether the school should be closed down, reorganized or continued as in the past. The complexities of the battle and the principles involved are not relevant here. The point is that Rockefeller believed it was important to save Lincoln School. He worked out a program for that purpose, but when he attempted to sell the program to the Parent-Teacher Association, of which he was president, he was frustrated at every turn. This was partly due to an honest difference of opinion that split the P-TA. But Rockefeller was sure the main reason was the action of a few Communists and fellow travelers who outtalked him, outwaited him and outmaneuvered him. Rockefeller was convinced that their purpose had nothing to do with education but was to discredit the dean of Teachers College, an outspoken anti-Communist. In any event, he got a lesson in tactics that he never forgot and, finally, he was so utterly defeated that he was forced to withdraw from the whole affair.

As a result, he began a serious study of modern Communism, its methods and its objectives. He became fully aware of the danger posed to capitalistic democracy by Communist methods. And once he became interested, he wanted to know everything. When he read *Das Kapital*, he reacted as if nobody else had ever heard of Karl Marx, and he insisted on giving copies to his chief associates with a strong recommendation that they become acquainted with dialectical materialism. He occasionally argued political philosophy with Lombardo Toledano, the extreme left-wing Mexican labor leader. One night at a private dinner party, he sat next to Mrs. Andrei Gromyko, wife of the Soviet ambassador, who had just made a trip to Cuba. She said the lot of workers in Cuba was "terrible" and that it would never be improved by capitalistic methods. America, she added, inevitably would turn to Communism. Rockefeller was fascinated by her partisan ideas and ended up by giving her a lecture on what the Institute of Inter-American Affairs had done to assist in raising living standards in Latin America. She was not impressed.

At no time was Rockefeller either intimidated or puzzled by Communism. He recognized the gravity of its threat to the democratic and capitalistic way of life. He knew that the "struggle for the minds" of men entailed a great deal more than mere preaching of a political philosophy; that it involved tremendous problems of economy and of national defense and of simply providing food for empty bellies. But he never doubted that the evolving system of capitalism under democratic processes was capable not just of withstanding the threat of Communism but of providing a better life for all than was possible under any system of duress and dictatorship. In an important way, Rockefeller represented a dynamic aspect of democratic capitalism as opposed to Socialist dictatorship.

"I believe that the United States can make democracy an idea that will be felt throughout the American Hemisphere as a force working for the interests and well-being of the people," he once said. "I believe we must do this from the point of view of capitalism as well as of democracy, and that we must frankly call it capitalism. A Russian friend of mine, who held a high Soviet office, once told me that the Russian leaders learned more about planning from capitalists in the United States than from any other source. 'The people in your great corporations,' he said, 'are the most effective and ablest planners in the world and why you don't plan together instead of working alone and against each other is something we Communists can't understand.'

"It seems to me the great stirring of peoples all over the world is not a result of Communism but of democracy. It is an indication that these peoples, for the first time, are conscious of their own destiny. We should welcome it and help them realize their destiny."

Rockefeller discussed the possibility of some kind of action in Latin America with many business friends and economic experts. Then one day, during a visit to Venezuela, Rockefeller called on a cabinet minister to discuss ideas that he thought might aid that country's economy. The minister listened with no great enthusiasm and, finally, reached over and pulled open a drawer on the left-hand side of his big desk.

"Señor," he said, "in this drawer I have all the money I need to do what is necessary." Then he reached over to the right-hand side of his desk and pulled out another drawer. "And in this drawer, I have more project plans than you can possibly imagine." He slammed both drawers shut for emphasis and exclaimed dramatically: "But what I don't have is the technical and managerial assistance to pull these things together and start an integrated program that will produce results!"

Most countries lacked Venezuela's big oil revenues, but the conversation illustrated one of the major problems of Latin America, and it was along this general line that Rockefeller, with the financial aid of his sister and brothers, began operations south of the border. He recognized that certain preliminary measures would be necessary. For example, social services, health and sanitation programs and educational facilities such as are normally provided by government in Western countries were lacking or were very primitive in the areas where he planned to operate. With this in mind, the Rockefellers set up in July, 1946, a philanthropic organization, the American International Association for Economic and Social Development and called the AIA. Shortly afterward they established the International Basic Economy Corporation, a private company to conduct business in Latin America, which will be discussed in a subsequent chapter.

The AIA was a nonprofit operation in partnership with local governments to provide social programs that were essential to general economic progress in underdeveloped areas. In a letter to his father explaining the founding of AIA, Rockefeller outlined a philosophy that strongly reflected the experiences of the Rockefeller Foundation in its work abroad.

Reasons for: very simply, I am convinced that the hope for future peace and security in the world depends on closer relations and better understanding between the peoples of the world, coupled with a rising standard of living and a steady improvement of conditions.

Objectives: to give leadership in bringing about cooperation which will result in helping people in other lands to help themselves in combatting poverty, disease and illiteracy. To strengthen, through the dissemination of technical knowledge, modern equipment and managerial experience, the self-sufficiency and independence of the individual, the basic forces which make possible the growth and development of the democratic system (as contrasted with the system whereby the individual is dependent on and subject to the control of the state.)

. . . Naturally, with the magnitude of problems which exist throughout the world today, it seems almost preposterous for a private group to enter the field. However, it is my feeling that the pattern can be set and that in a year or so it can be very materially expanded by public support growing out of a popular appeal. The ultimate hope would be that our government itself will recognize the importance of this field.

The AIA method was to work in contractual association with local governments which agreed to match AIA funds and to contribute personnel to carry out a program of training, educating and assisting rural workers and farmers in everything from public health to road building. A basic concept was that the contribution of funds by the AIA would be gradually decreased and the government contribution would be steadily increased until the programs were both operated and financed locally, enabling the AIA to withdraw or to use its resources to start other programs. Robert W. Hudgens, a former banker from South Carolina who had been in the Farm Security Administration in Washington, was made director of AIA and brought to it some of the successful farm credit procedures that had been developed by the FSA during the depression years of the 1930's. These techniques, combined with methods developed over the years by the Rockefeller Foundation, provided the basic foundation on which AIA was developed.

Rockefeller's activities in Latin America did not meet with universal approval in 1946 or, for that matter, in later years. The AIA had financial assistance from the oil companies, and this prompted charges in South American newspapers that the whole program was nothing but a false front to cover efforts by United States businessmen to exploit Latin American natural resources, particularly oil. Such charges were quickly seized upon by both left-wing and extreme nationalist politicians and would provide, through the years, the ammunition for countless political battles centered around Rockefeller's name. Typical of such attacks was an editorial in the nationalistic Brazilian newspaper O Semanario which described Rockefeller as "the Standard Oil magnate, king of the North American oil trust . . . the puppet-master who puts pressure on Brazil for surrender of its black gold, the No. 1 enemy of our country in the United States." The editorial made sure that no reader would misunderstand its viewpoint by adding that Rockefeller was a "representative of slave-colonialism, with his hands stained and dripping with the blood, sweat and tears of the peoples exploited by Standard Oil . . . a strangler of our economy, this cruel, rapacious and pitiless imperialist, this enemy of humanity. . . ." The intent of the editorial was to defeat a political candidate who had said that Rockefeller was "a good friend" of Brazil.

Meanwhile, the oil companies had demonstrated a great interest in improvement of local conditions and had put up $3,000,000 to assist a three-year AIA program in Venezuela—a program over which they had no control. Smaller contributions were made then and later by other businesses and individuals.

III.

Rockefeller had actually started his Latin American venture in Brazil, more or less on his own. At that time, he was not clear as to how to proceed. "I got my neck stuck out," he remarked later. "But we started some projects and we aroused a lot of enthusiasm among the Brazilians." The Brazilian projects attracted attention in Venezuela and, in 1947, Rockefeller was invited to talk to leaders of the Caracas government.

There were a number of reasons why Rockefeller was interested in Venezuela. He had liked the country from the first time he visited it in the 1930's. He and his family had been interested in the Creole Petroleum Corporation. Venezuela, after the war, had a population of about four million, with the highest per capita government revenues in the world derived almost exclusively from taxes and royalties on oil. Its agricultural and other production was so low that most staples had to be imported, the cost of living was possibly the highest in the world and the living standard of two-thirds of the people was very low. These conditions made Venezuela an ideal laboratory for the kind of experimentation Rockefeller wanted to undertake. But there was another thing that also interested him. There had been a revolution in Venezuela and the new President was none other than Rómulo Betancourt, the sharp-tongued left-wing politician and editor who had so bitingly attacked Rockefeller in the 1930's.

Betancourt and his government were trying to create a better economic balance in Venezuela by a policy of *sembrando el petroleo* (sowing the oil), under which 40 per cent of the country's revenues or about $250,000,000 a year were being plowed back into basic capital expansion. But he needed still more capital and technical assistance, and he was so happy to see the oil company heir whom he had once denounced that he sent a cabinet minister to the airport to welcome him to Caracas. A few hours later Rockefeller was in the President's office discussing the possibility of inaugurating projects in Venezuela. The about-face made by Betancourt was not ignored by his political foes. The anti-government weekly *U.R.D.* remarked that whereas Betancourt had once demanded that Venezuela

> liberate itself from the asphyxiating yoke of foreign capitalism, now it is required that we open our doors to the Messiah . . . and grant him the exploitation of hundreds of thousands of hectares of Venezuelan lands. God forbid that we think of Mr. Rockefeller as a bird of prey or a gangster—as he was called [by Betancourt] eight years ago—for he has come to our country to make us bigger and raise us up. . . . The people—though humorous about it— are confused.

Both Venezuelan and the Minas Gerais state governments in Brazil agreed to match the funds put up by AIA and in some cases to provide personnel and, in the next few years, the first eight programs were started. It is not intended here to attempt a review of the work of AIA in Latin America or its later activities in India, but a few examples will illustrate its methods. The organization, in a general sense, was trying to take the world's organized technical knowledge and step it down and apply it to the lives of people who needed help. The work was usually started by experts or specialists from the United States with local help, but one of the most important objectives was to train local personnel as rapidly as possible to take over and keep going on their own. Most of the programs were designed to spread information and educate people in simple fundamentals.

In the summer of 1950, for example, a resident of a mountain village in the Venezuelan state of Carabobo contracted smallpox. The people of the area were backward and superstitious. In the past, an outbreak of the dread disease—the plague—had often caused panic in such villages. The people were frightened and so superstitiously opposed to inoculation that they fled to the hills or rioted against the doctors and soldiers sent to vaccinate them, and an epidemic resulted.

But when smallpox was discovered in 1950 the reaction was quite different because the AIA experts were prepared to meet the emergency. Within a few hours, a bright yellow station wagon arrived in the village and cruised slowly through the streets broadcasting a message through a loudspeaker. The message was simple and friendly. "Everybody is invited to free movies tonight! Come to the plaza at dusk to see the movies."

Everybody in town was in the plaza at dusk. A motion picture projector was set up on the station wagon with the white-washed wall of the church used as a screen. A couple of comedy shorts were shown and then came an animated cartoon that explained, so even the children could understand, the dangers of contagious diseases such as smallpox and how vaccination could safeguard the individual. Later, a local official informed the people that there was a case of smallpox in the area and that it was important for all villagers to go to the doctor the next day for inoculation. An improvised clinic was set up the next morning and by nightfall practically everybody in the village had been inoculated. The danger of epidemic was past.

The bright yellow station wagon and the movies were a method of meeting an emergency but the vitally important work of the AIA was steady, day-after-day effort in many villages and in many phases of health and education. Programs were established, often at a very low cost, to provide instruction in nutrition, infant care, hygiene and cooking and sewing. There were traveling health clinics in trucks manned by a doctor and a nurse, who set up shop in village plazas, on the porch of the city hall or even under a large shade tree and examined or treated perhaps a hundred persons a day. The doctor urged the farm families to wear shoes for protection against hookworm. They were given vermicides to fight parasites. Dietary instruction was given to the women and local clubs were formed to disseminate information to the many who could not read. Vegetable seeds and plantings were introduced for home gardens to improve diets and a fundamental program of sanitary improvement was widely propagandized.

As local people and officials took over such programs, the AIA was able to turn to new projects. A series of educational comic books was produced to provide information on nutrition, improved farming methods and similar subjects. Radio programs and motion picture shorts were prepared and distributed to rural areas, and clubs were formed in the schools to give the children early training in improving food habits and better farming practices. After a decade of experience in Venezuela and Brazil, Rockefeller began seeking ways to extend the general idea of the AIA program to other Latin American countries. Financing was a difficult problem in some areas and it appeared most practical to attempt to work with established organizations. In 1958, a three-year project was set up with the Inter-American Institute of Agricultural Sciences, which has its headquarters in Costa Rica and to which all of the Latin American governments contribute. The purpose of the project is to develop and extend an information program in agriculture, food and related health fields throughout Latin America and to train personnel in mass communication so that the work may be carried on permanently by the institute. Experts on the permanent staff of the institute, as well as specialists from Costa Rica and elsewhere, assist in instruction of the students. The first course, lasting five months, was conducted in 1959.

Although programs to improve health and farm techniques were essential to Rockefeller's plans, it was also vitally important to establish credit facilities, particularly for farmers. Lack of credit was one of the reasons why South American small farmers were seldom able to improve their lot. Even where credit was available, the customary interest rate of around 20 per cent made it impossible for the ordinary farmer to borrow and, if crops were poor, he might have to sell half of his cattle to raise money for the next year's seed. As a result, even farmers with a couple of hundred good acres were often in financial trouble, unable to buy equipment or expand their operations or build modern homes with adequate sanitary facilities.

In 1948, Governor Milton Campos of the Brazilian state of Minas Gerais, invited Rockefeller to see whether something might be done to solve the problem, and the AIA came up with a supervised credit plan that became known as the "man-woman-and-a-jeep" system. The idea, as put into practice, called for establishment of an antonomous agency called the Associação de Crédito e Assistência Rural (ACAR), for which AIA and the state government each put up $75,000 a year. The money was not for loans to farmers but to establish and maintain the ACAR organization and its teams of trained specialists. Each team consisted of a young man, a young woman and a jeep, which was the only feasible means of transportation over the rough back-country roads. Each team—there were only four at first—established headquarters in an area approximately as large as a big county in the United States. With the aid of local officials, they held town meetings at which farmers and their wives were exposed to an information program, organized local clubs to promote improved farm and home practices and trained volunteers to teach everything from sewing to building a trench silo for storage of corn.

Their main objective, however, was to promote a practical credit system that would enable responsible farmers to increase and improve production and to raise their living standards. With the cooperation of Governor Campos, it was arranged for a state bank of Minas Gerais to make loans at the comparatively low interest rate of 8 per cent provided the ACAR teams recommended the borrower and certified that he was willing and able to cooperate in improving agricultural production. Most important, the ACAR teams carefully supervised the way in which the money was spent. For example, a farmer named Sebastião Onofre da Silveira owned a 140-acre farm but had no capital. He needed money for equipment, seed, additional cattle and to provide safe water and other sanitary facilities at his home. After investigation, the local ACAR team decided he was a good risk and went with him to the bank, where they drew up a specific plan for improvement of his farm and made application for a loan. The loan was granted but, to make sure that the money was properly spent, the bank honored Sebastião's checks only when they were countersigned by a member of the ACAR team.

The experts then helped the farmer buy fifteen dairy cows and two oxen of improved breed, material for fences and an outdoor toilet, insecticides, hybrid seed corn of proved quality and a plow. They convinced him he should start rotating his crops and that crops be properly sprayed. A cement floor was put in his house and the beds on which the family slept were raised from the floor. Sebastião and his wife attended community meetings at which all phases of farm and home life were discussed by trained personnel. At the end of the first year, Sebastião cleared 12 per cent more than his total loan, thanks to a big corn crop and to sale of milk. The health of his family had improved markedly. But the most important change, perhaps, was in his attitude. Instead of being a discouraged farmer with little hope for the future, he had become confident and proud of his ability to make his own way. He became a leader in local activities and a regular attendant at community meetings to discuss mutual problems and study new farming techniques.

The story of Sebastião and his family was repeated hundreds of times in various forms as the number of jeep teams in Minas Gerais state gradually was increased to sixty-one. By 1957, some six thousand loans had been made to farmers with less than one per cent defaulting. President Juscelino Kubitschek lent support to the system and similar agencies were organized in eleven other states where close to two hundred supervised credit offices had been established by 1959. Furthermore, the AIA was able gradually to reduce its financial support to about $50,000 a year while the local and federal government contributions were steadily increased from $75,000 in 1949 to around $350,000 in 1959.

In 1956, the credit and farm extension system that Rockefeller had started with four jeep teams in Minas Gerais became, with the encouragement of President Juscelino Kubitschek, a national federation—Associação Brasileira de Crédito e Assistência Rural— through which the local supervised credit agencies coordinated their activities, exchanged information and disseminated booklets, motion pictures and radio programs. In a decade, the system had not by any means reached all of the huge country of Brazil but it had provided a highly successful format for attacking a major problem and was growing rapidly.

In 1959, a report by John R. Camp, AIA vice-president for Venezuela, estimated that over a ten-year period Venezuela had improved agricultural productivity by at least 50 per cent. According to Camp's estimates the government programs in which AIA participated had contributed to the reduction of infant mortality by about 30 per cent, led to a large increase in the use of better seeds and planting stock, fertilizers and pesticides and farm machinery, tripled the number of apprentices for industry trained in trade schools and, through extension courses and schools, benefited at least twenty-five thousand rural families. AIA also aided in promoting more than forty rural community centers where methods of home and village improvement are taught, and had supervised the construction of some four hundred miles of low-cost farm-to-market roads. The organization also was instrumental in building up a system of two hundred rural youth clubs with four thousand members.

Meanwhile, the over-all programs in which AIA participated in Brazil and Venezuela in ten years had expended approximately $13,000,000, of which about half had been provided by the Rockefeller family and by businesses such as the Creole Petroleum Corporation, Shell Oil Company of Venezuela, Mene Grande Oil Company, International Petroleum Company, Ltd., and Socony-Mobil (Vacuum) Oil Company, Inc. (The oil companies contributed only to operations in Venezuela.) The other half was in direct contributions to the AIA programs by the Brazilian and Venezuelan governments, which already had taken over permanently three programs and were preparing to assume full responsibility for others. Thus, gradually one of the "little things" that Rockefeller initiated in Latin America became a guidepost to help the people find their own way toward the social and economic progress that is essential to the survival of democracy in a troubled world.

# THIRTEEN

# Troubles of a Good Knight

Rockefeller's great adventure in Latin America, his major hope that private enterprise could help raise living standards in under-developed lands was the International Basic Economy Corporation or IBEC, into which his family eventually put some $16,000,000. Whereas AIA was a philanthropic organization, IBEC was private enterprise for profit. As president of IBEC, Nelson Rockefeller set forth in 1947 somewhat like a well-heeled knight sallying from the castle gates to slay a dragon and bring prosperity and security to the land. He had a high purpose, great enthusiasm, considerable dollar armament and, unquestionably, an abundance of confidence and courage. Unhappily, he was under considerable pressure to move swiftly toward his objective, so that on several occasions he tripped over unforeseen obstacles, fell flat on his face and lost part of his armament. Even after the battle was joined, the wise money was on the dragon and, at the end of a dozen years, the beast was still definitely alive. On the other hand, the knight not only was still on the attack, but he was much wiser, his confidence was undiminished

251

and his successes represented one of the remarkable chapters in the history of relations among peoples of the Western Hemisphere.

Rockefeller's philosophical approach to IBEC was significant because it was developed at the end of World War II, when the Soviet Union was struggling to recover from the devastating effects of military conflict and when Communist imperialism was a comparatively small, if rapidly growing, shadow on the horizon. He believed it was essential to demonstrate that private capital could make an important contribution to international cooperation in a free world; that it was vital to the future of the United States to give underprivileged peoples positive evidence of America's spiritual and moral dedication to progress toward a better life everywhere under democratic processes. Such evidence, he believed, could be just as important to our national defense as demonstrations of military strength.

"Look at it this way," he summed up. "The United States is a rich and powerful country in a poor world; like a rich family in a poor town. The poor don't want charity, but they would like to be helped to stand on their own feet. Today, our welfare and security depend on the welfare and security of other peoples. We have to form a kind of partnership in which they are given the incentive and the means to progress. And, as good partners, we have to work together for mutual gain."

This social-economic theory might have been dismissed—and often was—as an echo of New Deal "do good" activities, except for the fact that the basic principle on which IBEC was founded in 1947 was that it would launch private enterprise businesses intended to return a profit for investors as well as contribute to the social betterment of the area in which it operated. The New York business community was not impressed by Rockefeller's theories but he sent economist Stacy May and two technical experts, John R. Camp and Fisher G. Dorsey, to Venezuela to ferret out the major factors that were retarding economic development and to recommend how the bottlenecks might be broken. Their report included a wide range of recommendations and pointed out that the first problem obviously was to provide more food at a reasonable cost to the consumer. To tackle this problem, IBEC established a subsidiary known as the Venezuelan Basic Economy Corporation (VBEC) to carry on business and farming enterprises. The oil companies invested something more than $10,000,000 in nonvoting preferred stock and the government acquired, temporarily, about $4,500,000 in nonvoting preferred stock. Offices were established in Caracas and Rockefeller provided a staff of experts to plan a program.

About this time, Mr. Rockefeller, Jr., gave some thought to his son's operations in South America and suggested that it would be wise to start on a small scale, see what problems developed and which ideas proved most feasible and then expand slowly as conditions might warrant. Rockefeller considered this advice but he decided——mistakenly—that there were sound reasons against limiting the initial projects. For one thing, his economists took the position that only by simultaneously starting several comprehensive businesses of an interrelated nature could VBEC make an impression on the over-all problem. Furthermore, Venezuelan government officials were eager to give the national economy balance by building up enterprises other than the oil industry and they strongly encouraged large-scale operations. Finally, Rockefeller was by nature in a hurry and he decided against accepting his father's advice to go slowly and cautiously.

VBEC started off with a great deal of enthusiasm and supervision from IBEC headquarters in New York. What IBEC—and Rockefeller—wanted was a program for establishment of model farms to show how food production could be increased, a wholesale food company to distribute products at lower cost to consumers and a company that would demonstrate how the fishing industry could be modernized in order to distribute and popularize food from the sea. These seemed to be scientifically planned and reasonable first steps toward solving the food shortage but, in fact, they served mainly to demonstrate how many unexpected problems IBEC would encounter.

A VBEC subsidiary known as Productora Agropecuaria, C.A.

(PACA), was established with capital of $3,000,000 to tackle the problem of introducing modern farming methods. It leased or acquired three properties—Central Bolívar, 7,800 acres in the state of Zulia, near the southern end of Lake Maracaibo, to be used largely for raising cattle; Monte Sacro in the Chirgua Valley, a plantation with 700 acres of tillable land near Valencia, to be used for truck farming and for raising corn and hogs; and Agua Blanca, 18,000 acres near Acarigua in the state of Portuguesa, for raising livestock, corn, rice and beans. Modern farm machinery—bulldozers, automatic potato diggers, power sprayers—were imported. The work of clearing and preparing the land was started—and trouble developed almost immediately.

The first big turmoil arose when the Rural Society of the State of Zulia passed a resolution denouncing IBEC's Central Bolívar farming project and calling on the government to prohibit it on the ground that "the high-powered North American enterprise" would soon drive local farmers out of business by unfair competition. Rockefeller was in New York but he cabled the society and made arrangements to meet with the farmers a few weeks later at Maracaibo. The founder of IBEC was astounded when he arrived at the big hall in Maracaibo and discovered that it wasn't large enough to hold the assembled and hostile crowd. Finally, everybody who could find a chair picked it up and the throng moved outside to a lighted tennis court so that all could hear.

The speeches were far from friendly to VBEC. "With modern methods the North Americans may increase production a hundred times and prices will fall so low that we will be ruined," one farmer shouted. Another added: "Yes, and they'll buy up our bankrupt farms and turn the whole area into a mechanized operation!" Other farmers were opposed to government participation in the VBEC projects and still others expressed fear that the oil companies were hatching some nefarious plot against them. All had different fears and all of them seemed to have a distorted idea of what VBEC was trying to do.

When Rockefeller arose he said that they were correct in believing that VBEC was set up to increase production. "Unless production is increased," he went on, "the country will never achieve an adequate food supply at reasonable prices. But don't believe for a moment that one group such as ours could increase production enough to have an important effect. If all of our plans worked out perfectly, which they won't, we might double production on our own land, but no more than that. And if we doubled our production we would still be producing less than three per cent of this state's normal food output. The only way we can do any good for Venezuela is to demonstrate to you farmers that if you adopt modern methods you can increase production and the entire countryside will benefit— not just the farmers but the merchants and the consumers!"

The audience was more attentive but still unconvinced. "What," one farmer shouted, "are your methods?"

"There is no mystery or magic," Rockefeller replied. "Some of our methods already are being practiced in this country and in this state. Others are urged on all farmers by the Ministry of Agriculture. We will gladly share our knowledge with all of you and we will make available the tools and the seeds and the fertilizers we use."

The fact that Rockefeller spoke Spanish and his ability to convince an audience of his sincerity began to have an effect. The questions became more friendly. With the tide changing, he shifted to an argument that he knew would appeal to the farmers. "The most important thing from our viewpoint," he said, "is that we learn from each other how to improve production. We have technical information, but the fact is that know-how is useless unless it is supplemented by knowledge of local soil and other conditions. You know those conditions better than anyone else can know them. If we have your help and if you have our help, we can progress."

The atmosphere had changed as Rockefeller explained the real purpose of the VBEC operations and there was a round of applause. But then a well-known Venezuelan Communist editor stepped to the platform and began speaking so brilliantly that the audience, including Rockefeller, was spellbound. The editor lost no time in making his point: Rockefeller, he said, was a wolf in sheep's clothing, PACA was an imperialist plot to get control of the nation's food supply and the Caracas government was so afraid that the small farmers would progress that they were promoting VBEC as a means of wiping out all independent farms and businesses. Everybody listened closely to his witty and pungent phrases and there was a thoughtful silence as he concluded. Rockefeller knew he could never match the editor's eloquence but he also knew he was better informed in regard to farming.

"Let me point out," he replied, "that VBEC projects are actually small, independent operations for the purpose of demonstrating what can be done, and we could not possibly become a monopoly. Our purpose is not to gain a monopoly of anything but to promote competition."

Patiently and in detail he went over his plans and explained how they would help raise living standards.

After a brief pause, the farmers stood up and cheered and when the meeting broke up at midnight the hostility toward VBEC, while not entirely eliminated, was comparatively slight. "It was a good example," Rockefeller said later, "of how fears and hostility are bred by misunderstanding and of how such feelings can be ended by a recital of the facts. The farmers and cattlemen of Zulia became our good friends."

II.

In 1948, the death of Mrs. Abby Rockefeller was a heavy loss to the family. Nelson Rockefeller had been very close to his mother and he would keenly miss her companionship and guidance.

Work was an antidote to sadness and he had plenty of that in Venezuela. By 1948, PACA had made a considerable impression on the Chirgua Valley by its truck-farming methods. At Monte Sacro plantation, to take a crude example, there were a few dozen old and gnarled orange and grapefruit trees which had not yielded fruit for years. As an experiment, the farm manager, in January, hooked up an automatic posthole digger to his tractor, quickly drilled several holes at the base of each tree and filled the holes with a mixture of soil and 20 per cent superphosphate. None of the local farmers missed a move and there was wide speculation until the following May when the old trees produced an extraordinarily fine crop of oranges and grapefruit. The fine crop did more than tens of thousands of words to demonstrate the importance of scientific use of fertilizers and, in one way or another according to their means, farmers in the Chirgua Valley applied the lesson profitably to their own lands.

Oranges and grapefruit were but a beginning. The local schoolhouse was a wreck and many of the fifty-three pupils eligible to attend classes were absent most of the time. Investigation showed that the children had only black coffee for breakfast and, if they had a long distance to walk to school, they were often too tired to get there. Further investigation disclosed that they lived on a diet of black beans and corn bread and were suffering from malnutrition. A new schoolhouse was built with a kitchen and lunchroom where all of the students were given a well-balanced lunch. Attendance picked up within a few weeks, and so did the morale of the children. A new church was constructed. Farmers were shown how to build inexpensive sanitary facilities at their homes. A system of irrigation, using light, movable aluminum pipes to draw water from deep wells, was installed to replace the antiquated irrigation by water from the river, which always failed in the dry season. Crops were sprayed both to keep down the weeds and to kill insects.

At the end of the first year, a record-breaking crop of vegetables was harvested and the Monte Sacro project should have been off to a wonderful start—but it wasn't. When it came time to get the produce to market, transportation facilities were entirely inadequate. Storage facilities were lacking. Most of what had been gained by improved farming methods was lost because produce could not be delivered to consumers before it spoiled.

The experience with vegetable crops at Monte Sacro illustrated, in an oversimplified way, the tremendous problems that IBEC faced in Venezuela and Brazil. There was extensive scientific preparation for each project, there was a heavy expenditure of funds and there was, usually, great enthusiasm and energy. But in areas which technologically and socially were far different from the United States there almost always were obstacles that could not be foreseen. At Agua Blanca farm, bulldozers cleared land for rice and corn crops in 1948 and spraying machines were imported to combat the insects that normally destroyed a good portion of local crops. That year the corn crops throughout the area were ravaged by "army worms" but the PACA spraying system saved not only the Agua Blanca corn but that of neighboring farms. Rockefeller also had ordered spraying equipment to kill the weeds that grew to great heights during the rainy season but it failed to arrive on time. The rains did arrive on time and, almost overnight, the weeds were higher than the corn. The corn crop was a financial failure. The rice crop was lost to weeds and heavy rains because of poor management.

A VBEC subsidiary known as Pesquerías Caribe, C.A. (PESCA), was formed with $1,500,000 capital, and an $800,000 refrigeration and ice-making plant was built at Puerto La Cruz in an effort to stimulate the Venezuelan fishing industry. With modern equipment, the experts argued, fishermen could go farther to sea and bring back a bigger catch, which could be processed and frozen and which would help solve the food problem. It was a fool-proof plan on paper but in practice almost nothing worked out. Some fishermen used their boats for smuggling. At another time and for an unknown reason they couldn't catch any fish. After many difficulties, conditions improved and owners of fishing boats who took part in the PESCA project increased their average earnings from $180 to about $450 a month. Crew members were up from $60 to $150 with fish reaching the Caracas market at the rate of about fifty tons a month, demonstrating that the plan was basically sound. The price paid the fishermen, however, was not as low as had been hoped—and PESCA couldn't make a profit.

Rockefeller's attempt to improve food distribution through still another VBEC subsidiary—C.A., Distribuidora de Alimentos, or CADA—started with a warehouse at Valencia to handle produce from PACA farms and from a local canning factory. Later four other warehouses were opened for the purpose of providing farmers with a wider market, of stabilizing prices and of reducing the cost of getting goods to consumers. But overhead costs were higher than had been expected and, unfortunately, the corner grocery store proprietor was not happy about passing his savings on to the consumer. CADA did help bring prices down slightly but it could not make a profit on its own wholesale operations.

In Brazil, a great corn-and-hog-growing country, IBEC established several large experimental farms designed to develop a hardy breed of pigs that would not be affected by a cholera epidemic that had wiped out half of the country's herds. A new, inoculated breed of hogs was imported and the experiment progressed successfully, but other problems arose. A severe drought skyrocketed the price of feed so that the farms could not make a profit. Then the Brazilian left-wing and nationalists newspapers opened a campaign against the project, charging that Rockefeller was trying to get control of oil lands and destroy the local meat-processing companies.

"Who is silly enough to believe for one minute that the great Rockefeller is interested in raising pigs?" one left-wing newspaper asked. "This whole farm business of his doesn't amount to a hill of beans: It is just a scheme to get hold of future oil lands."

Another Brazilian project was the Empresa de Mecanização Agrícola, S.A., called EMA, which Rockefeller established with $635,000 capital to introduce heavy mechanized farm equipment. In 1947, there were only 4,000 tractors in all of Brazil, and such work as clearing land was slow and costly. EMA imported almost a million dollars' worth of farm machinery in four years and made contracts with farmers to clear land, to plant and to cultivate certain crops that could be handled efficiently by machine methods. For half a dozen years, EMA was a great success. More than 100,000 acres of land were cleared at high speed and many other thousands of acres were worked by the company's equipment. Far more important, EMA demonstrated to Brazilians what could be done with modern farm machinery and inaugurated a highly important change in Brazilian farm economy. Furthermore, EMA made a profit on its operations—until inflation hit Brazil. Almost immediately, the cost of replacing machinery with imports from the United States rose to a point that made EMA's activities unprofitable, and continued inflation made them highly unprofitable.

This recital of IBEC reversals in South America might easily be taken to mean that Rockefeller's business adventure in under-developed areas was a multi-million-dollar flop, but, as will be shown, IBEC also had important successes. "We made mistakes, some of them big mistakes," Rockefeller commented much later. "We also had administrative troubles. Some of our people were not familiar with local conditions. There were some language problems. We had some incompetents and had to make costly changes in management. We didn't have enough experience—nobody had had much experience in this kind of pioneering work—and that includes me. We were constantly improvising to overcome unexpected obstacles, and at times we floundered in the field. But we learned and the most important thing we learned was not to try to start on too big a scale. We thought we had reasons for starting out big in various projects, but it was a mistake and we should have known it.

"For example: take our efforts to mechanize tropical agriculture. We went in thinking we would slay the dragon by introducing modern machinery and we flopped. We didn't know enough then to do the job. What was needed was experimental work."

About 1950, the early optimism in regard to IBEC had evaporated and, a little later, Rockefeller began liquidating various unprofitable projects. Chirgua Valley farm was taken over by Rockefeller personally for experimentation. The Agua Blanca property went to the government for experimental use and only the Central Bolívar livestock enterprise was retained by VBEC. The fishing company was liquidated at a loss. In Brazil, the heavy equipment owned by EMA was gradually sold to farmer cooperative groups, and the experimental hog farms were liquidated. In all, Rockefeller took a heavy loss—possibly $7,000,000 or more—in correcting the mistakes that were made in the initial stages of IBEC history.

But he wasn't in any mood to quit. Other IBEC projects in Venezuela and Brazil were making progress and, in some instances, making a profit. The lessons learned had been expensive but they had been well learned. In the 1950's, Rockefeller worked out a revised and a more "hard-boiled" formula of "good partnership," and he began putting it into practice with a high degree of success.

III.

Even when his business enterprises were faring badly, Rockefeller maintained his enthusiasm for Latin America. If government bureaucracy laid a heavy hand on his plans, he shrugged and shifted to some other approach to the long-range goal. If nationalistic newspapers denounced him as a buccaneer, he made a special point of greeting their editors warmly when next they met. If Communist demonstrators paraded with banners saying "Rockefeller Go Home!" he redoubled his efforts to meet and shake hands with as many workers as possible. His attitude toward the people, his direct approach to any problem that arose never failed to amaze his associates in Venezuela, Brazil and elsewhere.

Once when he was visiting a poor community on a little island off the Venezuelan coast he hired a taxicab for a journey through the countryside. The driver of the taxi, impressed by his distinguished passengers, began speeding down the narrow road, blowing his horn and dashing wildly through the little villages. In one village, his car struck and killed a pig but he ignored the accident and careened on down the road, until Rockefeller, sitting beside him in the front seat, furiously commanded him to stop.

"Why stop?" the driver asked. "It was only a pig."

Rockefeller made him turn back to the dead pig, get out of the car and ask who owned it. Nobody seemed to know but Rockefeller, still muttering in Spanish at the driver, finally located a woman who said the pig had belonged to her.

"How much was it worth?" Rockefeller asked.

The woman named a modest figure but then, sensing that she was dealing with someone out of the ordinary, tripled her price. She was paid and the party drove on, with Rockefeller's companions wondering why anyone should be so concerned about a stray pig.

On another trip into the interior, Rockefeller and several government officials planned to stay all night at a run-down little hotel some miles from Valencia. Approaching the end of their journey, they found the road blocked and traffic backed up for a distance of about half a mile near a crossroads. They sat in the motionless car for five minutes, which was the limit of Rockefeller's patience.

"I think I'll see what's the matter," he said, getting out and walking down the line of stalled cars in which the passengers waited patiently for traffic to start moving again. When he reached the crossroads, he found that a truck carrying cement had hit another truck carrying a load of steel. There wasn't much damage but the trucks were locked together, blocking the narrow road. The drivers were squatting at the roadside, looking at the trucks, and a dozen spectators were helping them look but nobody was doing anything about getting the trucks apart. Nobody recognized the North American.

"What are you doing about it?" Rockefeller asked one of the drivers.

"What can one do?" the driver responded. "It is difficult."

"Have you tried backing up?"

"Oh, yes, we tried."

Rockefeller walked around the two trucks. "I think they'll come apart," he said. "Come on. Get the motors started." He began giving instructions to the spectators to stand on one bumper and lift the other bumper. In order to see both sides at once, he climbed to the top of the cab of the cement truck and shouted orders. Everybody pitched in. The motors roared and, with a grinding bump, the trucks came apart. Everybody cheered. Rockefeller leaped from the cab of the truck to the center of the crossroads and began directing traffic. Ten minutes later, his companions drove up and he got into the automobile.

"You looked like a traffic cop on Fifth Avenue," someone remarked. "What happened?"

"Nothing much," Rockefeller replied. "Somebody had to do something or we'd have been there all night."

In the same spirit of getting something done, Rockefeller had made important progress with several IBEC projects from the time he started operations.

For example, a remarkable success was a company called Industria Lactea de Carabobo, S.A. (INLACA), which VBEC organized in collaboration with a group of Venezuelan milk producers. An old milk processing plant was modernized at a cost of around $500,000 and paraffinated milk cartons were introduced. At that time—1948— the daily output was 8,000 quarts of milk, and there was a severe shortage of pasteurized milk in the country. In two years the plant was selling 37,000 quarts daily and, as better roads were built, it steadily expanded until by 1959 INLACA was selling 132,000 quarts daily and delivering to more than 15,000 homes in 30 cities and towns. By then the company had a gross annual income of around $11,000,000. But more important, in Rockefeller's eyes, was the fact that the company had demonstrated what could be done in an important field. By 1959 there were 16 competing milk companies in Venezuela and production of pasteurized milk had risen from a few thousand to 400,000 quarts a day.

A successful Venezuelan business grew out of CADA, the unsuccessful wholesale food distribution project. When it was discovered that housewives were not receiving the benefit of CADA's lower distribution costs, a study showed the necessity of having retail outlets, and Rockefeller in 1949 introduced modern retail methods by opening a self-service supermarket at Maracaibo. The store was called Todos (Everything). It had handsome display and frozen food counters, neon lighting, pushcarts and all of the other equipment normally found in supermarkets in the United States. Todos was an experimental venture but its early success was more or less assured because there were many United States housewives resident in Maracaibo and they showed local women how to use new products. The next step, however, was more risky. A similar store (called Minimax) was opened at Valencia, where there were almost no foreign residents. The Valencia store attracted little business despite the fact that it offered food at lower prices. Housewives were curious but they not only were unaccustomed to self-service—they had no idea how to use the products, such as cake mix, that were on the shelves. The management finally realized that an educational program had to go along with the new stores and home economics experts were added to the staff to demonstrate the products. Within a few weeks, business began to pick up. Six months later the store was making a profit and thereafter it was a highly successful business.

Using the Valencia formula, five similar stores were opened in Caracas in the next few years, three more in the Maracaibo area, one in Judibana, one in Puerto La Cruz and one in Anaco. All of them were successful. It was also true that all of them were met with cries of protest from local storekeepers, who complained that they were being ruined by the North American monopolists. The local merchants, however, were not ruined. After a few cries of pain, they began remodeling their own stores and lowering prices in order to compete. Within a short time, supermarkets were common in the larger Venezuelan cities—Todos has six competitors, for example, in Maracaibo—and prices generally had been reduced by an estimated 15 per cent.

In 1958, the supermarket operations were combined with CADA, in which IBEC holds 51 per cent of the stock, and Venezuelan investors hold 49 per cent. (The VBEC organization, incidentally, was entirely absorbed by IBEC in 1955 and all government and oil company participation was ended.) The IBEC supermarkets in Venezuela, which now do $28,000,000 business a year, originally had to import about 80 per cent of their goods. The new merchandising techniques, however, had an impact on the national economy, particularly in establishing a steady and larger market for producers. As a result farmers and food processors were able to expand their operations, and by 1959 approximately 70 per cent of the goods sold in the stores was purchased in Venezuela and only 30 per cent was imported.

The success in Venezuela encouraged IBEC to extend its supermarket activities to other countries. By 1959 the total had grown to twenty stores with flourishing business in Puerto Rico, Italy and Peru, and plans were made for further expansion. In Italy, for example, four stores were doing a $5,000,000 business a year at Milan and four others were to be opened. These stores are jointly owned by IBEC and Italian investors but they proved so popular that a new chain wholly owned by Italian investors was quickly organized as competition.

IBEC also had important successes in Brazil, particularly in encouraging farmers to plant hybrid corn. In the 1940's, two Brazilian experts had developed a remarkably strong and prolific hybrid which was resistant to disease, wind and drought and had formed a small company that produced about twelve tons of commercial seed a year. In collaboration with these experts, IBEC organized a company called Sementes Agroceres, S.A. (SASA), in 1947, bought an 867-acre plantation in Paraná state and began raising hybrid seed corn. Only a few tons were harvested the first year and sold to farmers in the area. That summer there was a severe drought that destroyed much of the nation's corn crop but the farmers who had planted the new hybrid seed harvested a larger yield than normal.

This result so dramatically demonstrated the superiority of the hybrid that SASA could not keep up with the demand, although by 1950 its production was 1,250 tons or enough to plant about 10 per cent of all cultivated corn land in Paraná and São Paulo states. During this period, SASA realized profits of around 25 per cent, but in 1951, because of local overproduction, the company went into the red. A merger had been discussed earlier with the original Brazilian hybrid seed corn company, and at this time it was completed. The new company increased its total capital to $375,000 and launched a program to educate farmers all over Brazil to wider use of the seed. By 1959, SASA had six producing units in four states, was selling some 5,600 tons of seed annually, had developed several new hybrid strains and was the largest such company in Latin America. It was worthy of note that by then the company was entirely operated by Brazilians, the only United States citizen connected with it being a member of the board of directors.

There were, during the 1950's, numerous other successful IBEC ventures, ranging from construction of storage elevators for corn, seed, oil and other products in Brazil to the establishment of profitable soluble coffee plants in El Salvador and Guatemala. IBEC Housing Corporation also made a success of a new method for mass-produced concrete homes and in 1958 was one of the nation's largest builders of private houses. The company's main projects were at Margate, Florida (1,800 homes), and in Puerto Rico, where 3,273 houses were completed and work was in progress on 4,500 others. The houses were built under the National Housing Act and three-bedroom homes cost from $6,000 to $10,000. When Rockefeller first inspected one of the Puerto Rican housing developments—the $10,000,000 Villa Las Lomas project—he exclaimed:

"There aren't any trees! Let's plant some trees."

"But—" a cost-conscious aide began.

"I think we should plant a tree in front of each house," Rockefeller went on. "You can't have a treeless housing development. Let's put two trees on each street corner, too."

The trees were planted and after that nobody waited for the boss to suggest a little vegetation in the new developments. A tree was planted in front of every house.

These projects and others became an integral part of the IBEC pattern as Rockefeller's Latin American adventure gained strength.

> Things are going better for us from the business point of view [Rockefeller wrote in this period]. At first the Venezuela business community was afraid of us and thought we were going to crowd them out. Then, when we had trouble and lost money in various companies, they felt better about us and decided we were just human beings, although I think that they lost a considerable amount of respect for us as businessmen. However, now that we are coming through despite the adversities, there is a very friendly feeling on all sides, together with a restoration of respect but without the fear they had formerly. In a sense, we've become one of them.

The feeling of confidence was further strengthened in Latin America generally when experience convinced Rockefeller that the great economic problems in underdeveloped countries could be satisfactorily solved only if there was an improved system of attracting capital—big capital and little capital—for investment in industrial development. There was a stock exchange in Brazil, for example, but it failed to attract the necessary capital, particularly from small investors. As a result, most savings were hidden in the mattress or put into land and not nearly enough was available for new enterprises that would bolster the national economy.

In 1952, IBEC and the Chase National Bank of New York joined with a group of Brazilian banks to organize a financing company along the lines of modern investment banking. The company, Inter-American Finance and Investment Corporation, underwrote securities in the traditional United States manner. Not all of its securities (Brazilian companies and foreign subsidiaries operating in Brazil) were easily sold, the company lost its liquidity and the banks decided that they wanted to withdraw. IBEC bought all of the stock, changed the name to Companhia Distribuidora de Valores (CODIVAL) and transformed it into a sales company for an open-end mutual investment fund. A company called Cia. Empreendimentos e Administracão Ibec (CEA) also was organized to manage the fund and to encourage industrial growth by arranging financing for new enterprises in which foreign manufacturing companies may participate.

The investment fund, which is called the Fundo Crescinco, was something entirely new in Latin American financing. IBEC had an initial investment of about $100,000 and another $500,000 was put up by Brazilian banks and a few individuals. A diversified portfolio of stocks, including about $100,000 in United States securities, was set up and certificates were sold at a price based on the current asset value of the fund. Since a principal purpose of the fund was to attract small investors, the company spent heavily on advertising and sold certificates for as little as $33 or, on an installment plan, for $7 a month. Within a short time, the fund had attracted wide attention, some 200 salesmen were at work throughout the country and money began coming out of hoarding at the rate of about 40,000,000 cruzeiros ($250,000 in 1959) a month. By 1959, 7,000 investors had put in an average of around $500 each and the value of the portfolio, which originally was 30,000,000 cruzeiros, had grown to 1,000,000,000 cruzeiros. Cash distributions to investors were above 10 per cent per year and approximately 75 per cent of the participants were automatically reinvesting their earnings. So successful had the investment fund become in a few years that arrangements were made to start similar operations in Colombia, Argentina and Chile.

In some ways, Rockefeller believes that financing has become the most important method of aiding underdeveloped countries. The biggest problem, he points out, is industrialization which permits workers to produce more and therefore earn more, thus raising the standard of living. Industrial development requires big capital investments. Capital has to come from savings within the country or from abroad. The investment fund in Brazil was the first to encourage the funneling of small savings of many individuals into productive industrial development. In addition to the Brazilian investment fund, IBEC joined with a group of United States companies in 1957 to buy American Overseas Finance Corporation. The company, capitalized at $25,000,000, is designed to assist United States corporations in financing exports to international markets and thus to contribute to economic development of overseas areas that are in need of assistance.

"We expect to help experienced United States management to operate abroad and to help foreign companies buy United States goods," Rockefeller said in regard to American Overseas Finance Corporation. "IBEC has made a go of it in various fields and we now have the experience and the talent for progress. It can greatly stimulate underdeveloped countries and serve our purpose of bringing peoples closer together."

It is still not easy to assess the over-all achievements of Rockefeller in his Latin American enterprises. "IBEC in its own hard-headed way," said an article in *Barron's*, is running a kind of Point IV program. The significant thing is that it is doing so on a sound and paying basis. After some false starts, the organization now seems to be fulfilling the original concept: the investment of venture capital abroad, for a return. Its greatest contribution will be—and in this it is just beginning to succeed— in fostering an investment climate which encourages others to follow.

On the financial side, IBEC did business totaling roughly $80,000,-000 in 1959, when net income was more than $2,000,000.

The importance of IBEC and of AIA may not be measured, however, entirely in dollars and cents. Rockefeller set out to prove that private capital could render a service and still make a profit in lands that needed technological and managerial assistance. IBEC, despite its failures, demonstrated ways in which that objective could be achieved. But, far more important, Rockefeller with the assistance of his family used IBEC and AIA to pioneer vitally important advances in the economic and social structure of underdeveloped areas of the free world and, particularly, of the Americas.

# FOURTEEN

# Washington Revisited

The struggle between the Western democracies and the Communist states led by Soviet Russia was intensified during President Truman's second administration, and it was obvious to United States leaders that the policy of "containing" Communism by a series of military alliances was not enough. There had to be a policy of action to assist underdeveloped countries and to convince uncommitted nations that democracy was a positive force through which they could grow and prosper. Mr. Truman had this idea in mind even while the more urgent defensive policies—the Marshall Plan and the North Atlantic Treaty Organization—were being developed, and he once remarked that during this period he spent most of his time going over the big globe in his office, "trying to figure out ways to make peace in the world." In 1949, at a time when Rockefeller's IBEC projects in Latin America were well started, the President took a historic forward step by proposing what became known as the Point Four program of technical assistance to underdeveloped countries.

Although the Point Four program had "been in the minds of the

270

government," as the President said, for a couple of years, the actual launching of the idea was less a matter of planning than of improvisation. Ben Hardy had served in the press division of the CIAA during the war and had been impressed by what the coordinator's office as well as the later Rockefeller-founded AIA had done in Latin America. After the war, he went to work in the Department of State, where he was something of a crusader for the basic social ideas fostered by AIA, as distinguished from the much broader economic program Rockefeller was attempting to carry out through IBEC. Rockefeller discussed these programs with Hardy on various occasions, arguing that AIA represented only one part of the necessary program and that the technical and social services such as were sponsored by AIA could achieve only a limited goal.

When material was being prepared for President Truman's inaugural address in 1949, Hardy wrote a proposal that the President ask for an appropriation to launch a continuing program to help underdeveloped nations help themselves by sharing with them the technical "know-how" that had been developed in the United States. The theory behind this program was that the United States, by a comparatively small expenditure of capital and a large export of technical aid, could help to raise living standards, encourage worldwide prosperity and peace and provide an antidote to the spread of Communism. When material for the President's speech was assembled at the State Department, however, the section outlined by Hardy failed to arouse enthusiasm and it was entirely eliminated before the speech material was sent to the White House.

Mr. Truman prepared his inaugural address, which set forth three important courses of action for the United States in the critical postwar period. But when the speech was ready, a day or two before it was to be delivered, the President was not satisfied and was said to feel that it lacked punch. About that time, one of his aides, Clark Clifford, remembered the section Hardy had written and which Clifford had liked but which had been dropped by the State Department. He sent for the section and showed it to the President, who inserted it in his speech as "Point Four." Most of the top echelon of the State Department didn't know it was in the speech until they heard it delivered and then they still didn't like it.

The next morning Rockefeller read the speech in his newspaper and gave a yelp of delight when he came to Point Four, which Mr. Truman called "a bold, new program." Rockefeller had had no contact with the White House since the President fired him as Assistant Secretary of State, but he immediately wrote Mr. Truman an enthusiastic letter in which he said that Point Four was the most significant thing that had happened in foreign policy for decades and that it made secure the position of the President in the history books. In February, he wrote to an IBEC associate that he had attended a meeting on another matter in Washington, that the President had been present and had outlined the objectives of the Point Four program and "they coincide with ours 100 per cent." In March, he wrote in still another letter that

> for the first time, government and business are going to have to work together if we are going to be able to do internationally the job which needs to be done. . . . I am convinced that we can find [the] patterns which will permit the necessary and effective integration of efforts . . . in the best interests of the people of other countries as well as our own.

It seems reasonable to assume that Rockefeller would have been willing to be of any kind of service in promoting action in a field where he had experience and great enthusiasm. But there was no White House reaction to his letter. In June, 1949, the President asked Congress to appropriate not more than $45,000,000 to inaugurate the program, an extremely modest beginning. On several occasions, Rockefeller went to Washington to testify regarding the techniques which he had learned in Latin America and he was invited to a series of meetings to discuss plans for legislation carrying out the Point Four program. At these meetings, Rockefeller vainly urged that a separate agency not under control of the State Department be established. The Act for International Development finally passed Congress in the summer of 1950 as part of the general legislation for foreign assistance, but the appropriation for Point Four was whittled down to $35,000,000. On September 8, 1950, an executive order was issued delegating to the Secretary of State the responsibility for carrying out the program and establishing an International Development Advisory Board, which was to "consider" plans for achieving the objectives of the "bold new program." By then war had broken out in Korea and the United States was bearing the brunt of a United Nations "police action" to block the armed expansion of Communism in the Far East.

That summer, 1950, had been a busy one for Rockefeller. For one thing, the price of coffee from Brazil had shot skyward and there was so much complaint by consumers in the United States that it affected relations between Washington and Rio de Janeiro. Rockefeller went to Brazil, talked to government officials and to business-men and was so concerned over developments that, upon his return, he flew to Washington to discuss the situation with the President.

Mr. Truman listened attentively to his visitor's exposition of the deterioration of relations with Latin America. "The Latin American republics have supported your stand in Korea," Rockefeller said. "But a leader has to give recognition to his following and I believe, Mr. President, that you should make a speech to do this. If you just take off your hat to these people, they will be pleased."

Mr. Truman replied that he was just as enthusiastic about Latin America as Rockefeller was, if not more so.

"That's wonderful, Mr. President," Rockefeller said. "If you want me to, I could put together a few thoughts for you that might be helpful if you make such a speech."

The President said that the idea sounded all right to him but that Rockefeller should take it up with the Secretary of State and that he would follow the advice of the Secretary. Rockefeller did call on Secretary Acheson, who received his suggestions graciously. However, no speech was made by the President. The problem of relations with Latin America continued to bother Rockefeller, and later he went to see the President's special assistant, W. Averell Harriman, who stood high in the Truman administration. Harriman was sympathetic and immediately understood Rockefeller's concern. His attitude encouraged Rockefeller who, not long afterward, invited about a score of prominent businessmen to a dinner at which Harriman also was a guest. He hoped that they could plan ways and means by which the business community, in cooperation with the government, could take more positive action toward helping underdeveloped countries. The dinner was not a success. Harriman was preoccupied with broad problems of world economics and politics, and he seemed to feel that business leaders were not doing enough to help the government in its struggle to maintain its world position. For their part, the businessmen were harried by postwar problems and indicated belief that they could hardly carry out their own expansion plans, let alone participate in the Point Four program. The meeting—the whole series of events that summer—left Rockefeller discouraged about the future of the program as an antidote to Communism.

The administration, however, had made a start toward the President's goal when the State Department set up the Technical Cooperation Administration, headed by Dr. Henry Garland Bennett. The TCA began making arrangements with governments in Latin America, Africa and Asia to provide technical assistance, particularly to increase the food supply and to improve health conditions. This, as the President pointed out, was "the minimum machinery" for starting the program. Much remained to be done.

Then, in November, 1950, Mr. Truman appointed Rockefeller as chairman of the fourteen-member International Development Advisory Board to recommend policy in the execution of his Point Four program.

II.

President Truman gave Rockefeller to understand that he wanted the advisory board to prepare the ground for the assistance program in the same way that a committee headed by Harriman had prepared the foundation for carrying out the European Recovery Act (the Marshall Plan) to strengthen the Western powers against Communist expansion. Rockefeller accepted the chairmanship on the understanding that the advisory board would be authorized by Mr. Truman to study the entire problem of assisting underdeveloped areas rather than being limited strictly to the subject of technical aid, and that its report would paint a broad picture of the situation. On November 24, the President wrote him that "any adequate and sound program of international economic development must be both broadly conceived in relation to our national interests and so formulated as to lend itself to realistic and continuing cooperation between private enterprise and government, here and abroad."

The advisory board membership was: Robert P. Daniel, president of Virginia State College; Harvey S. Firestone, Jr., chairman of the Firestone Tire and Rubber Company; James W. Gerard, former ambassador to Germany; John A. Hannah, president of Michigan State College; Margaret A. Hickey, an editor of the *Ladies' Home Journal*; Lewis G. Hines, of the American Federation of Labor; Bertha Coblens Joseph, of Washington, D.C.; Thomas Parran, dean of the Graduate School of Public Health, University of Pittsburgh; Clarence Poe, editor of *The Progressive Farmer*; Jacob S. Potofsky, president of the Amalgamated Clothing Workers of America; John L. Savage, consulting engineer to the U.S. Bureau of Reclamation; and Charles L. Wheeler, a shipping and lumber company executive from San Francisco.

The board, with a staff of seventeen experts, worked for five months in rather remarkable harmony. One of Rockefeller's outstanding talents lies in getting together a group of divergent personalities who have had experience in various phases of a certain field of endeavor and bringing them into agreement on the best over-all method of approaching a common goal. He had certain specific ideas of his own in regard to the program. For instance, he did not believe the program could achieve its objective if it was limited to technical assistance and he did not believe that it should be under control of the Department of State. He made his viewpoint clear and the reasons for it, but his main efforts were directed toward bringing out all of the knowledge possessed by the various members of the board and melding their divergent ideas into a harmonious whole. The board consulted with leaders in the business world, with lawyers, with labor experts and many others who were especially equipped to offer advice. By the time the problem had been explored, the board agreed unanimously on all points to be included in its report, which was a far-reaching set of recommendations published under the title *Partners in Progress*.

> . . . The prevailing economic pattern of [underdeveloped] regions could be revolutionized through a consistent investment flow from the Western industrialized world of several billion dollars a year, if combined with local capital and channeled into genuinely productive enterprise. . . . What is really important is that we do now what can be done with the means available. To do nothing is to invite despair. To act is to hope.

The major recommendation of the board was for the centralization of all major foreign economic activities into one over-all agency headed by a single administrator reporting directly to the President. The revolutionary purpose of this proposal was to coordinate every phase of foreign economic policy and to prevent what was being done by one government department from being nullified by the acts of another department, as so often happened. It was suggested that the new agency be called the U.S. Overseas Economic Administration. The board proposed the establishment of regional institutes for technical assistance in the Middle East, Africa, South Asia and Southeast Asia similar to the Institute of Inter-American Affairs. The Point Four programs should require some measure of cooperative local financing, the report continued, and the United States should take the lead in creating an International Finance Corporation as an affiliate of the International Bank to encourage mobilization of local capital by making loans to private enterprise.

"One third of the people of the world have lost their freedom and are herded together under Soviet imperialism," Rockefeller said in a foreword to the report.

> The remaining two-thirds of the world's population is coming to see that the relentless pressures of military aggression from without

and political subversion from within cannot be ignored or appeased. . . . But the free people the world over are awakening to the fact that defense [of their freedom], in and of itself, is not enough—that there must be a positive force as well. . . .

Basic to defense and to human well-being and the promotion of free institutions is increased production—not in one part or country alone, but in all parts and in all countries. . . . Free men the world over must feel the surge of hope and faith that can only come from a united effort toward a common objective—the common objective can only be the peace, freedom and well-being of all. . . . As we worked, it [became] clear that . . . problems [of] defense and development . . . were indivisible.

While *Partners in Progress* was being completed in 1951, legislation was prepared to broaden the Point Four program, but some administration leaders indicated doubt as to whether it would pass Congress because Senate conservatives were not inclined to increase appropriations for foreign spending. Rockefeller had a wide acquaintance on the Hill and he discussed the proposed legislation with everybody who would listen to him, including such foes of spending as Senator Robert A. Taft, Senator Harry F. Byrd and Senator Eugene D. Millikin. He appealed for their support on the grounds that the United States was dependent on underdeveloped areas for raw materials and that we might lose such sources of supply unless those countries felt they had a community of interest with us.

After some intensive work, Rockefeller felt that there was a good hope of getting the necessary legislation approved, particularly when Taft indicated a favorable attitude. Rockefeller urged the Ohio senator to use his influence in behalf of the program on the grounds that it was not a partisan issue.

"All right," the senator finally said, "I will sit down with the President and a bipartisan group and, off the record, review the recommendations. I'll discuss with the President the means of getting the proper legislation to carry this out."

Feeling that he had gotten over the biggest hurdle, Rockefeller decided to tell Harriman the good news. Harriman, however, gave no indication of being pleased. Their conversation puzzled Rockefeller, who was so intent on getting congressional support that he had failed to notice a trend that was clear to his associates. They had observed that some Truman aides were doubtful about the ambitious and centralized program recommended by the advisory board and were concerned that the board's success in rallying nonpartisan congressional backing for a separate agency might interfere with the administration's efforts to get maximum political credit for a minimum foreign assistance program. It also seemed probable to some of them that Harriman believed Rockefeller hoped to become head of such an agency—as possibly he did—and had been building up support for himself in Congress. In any event, Harriman soon made it clear that he wanted to continue his European Cooperation Administration, which was supposedly a temporary assistance organization, and to broaden its scope instead of setting up the organization proposed by the advisory board to carry out the permanent Point Four program.

Rockefeller believed that such a procedure failed to present to the people of the United States either the problem or a workable solution. "The ECA has completed its work," he argued. "The new program is in our self-interest as well as the interest of others. It should be organized on a permanent centralized basis to meet the problems of an interdependent world. It is not a give-away program. It is the heart of our whole future security and well-being."

By this time, the report of the advisory board had been completed and the board instructed Rockefeller, as chairman, to present it to President Truman. The President, however, was resting in Key West and Rockefeller could not get in touch with him. He offered to take the report to Key West but Harriman objected. After considerable delay, Harriman finally took it when he flew to Florida to see Mr. Truman. Rockefeller's associates believed that because some leaders in the administration other than the President were not enthusiastic, the board's recommendations did not receive the consideration that otherwise might have been given them. On the other hand, Rockefeller was of the opinion that the President himself was both enthusiastic and open-minded about carrying out Point Four and that he might well have supported the board's recommendations if they had been presented to him in favorable circumstances.

Actually, the House Foreign Relations Committee, after hearing testimony by Rockefeller and Paul Hoffman, approved a bill very much in line with the board's proposals. When the Senate Foreign Affairs Committee considered the bill neither Rockefeller nor Hoffman was asked to testify, although both had offered to do so. With some difficulty, the administration representatives kept control of the Senate legislation and the final result was a bill that met their wishes rather than the recommendations of the advisory board for a single over-all agency responsible to the President. The TCA of the State Department continued to administer part of the program, while other parts were placed under the new Mutual Security Agency, which replaced the European Cooperation Administration. Harriman became director of the Mutual Security Agency on December 31, 1951.

The breadth and vision of the advisory board's report to the President was, perhaps, too much for the times; the board was seeking objectives not likely to be easily or quickly attained. The value of its work, however, was demonstrated in the next few years when several of its recommendations, passed over in 1951, were enacted into law. One such proposal in 1951 was that the United States take the initiative in creating an International Finance Corporation which, unlike the World Bank, would be able to finance privately-run enterprises without government guarantees of repayment. The board made the recommendation on the grounds that the greater risk involved would be compensated for by the fact that the corporation would share in earnings of the projects financed. Seven years later this proposal was enacted by Congress. The board also recommended establishment of an organization, affiliated with the World Bank, that could make loans repayable in local currencies. There are many multiple-purpose government projects in underdeveloped countries that might be financed in part by the World Bank if the government involved could raise funds to pay local labor and other local costs.

The board suggested establishment of an International Development Authority to make grants or loans in local currencies for that purpose. Nothing was done in 1951, but in 1959 the World Bank approved creation of an International Development Association with a capital of a billion dollars to serve such a purpose.

In general, Rockefeller believed that the advisory board's work made an important contribution by providing blueprints for future international cooperation. But when the administration's legislation, which he felt did not go far enough because it applied principally to technical assistance or "advice," was enacted in 1951, Rockefeller decided his usefulness as chairman was ending. He made an appointment to hand his resignation to the President, and arrived at the White House just as Harriman was leaving. The two men shook hands cordially, but perhaps with some reservations. There wasn't much doubt in Rockefeller's mind that the Point Four program was going to fall far short of the goals set by the advisory board and of the "bold new program" called for by the President.

"I'm just going in to present my resignation as chairman of the advisory board," he told Harriman.

"Oh, no!" Harriman protested. "The work is just beginning."

Rockefeller, nevertheless, told Mr. Truman that he believed his job was ended and showed him the draft of his letter of resignation.

"We had a wonderful talk," Rockefeller said later. "He couldn't have been nicer."

## III.

For two years after resigning from the International Development Advisory Board in an unhappy mood, Rockefeller pretty well managed to stick to his own home town. Now, as a co-owner of Rockefeller Center, he was more excited than ever to walk the streets of New York City and study its everchanging skyline. And the change that interested him most in 1952 was a great new tower that had sprung up along the banks of the East River—the strikingly handsome glass and aluminum home of the United Nations. Every time he looked at the United Nations building it gave him a little thrill of satisfaction because he had a perfect right to say—but never did —that it might not be there except for the fact that Nelson Rockefeller was a stubbornly determined man who regarded New York as the greatest city on earth.

Rockefeller and his family had long devoted a great deal of effort and money to the theme of international harmony, but the story of the United Nations building began in 1946 when Nelson Rockefeller was a member of the Mayor's committee that was working, without much hope of success, to have the world organization establish its headquarters in New York City. It had been decided that the headquarters would be in the United States but New York did not have a suitable site available and, despite the fact that the United Nations delegates preferred New York, other cities such as Philadelphia and San Francisco were strongly in the running.

Early in December, it appeared that Philadelphia might be selected as the United Nations site, and a final vote was set for December 11. Rockefeller was then in Texas but he flew home on December 9 to make a last effort in behalf of New York. Frank Jamieson had been keeping in touch with leaders of the United Nations, then temporarily situated at Lake Success in the New York suburbs, and he gave Rockefeller a pessimistic report.

"It looks as if it is in the bag for Philadelphia," he said.

A little later that evening, however, a New York newspaper reporter telephoned Jamieson and urged that Rockefeller keep trying. "The delegates," he said, "really want New York if only they can get a proper site."

The next day at noon, Rockefeller, Jamieson, Wallace Harrison and John Lockwood got together in Rockefeller's office just twenty-two hours before the deadline for bids.

"There must be something we can do," Rockefeller said. "What is it?"

"All I'm sure of is that we have to do it today," Jamieson remarked.

Various ideas were offered and finally Rockefeller asked: "What about Pocantico Hills?"

This explosive idea shocked the meeting into silence for a minute. The family estate at Pocantico Hills, some thirty miles from New York, was the spot that Mr. Rockefeller, Jr., loved probably more than any other in the world. It had been "home" to the family for three generations. Only a member of the family could fully understand the implications of the suggestion that it be shared for any purpose. Yet there seemed to be merit in the idea and Rockefeller decided to give it a try. He began putting in telephone calls to his brothers, who were at the moment scattered all the way from Wall Street to Virginia and South America. They were by no means eager to cooperate but once the situation had been explained to them they agreed to go along with the proposal. Then came the big problem. What about their father? Hesitantly, Rockefeller telephoned his father and explained their idea. Mr. Rockefeller, Jr., did not object. But a little later, when the group in his son's office was hard at work, he called back.

"Is this what the United Nations prefer?" he asked. "Is this the ideal location?"

For the next hour or so, the planners checked with United States and other delegates at Lake Success and despondently came to the conclusion that a site at Pocantico Hills, if offered, would be turned down. Just before dinnertime, Rockefeller called his father again and told him the results of their inquiries. "I guess they'd rather have some place in Manhattan, Pa," he said, wearily.

There was a brief discussion and Mr. Rockefeller referred to an area of several blocks on the East Side of Manhattan where a realtor, William Zeckendorf, was preparing to tear down a slum district and build skyscrapers. Harrison was familiar with the project and suggested that the property might be purchased for $8,500,000.

"Well," Mr. Rockefeller said, "I think that's all right. If you can get it at that price, Nelson, I'll give it to the United Nations."

"Why, Pa!" Nelson cried.

The next fifteen hours were frantic work. Rockefeller got in touch with city and federal officials to work out details while Harrison set out to buy the land from Zeckendorf. He finally found the realtor and his partner, Henry Sears, in a night club late that evening. Moving to another table, they spread out the blueprints of the East Side area and Harrison, raising his voice above the blare of the dance band, explained the Rockefeller offer. There was some discussion but in the end Zeckendorf picked up the red pencil with which Harrison had outlined the area and scribbled on the blueprint an option: "8.5 million—United Nations only. December 10 for 30 days." On his way back to Rockefeller's office, Harrison realized that he had talked himself out of a big fee because he had been scheduled to be the architect for the Zeckendorf skyscraper project.

It took a lot of work, but by ten-thirty the next morning the Rockefeller offer was presented to the United Nations and promptly accepted. None of the Rockefellers was present, but they felt a great deal of satisfaction not just because the United Nations headquarters would be in New York but because the family had worked together toward an end that they regarded as significant in the world's search for peace.

> It would be hard to express in words [Rockefeller wrote his father on December 14, 1946] what I felt all Tuesday evening concerning the authorization you gave us in connection with the site for the United Nations. . . . You've done many wonderful things in your life but I don't think that you have ever met any situation with greater courage . . . or with more vision.

Mr. Rockefeller's reply was a rather poignant summation of his relationship with his second son:

> . . . that you and I have so successfully supplemented each other, each bringing assets without which the other could not have gone forward, to me adds greatly to the joy and satisfaction of our joint accomplishment. You cannot, in all the kindness of your heart, begin to be as proud of me as I am of you.

# FIFTEEN

# Eisenhower's Appointee

The first Republican presidential election triumph in twenty years took Rockefeller back to Washington in 1952, almost before the smoke of political battle had cleared away. President-elect Dwight D. Eisenhower appointed him on November 30 to be chairman of the President's Advisory Committee on Government Organization to recommend ways of improving the efficiency and effectiveness of the executive branch of government. Rockefeller's interest in and his talent for government and politics had developed steadily over more than a decade and he was in high spirits at the prospect of working for the first time in an administration of his own political allegiance.

There were some remarkable differences between the young, inexperienced and impatient Rockefeller who set out to coordinate most of Washington and all of Latin America in 1940 and the forty-four-year-old Rockefeller who returned in 1953 as chairman of the President's advisory committee. After a dozen years, Rockefeller was familiar with the intricate twists and turns and the many blind alleys of the federal bureaucratic maze. He had a high respect for Congress and had proved his ability on many occasions to deal successfully

284

with its committees. He had a remarkably wide acquaintance in the executive branch and on the Hill and had reason to believe that his friends were many and his enemies, including some bitter ones, were comparatively few.[1] Even more important, however, he had learned that politics and government in the United States are the net result of a vast, amorphous and often tedious effort by many men and women to sift and evaluate and reconcile countless divergent ideas, and that exhaustive preparation and patience are essential to solid political achievement.

The ability to wait, to be patient, did not mean, however, that Rockefeller was any less industrious. He still could not find enough hours in the day to do all that he thought should be done. He still ate luncheon almost every day at his desk and expected staff members or visitors to keep right on with business while they shared his midday meal of a sandwich, ice cream and a chocolate brownie. At times, when he was concentrating on some problem, it seemed utterly impossible for him to understand why anybody in the office would want to take a whole hour off to go out to lunch. And so contagious was his enthusiasm that the staff ate more lunches at their desks, with only occasional complaints, than at restaurants. "It didn't seem fair to complain," one stenographer remarked later, "because he simply assumed that you were just as interested in getting things done as he was. And then he made up for it in other ways. He often did thoughtful things and I don't think I ever heard him say a cross word to the hired help."

There was no diminution either in Rockefeller's aggressiveness. "When he was convinced the time was right and he was on the right track," an associate commented, "he wanted action and, with experience in Washington, he knew a lot of ways to get action. If one thing didn't work, he would try another—and another. He reminded

[1] Even Senator Langer, who had harassed him and on various occasions had voted against his confirmation, expressed his approval when Rockefeller appeared as a witness at a closed session of the Senate Foreign Relations Committee. Langer said he wanted the committee to know that if another opportunity arose he would vote for confirmation, and this so pleased Rockefeller that "with some hesitancy" he mentioned it in an interoffice memorandum.

me at times of a whole passel of yellow jackets because he could stab away at you from all sides. Needless to say, this drove some bureaucrats crazy and, if they were powerful enough, they tried to cut him down."

Generally speaking, Rockefeller's services in the Eisenhower administration were less flamboyant, less spectacular in the eyes of newspaper reporters and the public than his activities in the 1940's. He was frequently frustrated. But, viewed at long range, his accomplishments were both solid and highly important, particularly in connection with the work of the advisory committee, which included Dr. Milton Eisenhower and Arthur Flemming, in setting up a new government department known as Health, Education and Welfare. Actually, Rockefeller worked on various government reorganization committees from 1952 until 1958. The experience was of great value because it gave him a remarkable knowledge of a wide variety of government operations which would be of importance later.

On two occasions, Rockefeller participated in surveys on reorganization of the Department of Defense. The first was at the request of Defense Secretary Charles E. Wilson, who had once remarked that "any time Nelson wants a government job he can have it with me." In 1953, a committee headed by Rockefeller and including a number of top military and scientific personalities investigated duplication and overlapping in the Defense Department setup. It was believed unlikely in Washington that the committee members would be able to reconcile their highly divergent viewpoints but they surprisingly agreed on a thirty-nine-page report which Wilson and Rockefeller took to the White House. At the door, the Secretary handed the report to Rockefeller and said: "Now, Nelson, you're more familiar with this and you better present the details to the President." Slightly stunned, Rockefeller found himself in the unenviable position of telling the nation's most famous soldier what to do about military organization. The President, however, seemed to be satisfied with the recommendations.

The advisory committee later recommended a second study looking to reorganization of the Defense Department after Wilson had resigned and Secretary Neil McElroy had taken over. A committee of experts was set up to make a study and recommendations to the President and Rockefeller was named as one of the consultants to the committee. The study was complicated and it immediately ran into strong feelings of rivalry among leaders of the various branches of the armed services, each of which was determined to hold its own ground in any reorganization.

Rockefeller favored far greater reorganization of the armed forces than was possible during the 1950's when Congress failed to overrule the recalcitrant service leaders. His attitude was indicated later by the report of a panel of experts in which he participated and which proposed that the three services be removed from the channels of operational command and that unified commands be organized to perform the missions called for by the nation's stategic requirements. The report suggested a reorganization of the Joint Chiefs of Staff on a unified basis under control of the chairman, who would be principal military advisor to the Secretary of Defense and the President. It also proposed that all promotions above the rank of brigadier general come from the Department of Defense rather than from the various services and that such officers be designated as officers of the armed forces rather than of a particular service.

Testifying before a Senate committee in 1958, Rockefeller said that it was "absolutely basic" to defense reorganization to amend the National Security Act of 1947 in regard to prohibition of any change in the combat functions assigned to the various military services. Until Congress acts, he once said, plans for unification are futile and "there will continue to be competition and duplication and confusion that will cost increasing billions in unnecessary defense expenditures and which could conceivably be catastrophic in case of emergency."

During the years Rockefeller served as chairman, the President's advisory committee recommended a total of thirteen reorganization plans. It was a measure of the work done that ten of the thirteen were approved by Congress and became law, effecting basic changes in the Defense Department, the Agriculture Department and the Office of Defense Mobilization, among others.

The work of the advisory committee covered the entire executive branch, giving Rockefeller an opportunity to exercise his skill in planning and to get an insight into several major problems which had not been solved when he resigned. He was, for example, tremendously interested in the various agencies that supervise interstate transportation facilities and came to the conclusion that they should be brought together under one tent as part of a comprehensive program to get public transportation on a more solid basis. The committee also studied reorganization of the office of the presidency, particularly for the purpose of taking some of the routine burden off the President and giving him more time for long-range planning and policy-making. Mr. Eisenhower was interested in White House reorganization and he frequently needled Rockefeller by asking:

"Well, when are you going to get around to working on the White House, Nelson?"

Eventually a plan for streamlining the White House operations was developed but it was not made public while Rockefeller was a member of the committee.

## II.

One of the first and most important jobs that confronted Rockefeller when he became chairman of the advisory committee was to plan the consolidation of the federal health, education and social security programs and agencies into a single cabinet department. It was not a new idea, having first been proposed in the Republican administrations of the 1920's and later by Democratic Presidents, but it was an extremely difficult undertaking because each agency was inclined to fight for its own independence and each one usually had supporters in Congress who could block a merger.

The committee devoted a great deal of time and effort to recommendations and legislation for creation of the Health, Education and Welfare Department (HEW), seeking to overcome as many as possible of the arguments against consolidation and to win the support of congressional committees interested in the various independent agencies. This was no easy task and the fact that the legislation was prepared and that Congress approved it in April, 1953, was regarded in Washington as a kind of minor political miracle. Mrs. Oveta Culp Hobby was nominated by the President as the first Secretary of HEW. Mrs. Hobby had been head of the Federal Security Administration. She had been impressed by Rockefeller's "skill, knowledge and patience" in the work of creating the new department, and she asked Mr. Eisenhower to nominate him as Under Secretary. Rockefeller had been impressed by Mrs. Hobby and he believed that it was of great importance to the Republican party, which had so frequently been stuck with a Wall Street label, to get the department off to a good start. He felt that it was essential to show that the sound innovations of the New Deal era—social security, for example—would not only be retained but improved by the Republican administration. Furthermore, most of the affairs with which HEW was concerned, such as education and public health, were fields in which he had had experience and in which he was intensely interested. When the President asked him to become Under Secretary, he accepted the job and became what Mrs. Hobby described as "general manager" of the huge department, in charge of a staff that numbered thirty-five-thousand persons. Under direction of the Secretary, he was responsible for administering the department's budget of more than $2,000,000,000 in addition to the handling of $4,000,000,000 in annual social security benefits.

Rockefeller "was bouncing a good many balls at one time when he moved to HEW," an aide remarked. "He was still deeply involved in the reorganization program and was devoting a good deal of time to plans for strengthening and unifying federal policy on water resources, which he regarded as vitally important. He had a lot of big jobs. The fact that he could handle so many things without getting into hot water was impressive. He has shortcomings as an administrator. He works amid considerable confusion. But he gets things done. He repeatedly showed that he could pick the right man for a job and he knew how to get work out of his associates. It soon became a common saying around HEW that Rockefeller would never get ulcers—he let other people get them by worrying about details while he concentrated on new and bigger objectives."

One of Rockefeller's first acts at HEW was to set up a chart room or briefing room. The heads of all principal agencies in the department were invited to "command performances" once a week. They thus became a kind of departmental council and each was required to use visual aids in making regular progress reports and explaining future plans so that all would know what was going on in the department. "Scratch a Rockefeller," one bureaucrat quipped, "and you'll find a chart."

Among other things, Secretary Hobby in the fall of 1953 developed a legislative program in which Rockefeller regarded changes in the social security law as most important. He arranged for Roswell B. Perkins, a young New York lawyer, to make an exhaustive study of the entire history of social security and this was presented, with the usual charts and graphs, at briefing sessions. Perkins later remained with HEW at Mrs. Hobby's request. Secretary Hobby and the staff then developed a long-range policy on social security. Rockefeller conferred repeatedly with leaders of congressional committees involved and legislation was drafted—and guided through Congress —to cover almost ten million additional workers by extension of social security benefits and to increase benefits substantially for retired workers and their families and for widows and dependent children.

Rockefeller also was instrumental in the passage of legislation expanding the federal-state vocational rehabilitation program, broadening the federal-state hospital construction program to provide more nursing homes and chronic-disease hospitals for aged persons. He helped develop legislation authorizing the White House Conference on Education as a major effort to foresee the future educational needs of the nation.

Rockefeller failed in an effort to reorganize the federal programs granting aid to states for vocational education, child welfare and other purposes. His study of the grant programs showed that the various agencies involved had different formulas for dividing federal money among the states and for requiring the states to match federal funds. The result was a hodgepodge that often failed to serve the purpose for which the funds were intended. Rockefeller proposed legislation to put the grant programs on a more uniform basis, to encourage the states to expand and improve their programs as circumstances might require in order to be eligible for federal funds, and to foster research into new and important fields. Five committees in the House and four in the Senate were involved in hearings on the legislation, and not even Rockefeller's sales talk could swing all of them to support of the various bills, which eventually were compromised to death.

During the final weeks of his tenure at the Department of Health, Education and Welfare, Rockefeller was instrumental in developing legislation to provide federal aid for school construction in localities without adequate resources to provide fully for their own building needs. This proposal became, after Rockefeller had left the department, President Eisenhower's first proposal for federal aid for school construction.

By the autumn of 1954, Rockefeller decided that HEW was a going organization and that his job was ended. He was interested in getting back into a foreign affairs job. The President was agreeable and, when Rockefeller resigned in December, 1954, Mr. Eisenhower asked him to become Special Assistant to the President for Foreign Affairs to give "advice and assistance in the development of increased understanding and cooperation among all peoples."

Before he left HEW, however, there were a couple of incidents that were typical of Rockefeller. When Halloween rolled around, the Rockefeller chauffeur appeared at the office with a carload of pumpkins, which were placed on the desks of secretaries and stenographers. Then the Under Secretary appeared and jovially announced that "the boss"—Mrs. Hobby—was gone for the day and that it was a great chance to devote a little time to a contest to see who could make the best jack o'lantern. He produced carving knives and everybody started to work, including the Under Secretary. Some fanciful pumpkin faces were produced and first prize went to one that, with a few frills added, resembled an elephant. Rockefeller's wasn't so easy to identify but majority opinion was that it resembled a Picasso painting and he was awarded a consolation prize.

Another Rockefeller idea that autumn was that the United States government should recognize Winston Churchill's eightieth birthday by striking a medal in his honor. The President approved and said he would be happy to present the medal to the British wartime hero. There were, however, complications. The medal would have to be cast by the United States Mint and that meant it had to be approved by the Treasury and Justice Departments. The Justice Department decided that there was no statute to cover such a medal but that Congress could pass an act authorizing it. Such complications were familiar to Rockefeller and he went about solving them with his usual energy. The medal was designed and cast by the mint, with a profile of Churchill on one side taken from a painting by Eisenhower. It was a handsome medal and the presentation to the former British Prime Minister was a noteworthy event.

But then more problems arose. Who was going to pay for the medal? The White House didn't feel up to footing the bill. If Congress paid, it would require special legislation and congressional leaders didn't want to get mixed up in that. Treasury Secretary George Humphrey balked at paying. Eventually, a bill for around $2,000 for one gold medal for Winston Churchill arrived on the desk of Under Secretary Nelson Rockefeller, who had had the idea in the first place. Without further ado, he paid it.

III.

Rockefeller moved over to the White House executive offices with a pocketful of ideas and, as usual, enthusiasm. His job basically was to assess the psychological aspects of United States foreign policy. The time had come, Mr. Eisenhower informed him, "for all of us to renew our faith in ourselves and in our fellow men. The whole world has been far too preoccupied with fears. It is time for people throughout the world to think again of hopes, of the progress that is within reach. . . ." Such words struck a highly responsive chord in Rockefeller's mind. Furthermore, the President asked him to attend meetings of the cabinet, the National Security Council, the Council on Foreign Economic Policy and the Operations Coordinating Board so that he would be in a position to know what was going on in all phases of foreign policy. And, most important of all, Rockefeller would report directly to the Chief Executive. For the first time, he reflected, there would not be any road block between him and the White House. Or so he imagined.

Rockefeller's most important effort in his White House job was the creating of a Planning Coordination Group (PCG) that was intended to serve as a review section for economic, information and other programs abroad. There already existed a Planning Board which funneled programs into the National Security Council and an Operations Coordinating Board which directed execution of the council's approved policies abroad. The Bureau of the Budget, however, had recommended the establishment of a new group that would review programs, ride herd on the implementation of policy abroad and coordinate the departments that were responsible for such endeavors. The task stirred Rockefeller's imagination and, in a short time, he achieved a great deal in a preliminary way, but he also ran into a number of road blocks and several major—as well as bitter—interdepartmental fights, particularly with Under Secretary of State Herbert Hoover, Jr., who was head of OCB and who resented the creation of PCG.

In his new job, Rockefeller had a staff of about twenty persons, including half a dozen liaison officials on loan from other executive branch offices such as Central Intelligence Agency and the Department of Defense, and a few of his own experts who were on his payroll in New York. His first problem, however, was an able executive assistant to take charge of the staff and he asked friends at the Pentagon to suggest a career officer who could do the job. They came up with the name of Major General Ted Parker, a West Point graduate who was stationed in Chicago in command of an antiaircraft outfit. Rockefeller's secretary, Donna Mitchell, telephoned

Parker and handed the receiver to the new presidential assistant.

"General," he said, "this is Nelson Rockefeller at the White House. I believe you've been informed about the job I'd like to have you do. Do you want to try it?"

He paused as Parker replied. Then Rockefeller said: "Oh?"

There was another pause in the White House office. Then Rockefeller's eyebrows shot up in surprise.

"Oh," he said again in a rather flat voice. Then he exclaimed: "Fine! What I want is an honest man who knows how to speak his own mind."

He hung up the receiver with a bang and turned to his secretary. "You know what he said? He said he would come to Washington if he was ordered to do it."

Several years later, when he was a lieutenant general, Parker recalled that he had told Rockefeller he liked his job in Chicago and didn't want to move to Washington. "But," he added, "I got my orders and I went to Washington and I must say I've never regretted it."

One of the first things Rockefeller wanted to do at the White House was to introduce some of the methods he had tried out in other executive branch offices, particularly the use of visual aids at conferences. A year or so earlier, he had had occasion to present a proposed project to the President and had used charts to speed up the discussion. The presentation had been scheduled for twenty minutes, and at the end of that time Roswell Perkins, who was in charge, paused and asked whether any further explanation was desired. Mr. Eisenhower urged him to continue and the presentation lasted fifty minutes. The charts enabled the President to grasp facts and figures and the basic idea of the project almost at a glance, Rockefeller said later, whereas the same problem presented in the form of a memorandum would have required several thousand written words. Mr. Eisenhower expressed enthusiasm for the method and, as a special assistant, Rockefeller hoped to use visual aides regularly at White House conferences.

Unfortunately, there wasn't any suitable briefing room in the White House offices. When charts were used on one occasion at a meeting of the National Security Council the space was so inadequate that they fell down and created something of a shambles. So what was needed was a briefing room where the NSC or the Operations Coordinating Board or any other group could meet and where apparatus could be permanently installed for use of the graphic system.

"Rockefeller began looking around for the right kind of a room," a friend said later. "It was awesome to see him prowling the White House and the executive offices, eying every wing and floor for a suitable chamber. His face lighted up when he spotted the White House bowling alley. It would be perfect for his purposes but, unhappily, the President didn't feel that the bowling alley could be torn out. Rockefeller kept on looking. He even eyed the White House swimming pool, although I don't know whether he was planning to get rid of it or just cover it over. Finally, he climbed to the top floor of the Executive Office Building (the former State Department) across the street from the White House. There was an old library there with a skylight, turret rooms and a complicated set of stacks for books all around the walls.

" 'Maybe this is it!' he said. 'We could clear it out and use the turret rooms for the various study groups and researchers.' His enthusiasm lasted long enough to make an investigation of problems that would be involved. The Secret Service promptly reported that it was impossible to provide proper security for the President in the maze of rooms and corridors on the top floor. And an engineering survey showed that the library floor was so old that, if its burden was increased, it was likely to cave in—and Rockefeller's office was directly underneath!"

It was not, however, obstacles of this nature that stopped Rockefeller. What stopped him was the top echelon of the Department of State. A word of explanation is due here because, throughout the period of his service in Washington, Rockefeller had frequently been in conflict with high officers of the department and it might seem that he was always out of step in regard to foreign policy. This was seldom true, nor was it at the root of the problem. The basic trouble was threefold. First, both President Roosevelt and President Eisenhower appointed him to jobs that, by their very nature, tended to infringe on the long-established prerogatives of the department and therefore to cause conflict. Second, Rockefeller usually wanted to go further on foreign aid than the department. Third, he had always strongly believed in people-to-people diplomacy—the idea that it was vitally important for the peoples of the various nations to know and understand each other in order to promote good feeling and cooperation and peace. Thus, in respect to the method and machinery for achieving an objective rather than in field of actual foreign policy, Rockefeller frequently did disagree with the traditional methods of experienced diplomats because he regarded foreign relations as far more than a strictly legalistic procedure between the various governments in power.

"You might explain it this way," a man who was a very close observer once said. "A diplomat and lawyer like Dean Acheson is wonderfully trained and disciplined. He is precise and legalistic. He reads and understands a document in exact legal terms. He believes in the rational man. Rockefeller never was trained to read or to speak in exact or legalistic terms. He does not see a problem in abstract terms but he intuitively understands it in human terms. He is like a painter who never learned to be a skilled draftsman but nevertheless can produce a good painting. You could say that the traditional diplomat would recognize Rockefeller's lack of skill as a draftsman and conclude—perhaps contemptuously—that he was no good. But Rockefeller would conclude that the legalistic diplomat knew nothing about how people felt or what they wanted."

In addition, one observant diplomat pointed out, Rockefeller resembles his paternal grandfather in that he "is a man who wants to have his own way."

He had sometimes had his own way in clashes with the department. More often he had not, but this did not discourage him from trying something else, nor did it cause him to feel resentment. To the constant bewilderment of his associates, Rockefeller almost always seemed to be convinced that his failure to put across an idea in which he firmly believed was due only to the fact that others did not fully understand the circumstances and that if the next problem were approached in a more sympathetic and thorough manner then everybody would be able to get together in a friendly and cooperative spirit and find the way to reach their common goal. This did not keep him from being a persistent fighter for his own ideas but it did often give his activities an accent of naïveté. A man who had crossed swords with him one day might, upon meeting him the following day, take an "on guard" position, only to have Rockefeller throw an arm around his shoulders and greet him like an old pal.

Rockefeller's efforts as Special Assistant to the President for Foreign Affairs, however, were inevitably doomed to put him in an unfavorable light at the Department of State, regardless of what he did or how he did it. Secretary John Foster Dulles was a man with a strong will and a determination to conduct the nation's foreign affairs in his own way. The idea of anybody being a Presidential Assistant for Foreign Affairs must have been repugnant to him and, for excellent reasons, he had no intention of letting Rockefeller get between him and Mr. Eisenhower. Obviously, he made this clear at the White House because Rockefeller found that he had to sell his ideas to the State Department. Dulles was away from Washington a great deal but in his absence the special assistant had even rougher sledding because Under Secretary Herbert Hoover, Jr., not only protected his superior's position but was definitely out of sympathy with Rockefeller's methods and ideas. Hoover was generally aligned with Treasury Secretary George Humphrey, Budget Director Roland Hughes and ICA Director John Hollister—known in Washington as the 4-H Club—to hold down government spending. Rockefeller not only believed in maintaining an adequate national defense but he was convinced that money spent wisely on foreign economic cooperation would save the taxpayers huge sums in the future. Hoover was in a position to stop him and he seldom lost an opportunity to do it in small affairs, such as setting up a chart room, or in large affairs, such as pushing the President's atoms-for-peace program. Some progress was made on the atoms-for-peace project but the champions of economy were not enthusiastic about the foreign aid program, particularly not along the lines Rockefeller believed essential. He argued in behalf of a loan for a $130,000,-000 program for expansion of the Tata steel works, a privately owned enterprise in India, at a low rate of interest and without an Indian government guarantee. The company planned to buy American equipment at a higher price than it might have gotten it elsewhere, but insisted that it could do so only if granted a low interest rate on a loan by the Export-Import Bank. Rockefeller urged the administration to agree as a demonstration of good will and support to private enterprise in an underdeveloped country but, at the last minute, Secretary Humphrey and others opposed the deal so strongly that it was abandoned.

There were other instances in which the "4-H Club" blocked proposals which Rockefeller believed would bolster United States foreign policy. He urged that funds appropriated by Congress for economic aid to Indonesia be spent to offset Communist efforts to infiltrate the former Dutch colony. Under Secretary Hoover believed such funds should be withheld until it could be determined whether Indonesia was pro-Russian or an ally of the Western powers. There was a definite division between a policy of action as opposed to a policy of inaction, and in the long run Rockefeller spent too much of his time at the White House in a fog of frustration. "Yet," said a man who followed these developments closely, "I never knew him to be vindictive against those who—rightly or wrongly—were blocking him. Not even in the privacy of his office did he ever berate anyone, although there were times at conferences when he had been the target of remarks so crude that almost everyone there was embarrassed. I am sure he was bitter but his strongest reaction to his staff would be to shrug and shake his head in a kind of despair."

Rockefeller began to realize that he was caught in a trap. Yet there did come a time when he was able to act effectively, and it was an important time.

IV.

In 1955 the cold war between the Western democracies and the Communist nations led by Soviet Russia had reached a point of crisis that prompted many statesmen to decide that only a meeting of opposing heads of state could relieve world tensions. This led to the first so-called Summit Conference at Geneva, with the United States, Great Britain, France and Soviet Russia participating.

While it was hoped that some concrete results might be obtained at Geneva, the conference obviously offered a perfect sounding board for propaganda, and the participating nations knew that all of the world would be listening to their words. Thus Geneva called for the best efforts of the United States' psychological warfare experts and especially of the President's Special Assistant for Foreign Affairs as well as the Planning Coordination Group.

The PCG accomplished no miracles but it gave Rockefeller a basis from which to work when plans were being made for the Summit Conference. He had received from the government information service abroad the raw results of surveys, made in European countries, of public opinion on the cold war. They showed that many Europeans felt the United States was just as much to blame for the cold war as Soviet Russia, that the atomic bomb should be banned and that United States bases in Europe should be abolished. The results indicated to Rockefeller that the Russians were doing a much better propaganda job than the United States, and he believed that our biggest problem at Geneva would be to counteract the idea that the Soviets were leaders in seeking peace.

To meet the problem, Rockefeller arranged through PCG for a kind of seminar of experts at Quantico, the U.S. Marine Corps base near Washington. Those attending were from colleges and private groups and government, all of them experts in international affairs and all of them cleared for top secret information. Accommodations at Quantico were less than luxurious and a bit crowded. An army officer who dropped by Rockefeller's suite the first morning was surprised to find him standing third in line among the five persons occupying the suite, waiting for a chance to shave at the single bathroom mirror.

The seminar, however, was a considerable success; out of the discussions came a proposal that the United States should make a dramatic peace gesture at Geneva by reviving an "open-skies" plan for international aerial inspection of all lands as a safeguard against secret preparations for atomic warfare. When the Quantico meetings ended Rockefeller had the proposal outlined in a one-page memorandum which he took to President Eisenhower. The President was immediately interested; very much interested, Rockefeller thought. He picked up the telephone and asked for Secretary Dulles.

"Foster," he said, "here's an idea." Then he briefly sketched the open-skies proposal and added that it had come out of Rockefeller's seminar.

Dulles replied that the State Department had a copy of the proposal, and that was about the end of the conversation. It was almost the end of the open-skies plan, too. A few days later, the President asked Rockefeller to attend a briefing with Dulles in the President's office. The Secretary of State seemed a bit surprised to see Rockefeller present but he promptly got down to business. He leaned back in his chair, placed his fingertips together on his chest, looked up at the ceiling and began speaking brilliantly and with the utmost clarity about plans for the Geneva conference. The net result of his remarks was that the important thing for the President to do at the Summit Conference was to identify the issues in the cold war. Then he should leave it up to the conference of foreign ministers, which was to follow, to work out the proper solutions, providing solutions could be found.

Rockefeller did not agree. "I believe, Mr. President," he said, "that you should make a pronouncement that will reassure the world as to the peaceful intentions of the United States. It is important that you destroy the idea some peoples have that the United States is a warmonger with an atomic bomb. You can be sure the Russians will attempt to make themselves out as leading the search for peace. The

Russian argument will be propaganda, but it will be important psychologically."

Dulles was strongly opposed and came back to his belief that the President should merely define the issues. He made it clear, too, that the nation could have only one Secretary of State and that, as Secretary of State, he did not appreciate interference in execution of the President's foreign policy. Rockefeller tried to get back into the discussion but Mr. Eisenhower suggested that perhaps the meeting had gone on long enough.

Rockefeller went back to his office and tried to take another look at the whole situation. He knew that the State Department had confined itself to preparing position papers for the President along the lines proposed by Dulles. He intuitively believed that when the time came such papers would not be enough. So he instructed his staff to go ahead with preparation of position papers along the lines discussed at Quantico, particularly in reference to the open-skies proposal. The State Department didn't want Rockefeller to accompany the President to Geneva, but after some discussion the President asked Rockefeller; Deputy Defense Secretary Robert B. Anderson; Admiral Arthur W. Radford, chairman of the Joint Chiefs of Staff; and Harold Stassen, who was the President's Special Assistant for Disarmament, to journey to Paris and there await further instructions.

In Paris, the four got together in an unhappy mood. Rockefeller had the position papers that his staff had prepared on the open-skies plan and in favor of freer world communications, and he showed them to the other exiles. Radford and Anderson were impressed. They consulted General Alfred M. Gruenther, then commander of NATO, and he, too, liked the idea. With nothing to do but wait, the group worked over the papers and suggested changes. Meanwhile, the chiefs of state and their foreign ministers were gathering at Geneva and the Russians, as expected, were making the most of the opportunity for peace propaganda. They appealed directly to the fears of Europeans, for example, by proposing the destruction of all atom bombs. The United States delegation started off by attempting to define the issues in the cold war but, after the first day, they appeared to be running out of steam in the contest for favorable world reaction.

These developments offered an opening for the Paris exiles and they sent a message suggesting that the President might desire to revive the open-skies proposal. On Wednesday, they were encouraged by the receipt of orders to move from Paris to a hotel in Lausanne. Then Rockefeller and Stassen were instructed to continue to Geneva. Several State Department officers appeared to be surprised when they encountered Rockefeller in Geneva. But the President had come to the conclusion that he needed to make a dramatic gesture to recapture the initiative at the conference and the open-skies plan still appealed to him as a way to emphasize the peaceful intentions of the United States. Stassen was given the job of drafting the proposal into Mr. Eisenhower's speech but, at the last minute, it was decided that the effect might be more striking if the President interpolated the plan in his prepared statement.

The climactic day—Thursday—of the conference was overcast and stormy. When his turn came, Mr. Eisenhower arose and began reading his prepared statement. But in the middle of his speech he laid aside his text and took off his glasses and looked around at the representatives of the most powerful nations on earth. There was, he said solemnly, a grave danger that, in an atomic age, the nations would destroy each other. The time had come to put the military blueprints on the table and open both Russia and the United States to unlimited aerial inspection by each other's airplanes. "I propose," he said, "that we take a practical step; that we begin an arrangement very quickly as between ourselves—immediately!"

Just at that moment there was a tremendous clap of thunder and the lights in the conference room flickered. Sitting directly behind the President, Rockefeller felt that the storm added an unexpected but welcome touch of drama to the speech and to the President's able presentation of the open-skies plan. The proposal was enthusiastically received by the Western delegates and hailed by the newspapers of Europe. Even Soviet Premier Nikolai A. Bulganin had a few kinds words for the proposal. But when Rockefeller walked out of the chamber with Mr. Eisenhower they encountered a short, bald and roly-poly man named Nikita S. Khrushchev, the powerful Secretary General of the Russian Communist party, and Khrushchev bitterly denounced the Eisenhower speech. The President more than held his own in the brief argument and then asked Rockefeller to accompany him to luncheon.

> There is no question but that President Eisenhower was the diplomatic figure at the conference [Rockefeller wrote to one of his children]. His integrity, his ability and his personality dominated the scene, and the Russians were fascinated by him. . . . He kept the initiative with them all the time. . . . [His] proposal took the Russians completely by surprise, and as you know made a tremendous impression around the world as to the sincerity of the President and the American people in their desire for peace. . . . Again on Friday, the President made another strong positive statement—this time a recommendation to reduce the barriers to remove those causes which prevent freer flow of ideas, people and goods between East and West. . . . The United States is indeed fortunate to have in this critical period General Eisenhower as President and Mr. Dulles as Secretary of State. They are uniquely able and informed, and make a wonderful team.

It was not, however, a team on which Rockefeller was going to find a satisfactory place.

Not long after Rockefeller had returned from Geneva, Defense Secretary Wilson came around to offer him a job as Deputy Secretary of Defense, a post that was about to be vacated. Rockefeller was very much interested and said he would be happy to accept if the President approved. He discussed the Wilson proposal with the President's chief-of-staff, Sherman Adams, and with Mr. Eisenhower, and both said they would approve if Rockefeller felt he wanted to move to the Defense Department. Then Secretary Humphrey learned of the plan. He did not approve of Rockefeller's willingness to spend money and apparently he didn't like the idea of moving him into the Defense Department. One day after a cabinet meeting, Wilson stopped to talk to Rockefeller and said that he was sorry but he would have to withdraw the offer of a job as deputy. Rockefeller didn't have to ask why.

At this time, Rockefeller had been away from family business affairs for more than three years and he felt there were urgent reasons for him to get back to his office in Rockefeller Center. One day he sat down and did a lot of hard thinking about the past and the future. His service in public office had given him unusually wide administrative experience and an insight into the intricate operation of the federal government that few men could claim at his age. As chairman of reorganization committees, as an Under Secretary, as the head of an agency and as a White House assistant, he had acquired a detailed knowledge of almost every executive department. He had had his ups and downs, too.

As the creator of CIAA, he had been a pioneer and, in the opinion of most observers, a successful if not a brilliant administrator. As Assistant Secretary of State he had been a center of controversy but he could look back on that period with a great deal of satisfaction. At HEW, he had taken a back seat but it was generally known that he had been the driving force in setting up the new department and getting it off to a good start. At the White House, he had promoted some successful ideas but, in general, he had failed and that was a bitter pill. The answer to all this, he decided, was that an appointed official was always subject to the policies and plans of his superior. Policy was made at a higher level and the appointed office holder had to stay within bounds. It was the elected official who was in the driver's seat because he had put ideas before the people and had won a mandate to act.

In December, 1955, Rockefeller told Mr. Eisenhower that personal affairs made it necessary that he resign as Special Assistant to the President. If he was discouraged, he didn't show it when he went around to his office at the end of the year to dictate a few final letters and pack his personal papers. Once he stumbled over a date while dictating and turned to his secretary to ask: "What year is this, anyway?" He roared with laughter when she replied: "Now,

Mr. Rockefeller, don't you clutter up your mind with what year this is. I'll take care of that."

But he was in a serious mood when he stopped to say good-by to General Parker, who was working on a record of their year in the White House.

"I'm convinced of one thing," Rockefeller said as he turned to go out the door. "You can't have a voice in your party unless you've proved that you know how to get votes."

# SIXTEEN

# The Politician

When Rockefeller returned to his private affairs in New York early in 1956 he made it clear that his brothers had been carrying the load of family responsibility for some years and that he was leaving public service because it was his turn to lend a hand at home. Some Washington political reporters predicted that he would eventually get into politics in one way or another. They pointed out that he had always been interested in public life and politics just as his Grandfather Aldrich had been. He had been taught from childhood that his most important mission in life was to be of service. It was unlikely, therefore, the Washington experts theorized, that he would remain in private business. Rockefeller, however, had no political plans and, for that matter, no particular prospects. Yet he would continue to be much interested in the national welfare and he had some definite ideas as to the need for better public understanding of foreign affairs and other national problems.

Rockefeller sometimes discussed these ideas with a few of his closest associates—Frank Jamieson, John Lockwood and Wallace

Harrison—and with his brothers. Harrison had been an important influence in Rockefeller's career since the 1930's, when he was one of the architects of Rockefeller Center. A tall, tireless and engaging man, he had interests as wide as the world and an ability to understand and clarify complex problems in a manner that was of invaluable assistance to Rockefeller during his service in Washington and in connection with his enterprises in Latin America. Lockwood's precise legal mind also had been important to Rockefeller's career since early in World War II. But it was Jamieson, perhaps, who had been most important to him in the political field. The slight, debonair former newspaperman brought a new note into the offices at Rockefeller Center when he established a rather elaborate research and public relations setup for all of the Rockefeller brothers after the war. He was a man who could plow through a lot of work, swiftly but so easily that it seemed no effort at all. He liked to laugh and he liked to get his feet up on his desk in moments of relaxation. And, unlike most of the Rockefeller associates, he was not a bit alarmed by the interest of newspaper reporters in the affairs of the family.

Jamieson and Rockefeller, except for an inner tenseness, were remarkably unlike. Rockefeller is broad-shouldered, stocky, with a kind of calculated disorderliness in the way he wears his excellently tailored clothes. He seems to be always in motion and usually a little behind the pace he sets for himself. His changing moods—gaiety, charm, earnestness, sincerity—are instantly reflected in an open face. As he talks, he goes through a restless, intricate series of gestures with his hands. Beside him, Jamieson was outwardly an almost nonchalant figure, a thin-faced man with white hair brushed smoothly back from his forehead, an easy smile and, often, a quizzical expression that made him pleasantly owlish behind his horn-rimmed glasses. Yet, the two men seemed almost from the beginning of their association in 1940 to complement each other in a remarkable way, to spark ideas and to generate action. "Their personalities rub off on each other," a politician once remarked. Jamieson had long been familiar with many areas of politics and public opinion that were important to his boss and he did not hesitate to make his viewpoint clear. The two men traveled together extensively in the United States and Latin America over the years.

## II.

One of the ideas that Rockefeller had when he left the White House job in 1955 was for a private study of major problems that would confront the people of the United States in the next ten or twenty years. Almost ten years earlier, he had felt the need for a better knowledge and understanding of the capitalistic system and had then arranged to make a comprehensive study of past, present and future political economy. The results of that study, showing drastic modification of the capitalistic system over half a century, had contributed to Rockefeller's education in economic affairs and may have influenced his attitude toward the use of his wealth. Then, as presidential assistant, he had been impressed by the success of the seminar of experts on foreign policy that he had sponsored at Quantico in preparation for the Summit Conference at Geneva and by a second Quantico seminar that studied and analyzed the results of the Geneva sessions.

When he returned to private business in New York he discussed with various friends and associates the possibility of using the "Quantico technique" to study major national problems and, particularly, to give the people of the United States a better understanding of economic, military, educational, moral and other situations they would be required to face in the future. Basically, the idea would be to look ahead to conditions in 1965 and then try to determine what could be done now to meet critical future problems. Rockefeller found the idea exciting and he suggested to his brothers that they finance a Special Studies Project under the title of *America at Mid-Century* in an effort to provide a blueprint for approach to future national problems. They agreed to do so through the Rockefeller Brothers Fund, a philanthropic organization they had set up in 1940 which had made contributions of more than $15,000,000 to many charities, civic organizations and educational endeavors. A group of thirty men and women recognized as leaders in all phases of American endeavor were selected as an over-all panel for the Special Studies Project and they, with a corps of experts, formed seven panels to study seven basic problems ranging from military security and foreign policy to education and the "moral framework of national purpose." Rockefeller had met Dr. Henry A. Kissinger of Harvard University at the Quantico seminars and, with some difficulty, persuaded him to take over as Special Studies director.

"The way Nelson puts things to you as a public duty makes it hard to refuse him," Kissinger remarked later to a friend. The panelists represented every phase of American life—General Lucius D. Clay; Lester B. Granger, of the National Urban League; Henry R. Luce, of Time, Inc.; Jacob S. Potofsky, of the Amalgamated Clothing Workers of America; Edward Teller, University of California nuclear expert; Frazar B. Wilde, of the Connecticut General Life Insurance Company; and Chester Bowles, former ambassador to India, among others.

Rockefeller acted as chairman of the over-all panel and worked extensively on writing the reports, but his main effort was directed toward achieving agreement among the panelists on a basic approach to the seven problems. This was no simple task. The panelists held widely divergent political and economic views. They were all individualists who had strong opinions and had risen to prominence by asserting them. It seemed most likely in the beginning that they would be at loggerheads and do nothing or that they would break up in a bitter controversy without agreeing on any report. "I don't think there are many persons other than Rockefeller who could have persuaded such a diverse group to put aside prejudices and work together in the national interest," one panelist said later. "He made everybody feel that it was important—not to give up our own opinions but to forget personal prejudices in favor of finding the best possible solutions to the problems posed. Even so, the whole effort might have flopped if it had not been for his persistence. He never gave up. He cajoled some and he prodded others. Briefly, he got the best effort from some of the finest minds in the country. And, surprisingly, nobody dissented from the seven reports."

The Rockefeller Brothers Fund reports attracted nationwide attention because they laid down blueprints for security, educational and economic programs at a critical time. The first reports were released at a time when Congress and the public generally were greatly concerned by Russian scientific achievements, such as the launching of the first earth satellites, and when there was widespread controversy over defense and educational expenditures in the United States. As a result the *America at Mid-Century* recommendations were given front-page attention by the country's newspapers and were widely studied by congressional leaders.

Meantime, there had been various suggestions, publicly and privately, that Rockefeller should run for Mayor of New York City or otherwise take an active political role in his home state. One nationally prominent Republican leader had offered to help him get a New York City political job as a step toward running for Congress, but Rockefeller wasn't interested. L. Judson Morhouse, chairman of the New York State Republican Committee, had talked politics to Rockefeller on several occasions. Rockefeller said he would "like to be helpful" in political areas but gave no hint as to how he might be helpful. Morhouse began thinking of him as a possible candidate for some office and, in 1956, suggested that he run for the United States senatorial seat being vacated by Irving Ives. Rockefeller declined. He felt he was temperamentally more suited to administrative duties than to a legislator's career.

At this time, however, Rockefeller did take advantage of an opportunity to make an exhaustive study of the affairs and the governmental structure of New York State. There was considerable demand for a convention to revise and simplify the state constitution. The question of calling such a convention had political implications. The Democratic administration under Governor W. Averell Harriman wanted to hold a convention because they hoped to reapportion the state and thus gain seats in the Legislature from upstate areas. The Republicans, who controlled the Legislature, were opposed to holding a convention because they had no intention of opening the way to reapportionment that would favor the Democrats. The Legislature did, however, create a Temporary State Commission on the Constitutional Convention to compile data on proposals for constitutional changes in preparation for a possible convention.

The temporary commission was divided between Republicans and Democrats, and it might have engaged in a political donnybrook that would fan the flames of politics. An early deadlock arose when the Republican legislative leaders and the Democratic Governor could not agree on selection of a chairman for the commission. Republican State Chairman Morhouse was still hoping to get Rockefeller into the political picture. Now he suggested that both the legislative leaders and the Governor could trust Rockefeller and that he be appointed chairman of the temporary commission. They agreed and Rockefeller accepted the job.

One of Rockefeller's first moves was to telephone a man he had never met, George Hinman, a quiet, highly successful lawyer in Binghamton with a vast knowledge of state politics and governmental affairs. Hinman was a bit startled to be asked to become counsel for the commission but, after he had met Rockefeller, he accepted the job. "I was surprised and pleased by his down-to-earth manner," Hinman remarked. "It wasn't just charm. He was completely bipartisan in his approach and he had picked an excellent staff of experts headed by Dr. William J. Ronan of New York University."

The commission over which Rockefeller presided held hearings in various parts of the state and listened to the recommendations of countless individuals and organizations. Rockefeller also arranged for professors from various state colleges to compile a series of studies of the background of the constitution, the way it worked under modern conditions and what should be done to improve it. In the end, the electorate voted against holding a constitutional convention but the commission's series of reports objectively brought into focus the entire problem of constitutional revision.

"He turned out to be a man who knew how to dissolve controversy," Hinman said much later. "Members of the commission and witnesses started out in an intensely partisan manner. Everybody had a political axe to grind. But the hearings never did develop in a partisan spirit. Rockefeller was seeking the answers to bipartisan questions and nothing else and he firmly refused to be led off the track. Everybody got a hearing but he never let the hearings deteriorate into political controversy. I felt that this ability could be a great attribute in public life."

III.

In March, 1957, Governor Harriman made a speech at the dinner of the legislative correspondents organization in Albany, in the course of which he remarked lightly that the Republican party should nominate Nelson A. Rockefeller to run against him in 1958. His remarks then and later indicated that he believed Rockefeller's political views were more liberal than those of state Republican leaders and that he would never get the nomination. Later, an insurgent Republican group in New York County, including John Roosevelt, set up a "draft Rockefeller" committee.

None of these developments, which amounted to no more than minor newspaper publicity, drew any reaction from Rockefeller. He did consult with leaders of the Republican party in his own county, Westchester, where Assemblyman Malcolm Wilson was a young and increasingly popular figure with many upstate friends. But the summer of 1957 rolled around and he was undecided about running for office. Occasionally, Morhouse or Hinman talked to him about the gubernatorial race, but without arousing much response. The fortunes of the Eisenhower administration in Washington were at a low ebb as a result of a business recession and a poor record in the 1956 congressional elections. Everybody kept saying that 1958 would be a Democratic year and that Governor Harriman, who had worked hard to win voters away from the Republicans upstate and who was regarded as a liberal politically, would easily be re-elected. That summer the state committee vice chairman, Jane Todd, convened a conference of Republican women upstate and Rockefeller was asked to be one of the speakers. He appeared on a hot, humid day when everybody was uncomfortable in the hall. He discussed the Eisenhower administration's budgetary position and bored most of his audience to the point of exhaustion. Morhouse, who had helped arrange for the speech, was despondent but he cheered up later when Rockefeller made a hit by chatting with the delegates informally.

In September, 1957, Hinman invited Mr. and Mrs. Rockefeller to his home in Binghamton, and asked William H. Hill, publisher of the Binghamton *Star*, to come to dinner. A slight, handsome man with white hair and a gracious manner, Hill was then eighty years old, retired from Congress but still the Republican leader of Broome County. He had been a power in upstate New York political affairs for many years and his newspaper editorials carried weight with state politicians. At dinner, the talk soon got around to the 1958 gubernatorial race and Hill indicated an interest in Rockefeller as a candidate. They talked generally about how a campaign might be launched but Rockefeller gave no indication of his own attitude; in fact, Hinman decided that he was definitely cool to the idea of running. The dinner with Hill was never made known, nor was a second visit by Rockefeller to Binghamton to confer with the publisher in November.

In the spring of 1958 several Republicans were angling for the gubernatorial nomination, including State Senate Leader Walter J. Mahoney of Buffalo, and Assembly Leader Oswald D. Heck of Schenectady, but the most active candidate was Leonard Hall, of Oyster Bay, a former congressman and recently retired as Republican National Chairman. Morhouse, however, had become convinced that Rockefeller was the party's best hope of opposing Harriman and the obvious national trend to the Democrats. He dared the wrath of other candidates and began moving around the state, urging county chairmen not to declare themselves but to wait until they had a chance to get acquainted with Nelson Rockefeller. The New York *Herald Tribune* published a poll of delegates to the 1954 Republican state convention showing that Rockefeller was the most popular choice for the gubernatorial nomination, with Hall running a close second. The New York *Post*, a strong supporter of Harriman, ran a series of articles about Rockefeller, including an interview in which he said that he was a Republican because "I think that as a party the Republicans have more competence organizationally and administratively" but "I'm not one to believe that one party wears horns and the other is exclusively composed of angels." He declined, however, to discuss New York State politics. Meantime, publisher Hill began a "draft Rockefeller" campaign in his newspaper and published the results of privately taken party polls purporting to show that Rockefeller would run better than other aspirants for the office.

The idea of seeking elective office posed many problems for Rockefeller. There was, first of all, his family to consider; not only his immediate family but the Rockefellers in general. He did not, at some particular time, put the idea of entering politics up to his family. Instead, the possibility that he might seek office emerged gradually in their minds and in their conversations and then slowly evolved into a distinct possibility. Mr. Rockefeller, Jr., was pleased with the idea but Nelson's four brothers were by no means unanimous in urging him to run for office. They were accustomed to the idea of public service but not of public service through elective office. Some members of the family definitely preferred to keep off the front pages and others wanted to think about the effect of a political campaign on the family generally. Nobody tried to tell Rockefeller that he should not run but, as the months passed, it was evident that the family position ranged from a cautious nonapproval to enthusiastic approval. Finally, there was never any given time when Rockefeller told them he had made up his mind. But the decision was made and, by a kind of evolutionary process, all of them became aware of it.

Of greatest importance to Rockefeller was the effect that politics might have on his immediate family. For some time, Mrs. Rockefeller had known that running for public office was on his mind. She apparently was not comfortable with the idea at first, knowing that it would mean a great change in the life of the family. Her own family were loyal Republicans without interest in public office, except for two cousins—Mrs. Eleanor Clark French, vice chairman of the New York State Democratic Committee, and Joseph S. Clark, Jr., a Democrat who became Mayor of Philadelphia and went on to the United States Senate in 1956. She herself had shown independence in her political views by registering in the Liberal party in New York several years earlier. But, except for her cousins, she was inclined to regard politicians in general without enthusiasm, largely because she had never had much contact with them. She had no intention of trying to influence her husband's decision, but she was somewhat concerned that a political career would mean difficult readjustments for the children.

The children, however, were delighted with the idea of their father seeking elective office. Rockefeller had always encouraged them to try new things, to learn about people everywhere. Mrs. Rockefeller often felt that he carried the spirit of adventure too far in urging the children to spend their summers in Brazil or Honduras or Europe, usually in some kind of a job, but these expeditions had always proved successful. Rodman, who had been graduated from Dartmouth, spent summer vacations as an oil company worker and as a farmhand in Venezuela before he went into the army for almost two years' service abroad. In 1953, he married Barbara Ann Olsen of Bronxville, N.Y. They have two children. In 1957, Rodman was working as a credit analyst for the American Overseas Finance Company in New York, and taking an active part in local political affairs.

Ann, who attended Brearley School and Wellesley College, went to London in 1953 to spend her vacation as a social worker in the city's most dismal slums, living in a $10-a-week youth hostel. While there she met Robert Laughlin Pierson, a student at the Episcopal Seminary at Nashotah, Wisconsin. He was ordained the next year and the couple was married in 1955. They have three children and live in Evanston, Illinois, where Father Pierson is vice-chairman of Christ the King Foundation, an educational organization.

Steven, whom his father calls "chief," worked on the Rockefeller farm in Venezuela during summer vacation while a student at Princeton prior to his army service. Michael spent a summer as a clerk in a supermarket in Puerto Rico during a vacation from his studies at Harvard, and Mary, while a student at Vassar, worked in a Cornell Navajo Medical Research project in Arizona.

One of Rockefeller's greatest pleasures always had been in taking his family—or as many of them as were available—on trips to the Far West and abroad, particularly to Mexico and South America. Then, in 1956, he decided they ought to know more about the continent of Africa, where there were widespread political unrest and mounting demands for independence from colonial rule. Mrs. Rockefeller and the children industriously read history books, travel books and guide books to prepare for the African trip but Rockefeller merely sent word to numerous friends that he was on the way. En route, Mrs. Rockefeller filled in his scanty background on the various countries they visited, particularly those along the Gold Coast and in the Congo River basin.

"But to father the important thing was what he could see and hear," a member of the family said later. "We went through fourteen countries and I don't think he ever stopped to rest. He wanted to see everything and to talk to everybody from the top government officials to the people working in the fields. He saw factories, churches, art galleries, theaters and farms, all at a terrific pace. He talked to political rebel leaders, merchants and Dr. Albert Schweitzer, to educators and artists and industrialists. And he came away knowing more about those countries—and remembering it—than I could learn in several years. What he really had were strong impressions—visual impressions—that would stick with him and be of use to him later."

The children enjoyed every minute of such trips with their parents, whether they were going to Yellowstone Park or to the Far East, and they were ready to join their father any time he wanted to try something new—like a political campaign.

A political campaign must have been very much in Rockefeller's mind by the late winter of 1958. He had made his own surveys of public sentiment in the state. He had listened to a lot of advice from friends and party leaders, some of whom strongly warned him that it was hopeless to oppose Harriman in that "Democratic year." He clearly saw that the odds were against him but his intuition told him just as clearly that now was the time to move, and he had great confidence in his own intuitive powers.

Sometime that spring—Rockefeller himself probably could not put his finger on the exact date—he decided to become a candidate for the Republican gubernatorial nomination. His closest associates claimed later to believe that he was undecided until late spring, probably in May. He never did announce his decision either to them or to his family, but "it just evolved—there came a day when we knew in our own minds that he was going to do it." Later, Rockefeller himself was inclined to give Hinman credit for getting him into the race but Hinman was no better informed as to his intentions than a dozen others.

For Morhouse, the day of decision came in June when the Republican party held its $100-a-plate dinner in New York. That evening he asked about fifteen leaders from all parts of the state to meet with him the next morning at the Roosevelt Hotel. When they were assembled, Morhouse set up ten charts that illustrated the results of polls and of his own investigations in key areas. He said that the party needed new leadership and that he believed Rockefeller was the man who could best provide it. He referred to Rockefeller's experience in state and federal government jobs, his business background and the initiative he had demonstrated in progressive and forward-looking endeavors such as the Rockefeller Brothers Fund reports.

"Look, gentlemen, I've been in this job for four years," he concluded. "I believe in this man. You can look at these charts and see that he will probably be a more popular candidate than anyone else we can put up. Now you know politics and you know that you've either got to be with the organization or against it. I say that the organization has to go for Rockefeller—and if it doesn't I will step out as state chairman."

Not all of the group was convinced. Some still wondered whether the Rockefeller name was a political liability. But, in the end, all of them decided to go along with Morhouse and the race was on. There was some effort at the time to spread the impression that Rockefeller was being drafted for the job; that a country lawyer named Jud Morhouse had "persuaded" him to get into the contest. No one, however, wheedled him into running. Rockefeller, once he had decided that the time was reasonably good, went after the job in a tough, competitive spirit that made the eyes of veteran politicians pop.

"He is an incredible competitor!" one of his new political friends gasped as he sank into an easy chair after a session in Rockefeller's office. "He's got drive and he's got guts, and anybody who thinks this fellow is a soft, do-good rich boy is crazy. He knows what he's doing."

The Rockefeller boom stirred no enthusiasm in the breasts of rock-ribbed Republicans. The right-wing *National Review* summed up old guard reaction that summer in an article denouncing high-priced publicity ballyhoo behind the boom, charging that Morhouse was circulating "phantom" public opinion polls and contending that Rockefeller was closer to New Deal than to Republican philosophy. New Dealer Harry L. Hopkins, the magazine said, would have

> understood the drive to secure the Republican gubernatorial nomination for Nelson Rockefeller. For he had a taste for what he used to call "tame millionaires." As early as 1934 he collected Averell Harriman, who had grown weary of Wall Street and turned eagerly to Ideology. . . . It is the *New York Herald Tribune* that has provided the chief ballyhoo for the Rockefeller buildup . . . with the result that its news columns have consistently magnified and exaggerated pro-Rockefeller developments. . . . Rockefeller's ties with the Liberal Party in New York are reported to be very close. His wife used to enroll in the Liberal Party . . . because she was "disgusted" with both major parties. . . . Nowhere does Rockefeller speak up for Republican principles of the free, non-statist society. His position seems to be that Republicans can do a superior job of implementing a Democratic philosophy of government.

On June 30th, Rockefeller called a press conference at his office on the fifty-sixth floor of No. 30 Rockefeller Plaza, where reporters gathered in a small modern library graced by the stark bronze bust that William Couper had sculpted of John D. Rockefeller, Sr., in his old age. Richard Amper, a former political reporter on the *New York Times*, had recently joined the Rockefeller organization and was serving as press secretary, and none of the reporters was surprised when Rockefeller said he "would welcome the opportunity of accepting the challenge should the Republican party choose me as its nominee.

"I have reached this decision," he continued, "because of my deep conviction that a new approach to government must be taken in New York State. Government must be given a new energy and efficiency to make it capable of solving the emerging and complicated social and economic problems of our times. . . . What we need is a transfusion of political courage to grasp the opportunities and the ideas of men who have convictions and creative talent and faith in the future. The challenge is to match the aspirations of the sixteen million people of this great state. Any man who accepts it must be mindful of the obligation it imposes."

Rockefeller's first goal, of course, was the rounding up of enough delegates to the Republican state convention to win the nomination. With his son Steven and Malcolm Wilson, he set out on an automobile campaign through the critical districts of the state at a thousand-miles-a-week pace. Morhouse, Hinman and other workers industriously paved the way. The Republican organization was discouraged by national reaction against the Eisenhower administration and had little hope of defeating Harriman. But Rockefeller exuded confidence. He was a new face and crowds responded to him enthusiastically, despite the fact that he was not yet a fluent public speaker. If the odds had been in favor of a Republican victory in November, Rockefeller's path would unquestionably have been rougher. But, without much hope of success, many county leaders were in a mood to try something different. They began lining up behind the new man. By the end of July, Mahoney and Heck were out of the race and on August 7 Len Hall announced that he was withdrawing as a candidate for the nomination.

"I probably couldn't have gotten the nomination," Rockefeller remarked later without convincing anyone that he was right, "if everybody hadn't believed that 1958 was a Democratic year."

On the evening of August 25, ten thousand cheering spectators in the great hall of the War Memorial at Rochester hailed the nomination of Rockefeller. While Mrs. Rockefeller, her five children and one daughter-in-law looked on, the nominee waved his arms in the glare of spotlights and denounced the Harriman administration as "short-sighted, vacillating and indecisive." He said that, if elected, he intended to create a climate for expansion of jobs, industry, business and agriculture, to meet the "challenge" of the state's educational needs, juvenile delinquency, health and welfare problems and the threat of organized crime. "The reason we are going to win," he shouted, "is the dismal record of vacillation and veto of the Harriman administration. The box score of these last four years has been: no hits, no runs—but, oh my! what errors!"

The correspondent of the New York *Herald Tribune* was moved to write that "an unmistakable spirit swept through the hall—the spirit of an army girding for victory." Most other correspondents present described it as a good political show and noted that the wise money was still on Harriman to be re-elected.

IV.

The contest between Harriman and Rockefeller was promptly dubbed "The Multimillionaire Sweepstakes." The tabloid newspapers, without much imagination, fumbled around for nicknames that would fit into headline type. They soon settled for "Rocky vs. Ave." Novelty manufacturers quickly produced a button labeled "Roll with Rock." The campaign attracted national attention from the start because, wrote columnist Marquis Childs, "that old John D.'s grandson should today be the Republican candidate for Governor of New York—and, what is more, a liberal candidate who has a chance to win support of left-of-center and minority groups—is one of the political miracles of our time."

Both Harriman and Rockefeller, however, ran into trouble in

their own ranks before the state conventions, held simultaneously, were ended. There was a political tradition that the two top places on the ticket should be divided between New York City and upstate. Rockefeller defied this rule when Wilson, a resident of Westchester County, was nominated as the lieutenant governor, partly because his conservatism was regarded as a balance for the gubernatorial nominee's liberalism. The most serious Republican problem, however, arose in regard to a nominee for the United States Senate. Tradition again dictated that the choice should be a man of Italian ancestry because there was a political myth that New York City could not be carried without an Italian name high on the ticket. Rockefeller wanted Joseph F. Carlino, a state assemblyman from Nassau County, for the post but the powerful Nassau party leader, J. Russell Sprague, was grooming Carlino as an eventual candidate for Governor and refused to approve, possibly because the prospects for a Republican victory of any kind in New York were so slight. Eventually, and with some difficulty, U.S. Congressman Kenneth B. Keating of Rochester was persuaded to abandon his rather secure seat in order to accept the nomination for senator.

At Buffalo, meantime, the Democratic State Convention had nominated Harriman for re-election and then run into even more trouble than the Republicans. Harriman wanted Thomas K. Finletter as the Democratic candidate for United States senator. So did most of the so-called liberal wing of the party, including former Governor Herbert Lehman and Mrs. Eleanor Roosevelt. But Carmine De Sapio, who had often been labeled the "modern" or "reform" boss of New York City's Tammany Hall, had been campaigning diligently to extend his influence to upstate New York and thus to become recognized as the party leader for the entire state. De Sapio had his own candidate for the senatorial nomination, District Attorney Frank Hogan of New York, and he decided to assert his political power to stop Finletter. He was successful in a long and bitter behind-the-scenes conflict that soon broke into open warfare and brought outspoken condemnation from Lehman, Mrs. Roosevelt and other prominent party liberals. After attempting to resist, Harriman rather apologetically accepted the nomination of Hogan, who had been an outstanding public servant but had no particular qualifications for the Senate, and thus opened the way for charges that he was dominated by Tammany Hall.

Rockefeller lost no time after the convention in getting organized for the campaign. His staff was growing, and most of the newcomers were young and enthusiastic. Dr. Ronan, who had directed the state constitutional convention study, headed the speech-writing staff and Roswell Perkins, having resigned from the HEW in Washington, took over direction of research. R. Burdell Bixby, a law partner of Thomas E. Dewey and an experienced political campaigner, came in to plan speaking schedules, Harry O'Donnell handled state committee publicity and another young lawyer, Charles M. Metzner, who had worked in Dewey campaigns, assumed charge of financial affairs. Rockefeller had never been particularly close to Dewey but the former Governor was consulted on several occasions and later made a statewide television speech in behalf of the ticket. The candidates' television and radio activities were directed by Tom Losee and Sylvester Weaver.

Rockefeller headquarters occupied the seventh floor of the Hotel Roosevelt and was repeatedly described by reporters who visited it as a huge, smoothly organized machine where scores of experts, politicians, speech writers, researchers, television and radio professionals, volunteer workers, secretaries and stenographers went about their business with efficiency and skill and no confusion or wasted effort. Nobody who worked there during the campaign agreed with these descriptions. Rockefeller's ability to keep a dozen balls bouncing at once as well as the amazing physical strength that enabled him to work at least eighteen hours a day kept the back rooms of the headquarters in a purposeful but chaotic kind of turmoil throughout the campaign. As in every campaign, the candidate frequently changed his mind at the last moment, speeches were rewritten an hour before delivery, and emergencies arose every hour on the hour. Over all the turmoil, Jamieson presided in a quiet, unexcited manner as a chief of staff to the nominee, keeping Rockefeller's ideas and objectives dominant in the minds of Morhouse and others who were directing the firing on the political battlefront.

Rockefeller was a demanding, hard-driving nominee, expecting almost as much of others as of himself. He wanted a Citizens-for-Rockefeller Committee established to attract independent voters. Headquarters was set up for the group, with General Lucius Clay as honorary chairman and with Oren Root, Jr., and Mrs. Russell Davenport—the former a veteran of the Willkie campaign—as co-chairmen. About a week later, Rockefeller complained sharply to an aide that he had driven a considerable distance around midtown and had seen only two places where citizens committee banners were flying and campaign literature was being handed out.

"Well, it takes a little time to get started," was the reply.

"We haven't got a little time," the candidate snapped. "I want to see those citizens signs all over town. Everywhere you go."

A week later the citizens committee had manned twenty vacant stores and plastered the store fronts with Rockefeller pictures and bunting, and more were being opened. A lot of Republican party workers accustomed to a leisurely pace suddenly discovered they were going at a rapid clip and not enjoying much sleep, but they also felt they were getting somewhere.

Rockefeller's board of strategy, meeting daily for luncheon at the Roosevelt Hotel headquarters, munched sandwiches and apple pie and agreed that the main problem was to take and hold the initiative in the campaign. Jamieson had no difficulty in seeing the most inviting target in Harriman's defenses—the hole opened by DeSapio's rough rejection of the liberal wing of the Democratic party in order to nominate Hogan. There was, however, considerable reluctance on the part of some Republican professionals to exploit the opening by attacking DeSapio and Tammany Hall.

"The only way Rockefeller can win," they argued, "is to cut into Harriman's support in New York City. The biggest bloc of voters in the city is of Italian descent. DeSapio is of Italian descent. Furthermore, we don't have a single Italian name in a top spot on the Republican ticket. If we attack DeSapio, we will alienate the Italian vote and we're sunk."

Neither Jamieson nor Rockefeller was impressed by this argument. Jamieson took the general position that Rockefeller had to be himself in the campaign and that he was not going to be hampered by political myths about voting blocs. The Republicans needed the support of independent and liberal voters to win and these voters were angry at De Sapio. Rockefeller, with the help of Rod Perkins' research staff, came up with an effective way to keep them from forgetting that they were angry. In a speech that was frequently repeated throughout the campaign, the Republican nominee recalled the 1924 Democratic state convention at which Tammany Hall attempted to force Governor Alfred E. Smith to accept its candidate for the United States Senate. Smith refused and, when the pressure was turned on, he retired to his hotel room and said he would renounce the gubernatorial nomination if the convention accepted the Tammany candidate. He stayed in his room for three days—until Tammany gave up. Rockefeller then compared the performance of Smith, a hero of New York liberals, to that of Harriman and charged that the latter didn't have the courage to buck Tammany corruption. In the draft of the original speech, Rockefeller stuck out the word "courage" and substituted the word "guts" but he reluctantly changed back to "courage" when some advisors suggested that he was getting too tough.

From the charge of Tammany domination, it was only a short step to the corrupt past history of Tammany Hall and to the so-called 1957 Apalachin crime convention—an assembly of sixty-three top-drawer gangsters from all over the country and from Cuba at the country home of a well-known racketeer in upstate New York. The convention, believed to have been called to divide up racketeering territory, was broken up almost by accident by alert state troopers, who arrested most of the participants but were unable to prove much against them except some long criminal records. How, Rockefeller asked, could racketeering be suppressed if the state administration was going to "knuckle under" to Tammany Hall? This line of attack may have been short on logic but it was effective. Harriman never really recovered the initiative. Then he made the error of attempting to campaign against the Eisenhower administration and tried, in vain, to force Rockefeller to defend the national Republican record. Rockefeller kept hammering away at charges that businesses—and jobs—were fleeing New York State, that educational facilities were neglected, that middle-income housing needs were ignored and that health and welfare laws could be improved.

But the real key to the campaign was Rockefeller himself. Having discovered that the candidate projected both charm and sincerity to an audience, the board of strategy pointed out that his biggest handicap was that the people of the state didn't know him. They brought in one of Madison Avenue's best-known advertising firms to direct a television and radio campaign that would give him "maximum exposure" to the people, and they recommended that he visit as many as possible of the state's sixty-two counties.

"Only sixty-two counties?" Rockefeller replied. "I'll visit all of them."

He did visit all of them—flying by seaplane into the last one, remote Hamilton County, near the end of the campaign. He traveled more than 8,000 miles and made 135 formal speeches in 103 communities. He made so many impromptu speeches and shook so many hands that nobody even tried to keep count. No farmer working his fields, no factory worker eating his lunch, no housewife doing the marketing was safe from the rumpled, smiling, bare-headed man who stuck out his hand and said: "I'm Nelson Rockefeller and I'm running for Governor." On street corners and in halls, the people gathered to see and hear a live Rockefeller in search of a job. "It's curiosity," the experienced politicians said. "It won't last." But it not only lasted, it gathered momentum. People came to see a Rockefeller and stayed to be convinced. The newspaper reporters got tired of quoting anonymous housewives as saying that "he's as easy to talk to as an old neighbor—and so sincere!" and the newspaper readers got tired of reading it. But it wasn't long before the political experts were saying they hadn't seen anything like it since Franklin Delano Roosevelt was Governor.

"Nelson does not just have a flair for politics," an old and loyal friend said. "He wants to make people understand he's interested in them. His mother had the same way of reaching out to people, of seeing the best in them and making them feel a kind of dignity. Nelson's been doing that all his life."

In addition, the nominee's family turned out to be good campaigners. Mrs. Rockefeller went with him almost everywhere and often they were accompanied by one or more of the children, who shouted encouragement when their father took a practice turn on the pitcher's mound at a Rochester Red Wings baseball game or donned a silk cap and drove a racing sulky down the track at a county fair or posed with a freshman beanie on his head at a college campus. Mrs. Rockefeller tried to keep the family's private affairs separate from her husband's political career. She could be tart and blunt when she thought reporters were too inquisitive and once when she was being questioned about her political background and was asked if she had ever been in Albany, she snapped: "No, I haven't—have you?"

But, because a political career "is what Nelson wants," she shook hands with enthusiasm up and down the state. She rose at dawn and was on the go all day and started out at dawn the next day and was amused and pleased one weary afternoon when a woman approached her in a crowd and said: "I thought I ought to tell you, Mrs. Rockefeller, that your stockings don't match!" She began, too, to appreciate the art of politics at the grass roots and to understand the tremendous effort her husband put into the campaign.

Rockefeller's stamina was a remarkable factor. His voice sometimes faded to a whisper in his office but when he got before a crowd he could speak up strongly. As his speaking improved, his confidence mounted and he repeatedly complained to his speech-writing staff that they were giving him "stuff that doesn't sound like me." Toward the end, he threw away the speeches and spoke from notes except on a few occasions. He was accompanied almost everywhere by his own motion picture cameraman and sound man, and short movie reels were made for distribution free to twenty-three television stations for use, if desired, on their news programs. Needless to say, such films always showed Rockefeller in a favorable light. "The secret ingredient of this campaign," one reporter cracked after touring with both candidates, "is money."

In the final drive down the home stretch, upstate polls showed that Rockefeller was doing well. He then concentrated on the New York City area, where the Democrats normally piled up a huge majority. His tactics were the same, and he shook hands along Seventh Avenue as vigorously as he had on Main Street. Plunging into the East Side slums, he made the grave error of remarking that he had never been there before but he ate blintzes and Italian sausage by the bucketful in delicatessen stores and lunchrooms and exuded good will. His appearance in a crowd of 300,000 at famous Coney Island beach touched off a friendly but intense mob scene that wrecked concessionaires' booths along the boardwalk. In the suburbs, he talked about the need for better school facilities, gobbled picnic lunches and signed autographs for children who, on one occasion, rushed him with such wild enthusiasm that he had to climb atop an automobile to escape being crushed. And he stayed there for half an hour writing his name on pieces of paper thrust up by youngsters. In Harlem, he appeared on a street platform with Count Basie's band and joined in the roar of laughter when the band leader shouted that "this man Rocky got so much money he could air-condition a cotton patch."

But it was in New York's Spanish-speaking districts, overcrowded with Puerto Ricans worried about rent control and welfare benefits, that Rockefeller received his most spectacular publicity. Thousands of persons jammed the streets to hear him speak at an outdoor "block party," cheered when he addressed them in Spanish and, finally, broke through police lines to lift him on their shoulders and carry him away with a big straw sombrero jammed on his head. It was a Rockefeller performance that would have seemed incredible to John D. Rockefeller, Sr., and one that, except for the publicity, didn't do the oil magnate's grandson much good. Of the 700,000 Puerto Ricans in New York City, comparatively few bothered to cast a ballot on election day.

Near the end of the campaign there were a couple of developments that attracted attention without having much bearing on the outcome. Vice President Nixon had taken charge of the Republican national campaign and made a series of bitter attacks on the Democratic party as he traveled around the country in an effort to rally despondent Republican forces. Nixon understood that it was politically wise for Rockefeller to avoid national issues in his campaign because he was trying to attract independent and Democratic votes. The Vice President had said he would cooperate and either come into the state or not come in as Rockefeller might desire. In October, when Rockefeller's chances of winning were increased, the New York situation apparently looked more inviting to the Washington strategists and, without consulting Rockefeller, Nixon decided to visit New York, ostensibly to help Keating and other congressional candidates. A date for him to deliver a television speech in New York City was arranged by the Republican State Committee, and various newspapers, aware of Rockefeller's attitude, began speculating on whether the two would meet.

Rockefeller was on a speaking tour upstate in his private plane when the Vice President arrived in the city and went to a hotel. Morhouse went around to pay his respects and found Nixon was working on his speech and somewhat miffed. Rockefeller was due back in the city late that afternoon but a storm blew up, delaying air travel, and it looked as if he might not return until the next day. Some of his advisors were hoping he would be delayed but the weather improved and his plane landed at Newark airport about seven o'clock in the evening. Rockefeller immediately telephoned Jamieson.

"What's the situation, Frankie?" he asked.

"Well, everybody's in a stew about what you're going to do in regard to Nixon," Jamieson replied. "I've been getting advice all day, half of it in favor of avoiding him if you want to get the independent vote in the city and the other half warning that the upstate Republicans will stay home on election day if you don't see him. Everybody seems to have a different idea."

"Oh, to hell with that," Rockefeller replied with the air of a man who makes his own decisions. There was a short silence on the wire.

Then he added: "He's the Vice President and he's here and he's going to speak and the only decent thing is to go see him. I'll telephone him right away."

He telephoned Nixon's hotel, only to be informed that the Vice President was working on his speech and couldn't talk to him. This gesture of irritation did nothing to change Rockefeller's plans. He said he would call again and, later, made a date to see Nixon the next morning. The Vice President's speech was an appeal for support of the Republican candidates, including a graceful reference to Rockefeller and the state ticket, without any remarks to which Democrats could take exception. Nixon poured a cup of coffee for Rockefeller the next morning at breakfast in his hotel. Both men smiled for the photographers and avoided any significant remarks.

The second last-minute development in the campaign came on the afternoon before election day when the final edition of the New York *Post* ran a front-page editorial signed by its publisher, Mrs. Dorothy Schiff. The *Post* had been a strong Harriman supporter throughout the campaign, although a weekly column written by Mrs. Schiff had frequently spoken favorably of Rockefeller. Then, in the final days, De Sapio seemed to sense defeat and attempted rather desperately to regain the initiative by launching a series of charges against Rockefeller. One of these concerned the activities of United States oil companies in Arab countries of the Middle East and purported to show that the Rockefellers were anti-Semitic. At that point, Mrs. Schiff abandoned Harriman and wrote an editorial urging the election of Rockefeller. The surprising last-minute shift was too late to have any real influence on the election but it left little doubt as to the outcome.

The outcome on election night was a resounding defeat for the Republican party across the nation but a victory by 557,000 votes for Rockefeller and election for Keating and all but one of his Republican running mates in New York State. About ten o'clock, with a happy crowd of party workers shouting for him in the Roosevelt Hotel ballroom, Rockefeller waited patiently until he received a telegram of congratulation from Harriman. Then he thanked the assembled party leaders, walked into his private office with the air of a man who had known it all the time and silently shook hands with Jamieson. A little later, behind a spearhead of police, he struggled through the roaring crowd in the ballroom, followed by Mrs. Rockefeller and the children, who were able to reach the platform only by joining hands and pulling each other along in Indian file.

About ten-thirty o'clock on New Year's Eve, 1958, the Governor-elect took the oath of office in the executive mansion at Albany with his hand on his Grandmother Rockefeller's Bible. The evening swearing-in is customary in New York because the retiring Governor's term expires at midnight. The next day Rockefeller broke his first precedent by doing away with the traditional top hat and frock coat inaugural costume in favor of a business suit when he was sworn for a second time at formal ceremonies in the assembly chamber of the state capitol.

"As this sixth decade of our twentieth century nears its end," Governor Rockefeller said in his inaugural address, "we are nearing, too, what could be the fatal testing time for free men—and freedom itself —everywhere. . . .

> . . . we see the world divided, the weapons of war perfected to deadly extremes and humanity seeming at times about to turn and prey upon itself. . . . The world . . . is divided, essentially, between those who believe in the brotherhood of men under the fatherhood of God—and those who scorn this as a pious myth.
>
> It is divided between those who believe in the dignity of free men—and those who believe in the monstrous supremacy of the totalitarian state.
>
> It is divided between those whose most potent force is their faith in individual freedom—and those whose faith is force itself.
>
> It is divided between those who believe in the essential equality of peoples of all nations and races and creeds—and those whose only creed is their own ruthless race for power.
>
> This division of the world—and this time of decision—leave no corner of the earth, no fraction of humanity, untouched. From this basic struggle, there can be no refuge nor escape . . . every

citizen in each community—all face a common challenge and share a common cause.

The graveness of the challenge is matched by the greatness of our opportunity to serve this common cause. Knowing this, we have no reason to fear—but every reason to strive.

For the spiritual resources of free men are unique, and the strength of free men is unsurpassed if united in common purpose. . . . For the first time in history, the revolution of science and industry makes possible the realization of man's ageless dream of individual opportunity and well-being. The commonwealth of humanity at large can be served now as never before in the story of man. Disease can be conquered. The hungry can be fed. The homeless can find shelter. . . . Through these means we can serve . . . the true end of freedom; not merely checking menace and peril to free peoples but assuring to free men of all nations the chance to nourish their spirit, enrich their mind, each to live a life of promise true to his chosen destiny. . . .

Let us unite in common cause with hope and faith and love, with vision and courage. Together we can thus work toward the goal of freedom of opportunity for men everywhere in a world of peace.

Some newspapers noted editorially the next morning that the speech sounded a bit more like the inaugural address of a President than of a state Governor. And it is quite possible Rockefeller intended it that way.

# SEVENTEEN

# The Governor

Governor and Mrs. Rockefeller moved into the ninety-nine-year-old executive mansion at Albany in the middle of the afternoon of the last day of 1958, a few hours before they were to entertain political and family friends at dinner. Mrs. Rockefeller supervised the unloading of trunks, and saw that preparations were in progress for the evening. Her husband began hanging favorites from his collection of modern paintings on the walls of the nondescript mansion that was first occupied by a Governor—Samuel J. Tilden—in 1874. The paintings should have looked out of place in the old house but Rockefeller has a good eye for space and color and a feeling for design. Walking along Fifth Avenue one day, he noticed that one of the trees planted at Rockefeller Center was slightly out of line with others. When he suggested that it be moved into line, the center's engineers insisted that he was mistaken because they had measured with the accuracy of surveyors when the trees were planted. Nevertheless, they received orders to measure again and the recheck disclosed that one tree was

332

about five inches out of line. Rockefeller has a passion for orderliness in such matters. Books on the table in his study must be perfectly aligned. A small primitive carving on his desk must be placed exactly so. He will get up from a conference table to adjust a picture that is a quarter inch awry on the wall of his office—or, for that matter, in any office he happens to be in. In the Governor's mansion, the hanging of modern paintings demanded a good deal of ingenuity but Rockefeller managed to achieve a reasonably harmonious effect. He was still in shirt sleeves, hanging the last paintings, when the first dinner guests arrived.

The town of Albany, as well as the executive mansion, is reminiscent of Victorian America and it has long been accustomed to strong personalities in the Governor's office. Since the time of President Tilden's tenancy, Grover Cleveland, Theodore Roosevelt and Franklin D. Roosevelt had gone on to the White House and several others, including Alfred E. Smith and Thomas E. Dewey, had been contenders for the presidency. Yet the man who took office on the first day of 1959 didn't fit into any pattern established by his predecessors. On the street, Rockefeller was a slightly rumpled figure in a shapeless hat, yet there was about him an aura of great wealth and he had just flown back from a vacation on his huge ranch in the far-away mountains of Venezuela. He was as easy to talk to as an old friend, yet he filled his home with strange, inexplicable paintings by artists named Miró and Picasso and Léger and Shahn. He presided over—and paid for—the biggest and fanciest inaugural ball of the century, but at other times he seemed to have the most fun when he invited everybody in his office to the executive mansion, lent a hand at rolling up the rugs and led the dancing to a Cab Calloway jazz band recording on a two-speaker high fidelity set. People didn't find it easy to think of him as a politician, but even before he reached Albany he was being hailed in newspapers across the country as a rare survivor of Republican disaster at the polls and as a potential nominee for the presidency.

Mrs. Rockefeller, too, lent a different touch to life in the executive mansion. She now had a handsome streak of gray in her brown hair—

"the *gray* is natural," she once retorted to an inquisitive reporter. She was expert at cultivation of exotic flowers. She supervised relandscaping of the mansion's grounds and the building of a garden for outdoor entertainment. She presided gracefully and efficiently over official functions, and she coped with the threats of an excellent but temperamental chef to quit on the spot when the Governor arrived for luncheon with fourteen guests instead of the expected three. She participated in an endless round of Republican women's meetings with a kind of no-nonsense-let's-get-things-done air that pleased most of her co-workers. She discovered that politicians were people and often admirable people when you got to know them. At an office party, she demonstrated how the Charleston was danced in the 1920's. She didn't develop any great enthusiasm for newspaper reporters but she cooperated with them and, because she is five feet, ten and one-half inches tall, she once kicked off her high heels in order not to tower over a group of women reporters with whom she posed at the mansion. She later regretted it when she saw the picture in the newspapers because the photographers ignored the group and snapped the Governor's lady in her stocking feet.

In the huge granite state capitol on a hillside overlooking Albany's business section and the Hudson River valley, Rockefeller showed himself to be little concerned with tradition and precedent. Joseph Zaretzki, Democratic leader of the Senate, gaped in surprise when the Governor barged into his office to talk over a legislative problem. House Speaker Oswald D. Heck was pleased when Rockefeller insisted on coming to his office for Republican conferences because the Speaker was still feeling the effect of an illness. The Governor listened attentively to the experienced Republican leaders, most of them conservatives, but after Heck died he was content to see Joseph Carlino, a youthful liberal Republican from Long Island, elected to the Speaker's job. "Rockefeller was smart from the beginning in the way he handled the Democratic leaders as well as the Republicans," one Democratic senator from an upstate city commented. "He conferred with them and he kept them informed in regard to his general plans. They'll fight him publicly, of course, but privately they acknowledge respect for him and think he's a pretty good fellow. So do I, although I usually vote against him."

Once the Governor broke precedent by quietly taking a seat in the Senate gallery during debate on a bill in which he was particularly interested. And any day the Legislature was in session he was likely to be seen surrounded by a dozen visiting schoolchildren in the corridors or trotting down the capitol's famous "million dollar" staircase because he didn't have time to wait for an elevator or talking earnestly with an assemblyman whose arm was caught in the Governor's friendly but firm grip.

Rockefeller has a small office but he also often uses the imposing executive chamber, a room sixty feet by forty feet on the southeast corner of the second floor. The walls of the chamber are wainscoted to a height of sixteen feet with red mahogany, surmounted by a carved molding, and the ceiling is covered with Spanish leather. There is a big, carved stone and oak fireplace on one wall. In recent years, the chamber had been used primarily for public ceremonies and hearings. Rockefeller moved six portraits from an outside corridor into the chamber, including those of Hamilton Fish, General Lafayette, Governor Theodore Roosevelt, President Martin Van Buren, Chief Justice Charles Evans Hughes and the first Governor, George Clinton. Visitors at first tried to read some significance into the portraits he hung in the chamber, only to discover that his choices were based solely on the ground that they were the better paintings.

As Governor, Rockefeller continued to save time by eating at his desk and continued to be entirely indifferent to what he ate, which was usually a sandwich from a nearby lunchroom. "He never says he wants any particular kind of sandwich," his secretary, Ilene Slater, once remarked, "and he occasionally gets some odd ones. But, except for one occasion, I never heard him complain or say not to bring that kind again." Rockefeller spends most of his time in Albany during legislative sessions but during the remainder of the year he commutes in his private plane to New York, usually accompanied by key members of his executive staff. He established new offices in a converted private house on Fifty-fifth Street after becoming Governor and seldom went to his Rockefeller Center office, which he left in charge of his efficient personal secretary, Louise Boyer.

"There are obviously certain advantages to having a lot of money when you're Governor," a newspaperman remarked wryly not long after Rockefeller took over at Albany. "The Governor was supposed to go to New York last night to have dinner with a dozen friends but at the last minute he couldn't get away. So, did he cancel the dinner date? Of course not. He sent his plane to New York, picked up his guests, flew them to Albany for dinner and flew them home again before midnight."

The newspaperman might have added that there also are some disadvantages. Just before moving to Albany, Rockefeller bought a new limousine, a handsome black number with much special equipment, including an air-conditioning unit. He was pleased with the new automobile and, exercising the inalienable right of a state's chief executive, he instructed his driver to have the No. 1 license plates put on the vehicle. A little later the driver showed up with a red face.

"Sorry, Governor," he said, "but the Motor Vehicle Bureau tells me the No. 1 license plates can't be put on private cars. The law says they have to go on a state-owned car. You can have them for your official automobile."

For a man with only a moderate fortune, that probably would have ended the matter. But Rockefeller didn't want the No. 1 plates on his official car; he wanted them on his new limousine. He thought the problem over and, with a sigh, decided to give his new limousine to the state for use by the Governor.

Sometimes having a lot of money is expensive.

II.

Rockefeller wasted no time in taking command. His aggressiveness, his ability to look ahead and his willingness to face up to big and difficult problems demonstrated an eagerness to lead from the day he took office. Veteran party leaders in the Legislature who expected to influence and guide him discovered that he welcomed their advice and that he made up his own mind. Die-hard political foes discovered that there were many areas in which he preferred to cooperate but that, in a showdown, he had a professional grasp of political maneuvering and in-fighting. "His tools," one political correspondent noted, "were patience and persuasion. He didn't twist arms, he patted them." He recognized the necessity of meeting political patronage problems, but in major affairs affecting the state he frequently ignored partisanship and the protests of Republican leaders in order to appoint the best-qualified man. By the end of the first month of his tenure, nobody in Albany had any doubt who was running the state or who was leader of the Republican party in New York.

Just where he was leading the party was another matter. "Rockefeller is a new type of politician, as yet undefinable," wrote one newspaper correspondent.

> He does not fit into any bracket. He insists that labels are meaningless as far as his approach to his job is concerned. Such terms as liberal and conservative, right and left, annoy him deeply. . . . They are out of date and have no application to present day problems, he says with feeling. He seems to be one politician who is genuinely uninhibited by any kind of dogma, Republican or Democratic.

Other political correspondents suggested that Rockefeller's leadership was modifying the traditional attitude of the Republican party in the state. The *New York Times* said there was

> a growing realization among Republican leaders upstate that fashions in politics are changing. . . . The election results are convincing some local leaders that they need Mr. Rockefeller's help in retaining control of their county and town administrations far more than he needs theirs for his legislative program.

Rockefeller's program was big. He set out to achieve the most thorough overhaul and modernization of state government since the days of Alfred E. Smith. He proposed to raise taxes to make up for a prospective budgetary deficit. In line with his rather extravagant campaign promises, he proposed action to revitalize the state's economy, to increase agricultural research, to create an Office of Transportation to attack the New York commuter transportation crisis, to expand educational facilities, to strengthen civil rights procedures, to improve social insurance programs, to transfer pension rights of workers who change jobs, to help safeguard union funds from abuse, to improve basic health insurance coverage for retired persons and for unemployed persons, to mobilize "all the forces of our communities" to reduce juvenile delinquency and to stimulate "a major flow of private capital in the field of middle-income housing in urban areas."

Some of these proposals were a continuation or expansion of programs initiated by the Harriman administration, and others, admittedly, were not likely to be carried out in the immediate future. Yet, there was much in the program that was new and dynamic, representing goals toward which Rockefeller intended to work. Furthermore, progress was made before the Legislature adjourned. For example, the Legislature:

> Enacted a labor law regulating the fiduciary status of union officials in the use of union funds and putting curbs on conflicts of interest in their financial and business transactions. The bill made union leaders legally responsible for the funds they administer and required unions and employer associations to file annual financial reports to help safeguard union funds and eliminate financial abuses.

> Enacted legislation providing for a "tapering-off" of extended unemployment insurance benefits so that recipients would not have benefits cut off, irrespective of federal action.

> Enacted legislation for building up of a revolving fund from which workmen's compensation awards can be paid promptly even if the employer has failed to carry workmen's compensation insurance and has failed to make payments to the fund.

> Established statutory basis for studies by Industrial Commissioner of the impact of automation on employment and the need for retraining programs.

> Provided tax relief for railroads and made it possible to purchase

That daring young man must have New Yorkers dizzy on their flying trapeze!"

Rockefeller's biggest and most difficult and most significant achievement in his first year as Governor, however, was none of these things. It was his politically daring move to put the state's fiscal house in order by a tax boost of $272,000,000 to pay for improved state services. For a while, it looked as if his political balloon was going to collapse before it got off the ground.

III.

There is a familiar saying that it is impossible or at least very difficult to be a bad Governor of New York because Alfred E. Smith, in the 1920's, put through a reform program that, among other things, made a balanced budget mandatory. Rockefeller charged in his campaign speeches, however, that the state had been living beyond its income in recent years because it had been borrowing and tapping accumulated reserves to pay for social services, highways, aid to education and similar items that were both required and desirable in modern society. As a result, when he took office he declared that, with the state reserves down to $47,000,000, the government faced a $700,000,000 deficit and "the most serious fiscal problem in more than a generation."

The last Harriman administration budget was $1,800,000,000. By the time Rockefeller had totaled up his first budget, including almost $200,000,000 of additional mandatory or obligatory spending, he proposed to expend a total of $2,041,000,000, an increase of about $240,000,000 and $424,000,000 more than expected revenues. This was bad news on the political front but Rockefeller had before him the disastrous examples of other states that had failed to maintain fiscal order and he had no intention of evading the issue. He announced that he expected to put the state on a pay-as-you-go basis as soon as possible. Meantime, he proposed to meet the 1960 budget figure by borrowing $100,000,000, by using $47,000,000 left in the reserves and by calling on the Legislature to approve a whopping tax increase of $277,000,000. A little later, he added a proposal for a withholding tax system of collection. He also ordered a drive for maximum economy and efficiency in all departments of the government.

The cries of protest against the tax program started immediately and swelled to a state-wide chorus as details of the increase became known. More than two thousand letters and telegrams a week, virtually all of them protesting any tax increase, were received at the Governor's office. Democratic legislators and politicians led the verbal assault, concentrating on the Governor's proposal to lower state income tax exemptions from $2,500 per couple to $600 per individual. "It's a soak-the-poor plan," they charged. "Rockefeller is a rich man and he has no conception of what a difference the increased tax will mean in the food and clothing budget of a working man's family." At one public appearance in New York City, the Governor was greeted by a chorus of boos. He took it with a grim smile and remarked that he didn't "expect anybody to dance in the streets because they have to pay more taxes." To a group of indignant Republican politicians in an upstate city, he said: "I know how you feel. Somebody said my grandfather spent the last years of his life giving away dimes—and here I am trying to get them back again, all at once." Everybody laughed but it was uneasy laughter.

It was no joking matter with Rockefeller. He was in favor of the services the state was providing; in fact, he hoped to expand them. But he saw no point in closing his eyes to the fact that they had to be paid for. The Governor argued that the tax increase was evenly distributed among poor and rich, and his charts showed that actually the percentage increase would be very slightly greater for taxpayers with incomes over $6,000 annually. But this was far from enough to offset the protests which created alarm among a pivotal group of Republican legislators. Another factor also was bothering the Republican legislative leaders. They did not want to create a public impression that they were prepared to rubber-stamp whatever program the Governor proposed. As a result, the majority leader, Senator

Mahoney, undertook to make some compromise adjustments that reduced budget expenditures by $35,000,000 and slightly reduced the tax boost for married couples. A small group of Republicans under pressure from their home areas organized a "revolt" against the tax increase and claimed they had enough votes to block it.

Rockefeller did not want to crack down in order to get his program passed. When some of his advisors became alarmed, he went on television to explain the tax increases and to argue for them. He called the tax rebels to his office but instead of swinging a whip he urged upon them the wisdom of fiscal solvency. He gave a little, unimportant ground but, when the going was roughest, he became increasingly firm against compromise. One day when the newspaper headlines said the tax bill was in danger of defeat, he stalked into his office with a grim expression on his face and said to a friend: "This bill may be poor politics but it's good government and I'm going to get it through come hell or high water." Softly but firmly, he began putting on the pressure. On the evening of March 9, with newspapers predicting a close vote, he cleared off his desk, shrugged his broad shoulders into a wrinkled topcoat, perched an old hat on his head and walked through the adjacent office of Press Secretary Richard Amper on his way home. Amper and several reporters were discussing the bill's prospects, and they were not optimistic. For a moment, they didn't notice the Governor, who might well have been mistaken by a stranger for another but less distinguished-looking newspaperman. Then everybody turned to him.

"Don't worry, fellows," he said. "It's in the bag."

He went on out the door. "At least," one reporter commented, "you can't ever say he lacks confidence."

The next day, the Republican leadership conferred with the rebels for two hours. The tax bill was reported out of committee and on March 11 the measure, very slightly modified, passed the Senate by a vote of 31 to 25 and the Assembly by a vote of 78 to 69, just two votes more than the required majority. All of the Democratic legislators voted against the bill.

"He's tough, this Rockefeller," a Democratic assemblyman muttered to a reporter as the session recessed. "He knows how to get what he wants."

Whether Rockefeller got what he really wanted remained to be seen. He certainly failed, despite his detailed statements and television speeches, to get across to the voters his contention that the tax boost was vital to their own interests. His popularity with the general public plummeted downward in alarming fashion in the following weeks. On the other hand, his national prestige did not suffer and, in certain ways, it increased. He had demonstrated that he was a strong leader in control of a difficult political situation. He had gotten his most unpopular task out of the way in a hurry, the state's finances were in good shape for the remainder of his term and there would be time, perhaps, for the voters to forget.

"Rockefeller demonstrated a political grasp to match any professional," wrote James Desmond, political correspondent of the New York *Daily News.* "He . . . exhibited . . . audacity in his proposals, toughness in sticking by the main objectives, resilience in giving a little here or there to achieve the over-all goal and, of course, patience in waiting out recalcitrants." The chief correspondent of the Gannett newspapers, Emmett N. O'Brien, added that the victory "establishes him as a real leader of his party, a man 'who can get things done,' and . . . an administrator who is unafraid to tackle the tough problems of government." Rockefeller, commented the *New York Times,* "succeeded in this momentous test of leadership. . . . He thus set a standard for fiscal courage . . . at a time when deficit financing and deferred reckoning have become so habitual as to be accepted as orthodox government."

> Eyed in the most favorable light, the Rockefeller administration is seen as bold in advocating an unpopular rise in taxes, effective in welding together dissident sections of the GOP majority, and responsible in fostering legislation which fulfills campaign promises [R. Stafford Derby wrote in the *Christian Science Monitor*]. This was a major exhibition of leadership. It was so accepted outside the confines of the state. Plaudits from other areas where governors

had failed to show such courage and state finances were in very bad shape received notice in local and syndicated news stories.

Although these comments generally indicated the tenor of reaction to Rockefeller's first legislative session, there were exceptions. The Democrats had no intention of letting the voters forget that the Governor had "unnecessarily" saddled them with new taxes and they bore down on the charge that he had soaked the poor and favored special interests, such as banks and stockbrokers, in connection with special taxing powers granted to New York City. There was a plaintive note of criticism, too, from a source that seldom found itself in the same political corner as the Democrats in New York City. The legislative representative of the Real Estate Board of New York, Inc., wrote in the organization's weekly publication that

> despite the fact that [Rockefeller] has interests in a realty company which owns $150,000,000 worth of improved property in Manhattan, the Governor . . . has shown no concern with the problems of the real estate industry. His pledges all through the state campaign last year indicated sympathy for every state undertaking which would add to realty's burden. With the Governor determined to keep these pledges, there was little chance of fending off the inevitable attacks on property during the recent [legislative] session.

Relaying this "unconscious tribute to Rockefeller. the property owner" to its readers, the New York Times commented: "It looks as though the Governor has lost the landlord vote.

### IV.

In the spring of 1959 the fortunes of the Republican party were at a new low outside of New York State. A poll of Republican party members showed that 44 per cent believed a Democrat would be elected President in 1960 and another 13 per cent were uncertain. Vice-President Nixon, who had presided over the 1958 election catastrophe, was still urging the party to get up off the floor and fight. He had secured a strong grip on the party machinery and was generally conceded to be all but certain of the presidential nomination in 1960. There was, to be sure, talk about Nelson Rockefeller. The liberal wing of the Republican party, which had little enthusiasm for Nixon, watched the New York Governor with increasing interest. Others emphasized the fact that any Republican presidential nominee had to capture a heavy Democratic vote to win and, because of his battering attacks on the opposition, it seemed unlikely Nixon could raid the majority party as Rockefeller had done in New York. On the other hand, Nixon was known everywhere as a result of numerous campaigns across the country whereas Rockefeller was little known to the people outside of a few Eastern states. In April, a group of young Republican business and professional men formed a "California-for-Rockefeller" organization in Nixon's home state without causing any alarm among party professionals. In June, Nixon was estimated by professional pollsters to be the choice of 63 per cent of Republicans and Rockefeller of only 20 per cent.

The summer brought further gains for the Vice President, particularly in connection with his visit to Russia, where he opened the United States exhibition at Moscow. Soviet Premier Nikita Khrushchev at that time was vigorously pressing his campaign to soften the cold war, to promote a state of "peaceful coexistence" with the Western democracies and to bring together the heads of the Big Four powers in another "meeting at the Summit." He had also, presumably as part of his maneuvering toward these goals, threatened to create a grave international crisis by unilaterally breaking up joint Big Four control of the city of Berlin. In these circumstances, Nixon's Russian visit attracted world-wide attention, particularly when he favored a visit by Khrushchev to the United States. Nixon also engaged in an ideological debate with Khrushchev at the public opening of the United States exhibition. What, if anything, the debate proved was less important in the public mind than Nixon's blunt manner in confronting the Russian dictator with the advantages of the American way of life. The Vice President's visit was a political triumph that increased his prestige at home.

Throughout the first half of 1959, Rockefeller tended to his business as Governor of New York. He had developed a friendly and often witty manner of turning aside the questions of reporters in regard to his presidential ambitions. As such questions became more frequent, Press Secretary Amper placed on his own desk a huge campaign button on which was inscribed: "As he said, my interest is in doing a good job for New York." This did nothing to stop the questions. Reporters had learned that the Governor had a weakness for off-the-cuff conversation. He wanted to keep them informed of what was going on in his administration. "He's candid with us," one Albany correspondent commented. "He likes to 'level' with us and we don't get many no-comment answers." Rockefeller's press advisors often thought he was far too candid because his ready answers created political problems that might easily have been avoided. Once, before a press conference on an important state issue, they strongly impressed on him that he must not reveal that he intended to take a certain action. The conference went off smoothly, the reporters got their story and Rockefeller did not say anything about his intended action. Then he and an aide flew to another city for a political meeting. As they got off the plane, a local reporter greeted the Governor and asked:

"Are you going to take such-and-such action?"

"Yes, I am," Rockefeller replied, while the aide shuddered.

When the reporter had gone, the press secretary asked: "Why didn't you say you had no comment? Why did you tell him 'yes'?"

"Well," the Governor replied, "he asked a question, didn't he?"

In regard to the presidential campaign of 1960, Rockefeller managed for a long time to avoid any definite statements but he did nothing to discourage newspaper comment. Political columnist Joseph Alsop wrote that Rockefeller's phenomenal rise

is in fact an essay in modern conservatism. It is a test of the "progressive conservatism" that President Eisenhower used to talk about, before he finally began to see the nation's problem exclusively through the eyeglasses provided by George M. Humphrey. In the most literal sense of the word, it is obviously unconservative to stint the nation's defense in a time of great danger. In the same fashion, it would have been unconservative of Rockefeller to stint New York State's essential services instead of raising taxes . . . it is equally unconservative not to raise the money to meet the bills as they come in.

. . . The Rockefeller [political] problem is simple. After riding very high at the time of his great victory in New York, Governor Rockefeller dropped behind Vice-President Nixon . . . when he presented his program to increase New York state taxes. Still running second, he cannot exploit the "Nixon-can't-win" slogan. If he waits to make his Presidential bid until next year . . . it may be too late.

The political correspondent of the liberal New York *Post*, William V. Shannon, spent three days touring the state with Rockefeller and wrote that

he has established mastery over his Legislature and his party. Although money, ideas and political organization have all played a part, this has not been a triumph of money nor intellectual power nor political skill. It has been singularly a triumph of personality. Nelson Rockefeller personally took the politicians and the voters by storm. He is a winner. . . . Rockefeller clearly has the basic good health, the sure self-confidence, the ready energy and the mental poise which high public office demands. . . . Most [politicians] are too guarded to be witty. Rockefeller, alert yet relaxed, is excellent on the quick comeback. To put the matter simply, he is fun to be with. . . . His cabinet appointees . . . as a group . . . insure him a competent administration. . . . He has established successful personal relations with his legislative leaders, some of whom are old guardsmen who might have caused him much trouble. . . .

. . . but can the Republican party possibly be a vehicle for liberalism? . . . There is little doubt that Rockefeller . . . would make a better conservative President than Eisenhower. The case being made for him, however, goes beyond this. It is argued that Rockefeller would also be a success in liberal terms. . . . The fundamental argument against believing in this conception of a drastically liberalized Republican party headed by a figure like

Rockefeller is that the GOP is a party of business. Conservative businessmen would not permit their party to become for very long the vehicle of liberal programs. . . . To think otherwise is to indulge in romantic sentimentality. Rockefeller may have Franklin Roosevelt's personal charm, but FDR constructed the New Deal on a social and political base that Rockefeller as leader of the business-men's party will not have.

In June, the *New York Times* political writer Leo Egan reported that Morhouse was under heavy pressure to get a presidential campaign started in Rockefeller's behalf but that he was keeping the drive in "low gear." And the following month, Donald Grant of the St. Louis *Post-Dispatch* traveled around with Rockefeller and concluded that he

is no Hamlet, unable to make up his mind; he would like to be President of the United States both because he enjoys politics and because he believes that as President he would be able to accomplish certain things in the general public interest that even a Rockefeller as a private citizen—or as a state governor—cannot accomplish. . . . The volume of mail reaching Rockefeller from all parts of the country is increasing daily—most of it urging him to run for the presidency. . . . The things that concern [Rockefeller] most [are] a life of purpose and meaning and equal opportunities for all Americans, peace in the world and an extension of the community of mankind—"the commonwealth of humanity at large" is Rockefeller's phrase—around the globe. On one occasion . . . he said: "We live in an age that requires bold dreams and great visions, for we have learned that our imagination may be more of a limiting condition than technical problems." . . . Nor does he think the problems that face the nation today can wait. In Nelson Rockefeller's view we already have been drifting too long.

Only a couple of times during the summer, however, did Rockefeller's name figure prominently in the nation's headlines, and on one of those occasions he was in a distinctly secondary role. In August, a Reuter's news dispatch from Soegne, Norway, said that the Governor's second son, Steven, was in town and romancing a pretty, blonde Norwegian girl who had once been a maid in the Rockefeller household in New York. Her name was Anne-Marie Rasmussen, and her father was a retired fish merchant and owner of a small grocery store. The newspapers and news agencies were quickly in full cry after a "Cinderella love story." Rockefeller gave them no assistance, referring all questions to Steven, who was spending most of his time touring the Norwegian countryside with Miss Rasmussen on a tandem motorbike.

Actually, the Rockefellers knew all about Steven's trip to Norway, but they weren't absolutely sure that Miss Rasmussen had said "yes." The Norwegian girl had come to New York in 1956. At that time, she spoke the language poorly and about the only job she could get was as a maid. After she learned to speak more fluently, she got a secretarial job, but by then Steven had fallen in love with her. In 1959, she went home to see her parents and Steven followed her after telling his parents that he hoped to marry Miss Rasmussen. Governor and Mrs. Rockefeller said they were delighted. "I couldn't be happier," Rockefeller said when he and his wife and children arrived for the wedding in the little Norwegian town. There were only 180 guests in the church but 5,000 persons gathered outside to cheer as the couple emerged after the ceremony to face 100 reporters and a battery of motion picture cameras. Mrs. Rockefeller thoroughly disapproved of the hullabaloo stirred up by the press, which she regarded as an unwarranted invasion of the couple's privacy.

Governor Rockefeller's other news-making trip was to Puerto Rico to attend the Governors Conference as chairman of the civil defense committee. The committee's report, however, received less attention than a party Rockefeller threw for all of the governors and their wives at a plush new Puerto Rican golf club resort, built by his brother Laurance, and a press conference at which the Governor's candor outweighed his political judgment. In more than an hour of give-and-take about the 1960 presidential race, he finally made the error of referring to impending public opinion polls as being a factor in deciding what he would do about seeking the Republican nomination. His political advisors were horrified the next day when they read news stories giving the impression that the Governor would decide whether to seek the nomination on the basis of his showing in polls to be taken in November rather than on the basis of a fighting campaign for the job. Rockefeller had to call a special press conference in Albany to get off the hook, pointing out that he had not hesitated to run for Governor when nobody thought he could win and he would not let polls decide what he would do about the presidential nomination.

With the end of the summer, Rockefeller and his board of strategy realized that, while it would be poor politics to announce his candidacy, he had to get busy if he hoped to be in the running in 1960. On September 25, he addressed the annual meeting of Associated Industries of New York State, Inc., reviewing action by his administration to create a more favorable climate for the growth of business, industry and agriculture. But, he added, that he thought

it only fair to point out that every segment of our economy bears a responsibility toward the achievement of our common goal. Therefore, I would like to suggest . . . the role that you in industry can and must play. This role might be called "industry's responsibility to the community," but I prefer to think of it as your role in our common effort to achieve a sustained economic growth. . . . We need your talents and vast experience in government. . . . You and your employees are in a position as individuals and as corporations to participate in every phase of public life. . . . You can encourage your people to take an active part in the local political organizations . . . to run for public office . . . to take appointments in government and on commissions at all levels where their talents are so badly needed. And you can encourage them—and most importantly—by setting the example yourselves in participating in all manner of community activities that are the backbone of citizen participation in our free society.

When Russian Premier Khrushchev made his remarkable visit to the United States in September, both the Soviet and the United

States governments put great emphasis on the necessity for an ac-
commodation that would assure international peace as the only
alternative to world suicide by atomic warfare. Rockefeller had no
official role in the Khrushchev visit except to cooperate with the
State Department's arrangements and to extend a formal welcome
to New York. This he did in a private call on the visitor, but he
also took advantage of the opportunity to give the Communist
dictator some pointed advice on the democratic way of life by reminding him that the people of New York or their ancestors had

> all come here from other lands—many to escape persecution and
> all to find freedom and opportunity. While we are proud of our
> great productive capacity and high standard of living, even though
> much is left to be done, I hope [you] will sense and feel more
> intangible values which are of even greater significance to an un-
> derstanding of America—the values in which we believe as a
> people—freedom and dignity of the individual, equal opportunity
> for all to develop their intellectual, spiritual and cultural capacities
> to the fullest, as well as equal opportunity to meet their material
> needs. . . . These values grew out of our basic spiritual beliefs in
> the brotherhood of man under the fatherhood of God. . . . These
> values, we are convinced, reflect the deepest aspirations of all man-
> kind and we, as a people, are dedicated to their universal realiza-
> tion.

Rockefeller had no reason to doubt that Khrushchev was interested
in promoting a relaxation of international tensions, but he had
serious questions whether the Soviet Union wanted "peaceful coexistence" on any terms except those that would further its goal
of world Communism. On October 8, the theme of the annual
Gold Awards dinner of the New York Board of Trade, Inc., was
"world peace through world trade and world travel." President
Eisenhower sent a message of greeting to the fourteen hundred guests
saying that international understanding through increased trade
and travel would help the people of the world thrive. As the principal speaker at the dinner, Rockefeller was thoroughly in favor
of world trade and world travel but he struck a disharmonious note

by warning against accepting Communist methods of using discriminatory trade practices to further their political strategy.

> The real problem and the real issues . . . [lie] precisely in the highly discriminatory system in accordance with which the Soviet bloc conducts its trade with the rest of the world. . . . On the present basis any increased volume of communist trade will add in direct ratio to their power to disrupt and dominate the world trade by Trojan Horse tactics. The best way to deal with a Trojan Horse is to see that it carries no lethal weapons before it is allowed through the gates.

He charged that the Russians repeatedly used their own economic wealth to "disrupt vulnerable economies" for political purposes. For example, they sent arms to Egypt in exchange for cotton and then dumped the cotton in Egypt's European markets at less than Egyptian prices.

> Even in its present small dimensions [he added], communist bloc trade can cause serious dislocations to free world markets if we allow it to be conducted on communist terms. If this trade were to continue on the present basis, it might well become sufficiently large ten years from now to become a real menace. . . . Let us insist that if the Soviet Union really wants to normalize its relationships with the great community of nations, it must observe the rules and practices which have been adopted by the free peoples of the free world.

Three weeks later he returned to the question of Russian intentions at a time when the United Nations was considering a proposal by Khrushchev for complete world disarmament. Appearing on a question-and-answer television show, he said he "personally" favored resumption of the underground testing of nuclear weapons, which President Eisenhower had suspended in 1958. "I think that we cannot afford to fall behind in the advanced techniques of the use of nuclear material," he said. "I think those testings could be carried on, for instance, underground where there would be no fallout."

How long, a questioner asked, did he believe the United States and the Soviet Union should go on "not trusting each other"?

"Oh, I think you can trust them all right," Rockefeller replied, summing up his attitude toward the Communist leaders. "I think you can trust them to try and carry out their stated objective of the domination of the world."

v.

After more than a year of direct action in the field of politics, Rockefeller was neither disgusted (as some friends had predicted he would be) nor discouraged. He gave observers the strong impression of a man with a mission—a man performing a service in which he believed and enjoying every minute of his incredibly busy life. He had been since childhood intensely serious about anything he undertook and to this he had added a steadiness of approach without sacrificing either spontaneity or enthusiasm. He could still exclaim that a routine, boring political session was "great fun" or that a set of budgetary figures was "wonderfully exciting!" He had become, on most occasions, a skillful politician and if he sometimes seemed to overdo the backslapping, the handshaking and the hugging of small children, it was a fault that was utterly natural to him and one easily forgiven by voters whose backs were slapped, whose hands were shaken and whose offspring were swept up in the Governor's arms.

But more important, Rockefeller's first year as a professional proved to his own satisfaction that politics—successful politics— could be the highest and most honorable calling. Something of this conviction he expressed on October 22, 1959, at a memorial dinner for former Governor Alfred E. Smith.

> We need, as a people and as a nation, to be one thing—and one constant and honest thing in the sight of all. . . . There can be no safety in preaching one thing while practising another. . . . We cannot preach of equality or of freedom to the world of nations, if we do not fully practice freedom and respect equality in the cities and in the lives of our own nation. We cannot win the respect, and trust, of black men in Nigeria or Ghana until we have

honored the citizenship of Negroes in Georgia or Alabama. We cannot stir and summon the hopes of millions who are stifling in the slums of Calcutta or Djakarta if great American cities are too lazy, too fat with pride, to clean the slums from their own earth. We cannot inspire the admiration of a score of new nations hungry for ways to speed their own economic progress if the economic growth of America slows or falters. . . .

Within our own politics, the same rules . . . apply with equal force. And if any young man caring about politics, as he should, were to contemplate a life in politics and were he to come and ask my first counsels and warnings, I would tell him these equally plain things. You can only be one thing to all citizens, wherever you go, whatever you say, whatever you seek. You cannot trim your principles to fit your ambitions or change your convictions as you change your audiences. You cannot cheer loudly for civil rights in one part of the nation, and speak softly and evasively of them in another. You cannot promise to fulfill the most lavish hope of every group or sector—for then you are only pretending to be independent of each by the strange method of becoming the slave of all. . . . Neither hopes nor votes can be won except, finally, by the truth, not just openly spoken, but honorably lived. . . .

We dare not—we cannot—live as a nation in repose, calmly waiting for each new challenge to emerge on the far horizon, advance slowly and implacably toward us, finally confront us in the grim shape of crisis. We live in an age of revolution and explosion. . . . And, in such an age, we . . . shall learn to be the masters of circumstance or we shall be its victims. . . . We need a sense of full purpose—a dream if you will. We need such a dream in order to live the waking life in this tormented world. For without such a sense of purpose . . . we could only be a nation of sleepwalkers stumbling toward ever deeper darkness.

In the last months of 1959, Rockefeller carried his plea for "a sense of full purpose—a dream if you will" to a wider audience by making speaking tours to the Pacific Coast states, to Indiana, Missouri, Minnesota, Wisconsin, Oklahoma, Texas and Florida. The purpose of these whirlwind trips was to sample political sentiment, particularly within the Republican party, preliminary to deciding whether he would oppose Vice President Nixon for the Republican presidential nomination in 1960. He put much emphasis in his speeches on party unity and teamwork. He also sought to define issues on which he might challenge Nixon's strong grip on the party machinery. He urged, for example, a more coherent, consistent and concrete foreign policy program as well as a revised long-term land-use program and a system of stabilization supports (based on production costs and farmers' net income) to relieve the problem of huge farm surpluses.

His tours attracted national attention. His reception varied from unexpectedly large and enthusiastic public turn-outs in some cities to very cool reaction in other cities, particularly where party leaders were firmly committed to Nixon. The net result, however, was successful enough to convince political and newspaper observers that he would strongly challenge Nixon for the nomination. But Rockefeller had other ideas. On the day after Christmas, he surprised the nation by a "definite and final" announcement that "I am not, and shall not be, a candidate for nomination for the Presidency. . . . Quite obviously I shall not at any time entertain any thought of accepting nomination to the Vice Presidency."

The decision, he said, was dictated by the conviction that "the great majority of those who will control the Republican convention stand opposed to any contest for the nomination" and that "any quest of the nomination on my part would entail a massive struggle . . . demanding so greatly of my time and energy that it would make impossible the fulfillment of my obligations as Governor of New York." He added that he intended to continue to devote his efforts to strengthening and invigorating the spirit of the Republican party, and expected to support its nominees and programs in 1960.

> As to our country: the national and world issues before us, I deeply believe, hold omen of both menace and hope, both danger and opportunity. . . . Every one of them invites scrutiny. . . . For such a time as this calls for a profound and continuous act of national self-examination. I shall contribute all I can to this political act. I shall speak with full freedom and vigor on these issues that confront our nation and the world.

In view of all the circumstances, it was not surprising that many political observers read the statement skeptically, looking for some hidden meaning or some devious political maneuver. The fact was, however, that Rockefeller had followed his customary practice of the direct approach. He had, as usual, faced the facts and made a decision, and he had explained both the facts and the decision as frankly as possible.

Commenting on Rockefeller's statement, the *New York Times* said editorially that "he still remains a nationally important figure. No one in his party has spoken with more eloquence or conviction. . . . He has undoubtedly increased his influence and his stature." Political columnist Walter Lippmann commented that the Governor of New York had shown by his past actions that "he is not afraid" to face great and grave national problems, and concluded that "in these fundamental matters, Rockefeller is a man of the future."

# ... 11:34 a.m., Wednesday, January 13, 1959

The Governor's plane circled monotonously through dirty gray clouds as the pilot awaited control tower orders to drop blindly down toward the airport runway. Inside the cabin, the noise of the engines had subsided to an impatient hum.

"Governor, you've said we have to have a sense of purpose—maybe some people would call it a dream. Just what are we going to aim at as a nation?"

"First, remember we're living in a world that's in a kind of revolution—scientific, political, everything," he replied, his hands moving restlessly on the writing table as if he were reaching for the right words. "We've got to be a part—an influential part—of that world, a generating force, you could say, to help guide this revolution along democratic principles and create an orderly world community. We can't do that unless we show that our system will help peoples who are trying to raise their own social and economic standards."

"Do you mean the government must spend a lot more money to help these underdeveloped countries?"

"I mean the government must pave the way by measures, including technical aid, that will enable business, labor and capital to do the main job of providing managerial and scientific knowledge and funds. It is realistic in an inter-dependent world and it is in our own self-interest. If we help step up the buying power of other countries our own economy benefits in the long run."

"These are broad ideas, Governor. Do they mean much to the average citizen?"

"Well, world peace is a broad idea but it means a lot to everybody. We've got to understand the kind of world we are going to live in if we expect our kind of life to survive."

"Survive in competition with Communist Russia?"

"I'm not forgetting the Communists. We're not going to surrender our values to any kind of totalitarianism. But if Soviet Russia were to disappear tomorrow, the problems of the world community would remain. It is not what we're *against* that counts. It's what we're *for*."

At the front of the airplane cabin, the fasten-your-seat-belt sign blinked on. The tempo of the engines picked up to a steady, urgent beat. The gray world outside the windows thinned to cottony white as the plane came on course and thrust its groping electronic fingers down toward the unseen airport runway.

"Of course," the Governor said, "our national purpose has to start at home. If we don't preserve our social gains and guard the rights of our citizens and move on to new levels of well-being at home, then we'll have no say in the future of the world community. And you can be sure of one thing: we've got to work and we've got to get rid of our softness and indifference. Only our best will count in these days."

The wheels touched down on the runway with an angry but comforting hiss. The Governor raised his clasped hands above his head and shook them in a silent gesture of congratulations toward the cockpit. The cloud ceiling seemed almost down to the top of the airport control tower. Across the Potomac River, even the Washington Monument was hidden by a pearly curtain of mist.

*January 30, 1960*
*Guilford, Conn.*

# Index

History, US, Bk 3 Reel
Political